PRAISE FOR *CLASS NOTES*

"[*Class Notes* is] a journey into the heart of a famous family. Lively and colorful...the narrative at times takes on the breathless, cheerful chaos of a touch football game at Hickory Hill..."

—EDWARD WOLF, writer and policy advocate

"Olympic champion, emerging teacher, governess to American royalty: Carolyn Wood crammed in more living before her mid-twenties than most folks manage in triple that span. *Class Notes* is a splendidly observed, tender-hearted story about coming into one's own in a mind-boggling environment. It's like being led backstage through a specific moment of history by a sharp-eyed and cool-headed tour guide."

—SHAWN LEVY, author of Paul Newman: A Life
and The Castle on Sunset.

"In *Class Notes*, the Olympian, Carolyn Wood, blends literary and musical references, the dreams and sensibility of a young adult, and insights into a family the media made Americans believe we knew. In her deft prose, she offers the complicated nature of parenting, faith, politics, and most importantly, grief. *Class Notes* is an intimate, complicated, and kind portrayal of American royalty."

—KATE GRAY, author of For Every Girl and Carry the Sky.

"Two weeks before his death, RFK met and saw something extraordinary in a young Carolyn Wood. You will too, in this detail-packed memoir of an exhilarating and taxing year with the Robert and Ethel Kennedy family. Sprir over the ensuing 53 years, the universality of a young woman's desire to live a meaningful life will inspire you, even as you are awed by the rarified details of life with the Kennedys."

—LAURA O. FOSTER, *Portland Stair Walks.*

"When I picked up Carolyn Wood's memoir, *Class Notes: A Young Teacher's Lessons from Classroom to Kennedy Compound*, I couldn't put it down; it carried me through a young woman's first year as an English teacher in Oregon to her time serving as a governess to Robert Kennedy's children immediately after his assassination. Wood becomes a servant to this famous family and her memoir explores not only issues of class and privilege, but the way grief permeated the children's lives in silent and sometimes devastating ways. Wood writes with insight and self-awareness about her own, and our nation's, starry-eyed view of the Kennedys and her revelation of their humanity."

—PERRIN KERNS, creative writing instructor and filmmaker

"I was one of those students who begged Ms. Wood to share her tales of the Kennedys with our class. She wouldn't. But twenty years later I'm finally able to read the amazing and thoughtful story of her time in Hyannis Port. It was worth the wait."

—BOAZ FRANKEL, co-author of *Let's be Weird Together.*

"As a longtime fan of the Kennedys, reading this detail-packed memoir feels like hiring a time-travelling spy to live these experiences and tell me about them so vividly that it feels like I was there. I'm grateful this beautiful story exists."

—BROOKE BARKER, author of *Sad Animal Facts* and co-author of *Let's Be Weird Together.*

CLASS NOTES

For Debra —
fellow yogi —
Cheers to our
teachers

Carolyn Wood

CLASS NOTES

A Young Teacher's Lessons from Classroom to Kennedy Compound

A Memoir

CAROLYN WOOD

WHITE·PINE·PRESS

Portland, Oregon

Class Notes: A Young Teacher's Lessons from Classroom to Kennedy Compound
White Pine Press, Portland, OR, 97225

Line editing, proofreading, cover design, and interior book design provided by Indigo: Editing, Design, and More:

- Line editor: Ali Shaw
- Proofreaders: Kristen Hall-Geisler, Sarah Currin
- Cover designer: Olivia Hammerman
- Interior book designer: Vinnie Kinsella

www.indigoediting.com

ISBN: 978-0-9977828-2-0
eISBN: 978-0-9977828-3-7
LCCN: 2021914521

To all my teachers and students,
in gratitude for a lifetime of lessons

"Here is life, an experiment to a great extent untried by me…"

—HENRY DAVID THOREAU, *Walden*

CONTENTS

PROLOGUE

"Tell us about the Olympics, Miss Wood." "What was it like in Rome?" Students peppered me with questions in those early years of teaching. "How did it feel to win gold?" Or someone might say, "Tell us one story about the Kennedys, Miss Wood. Did you really get to meet Jackie?"

As a first-year teacher, I already knew the bird-track tricks of students, remembered how all you had to do to get some teachers off and running would be to say, "Tell us about the war, Mr. X," or "What was it like in Mallorca, Miss Y?" or "What were the Russians? Germans? Japanese? Koreans? Spaniards really like, Mrs. Z?" For the first seven years teaching at my alma mater, I fended off the questions with "Tell me about the reading you did last night." Even toward the end of my career, especially during Olympic years or when one or another of the Kennedys appeared in the news, someone would ask again, because they always knew my backstory. A teacher's history and reputation are passed along among students and siblings; after thirty-five years in the classroom, children of former students had begun to show up in my classes.

Still aware of the get-the-teacher-off-track trick, I had a different response. "I'll write it all in my memoirs when I retire. If any of you get published first, I'll follow you as fast as I can. We'll buy each other's books," I told them.

YEARS AFTER I RETIRED FROM teaching, while emptying the attic for new insulation, I pulled down the swimming scrapbooks my mother had so carefully kept throughout my racing days, and I set to work telling that story. It became the memoir *Tough Girl: Lessons in Courage and Heart from Olympic Gold to the Camino de Santiago,* an account of training and competing in the 1960 Rome Olympics and reflections while walking the Camino fifty years later.

I found another container up there in the attic, a long red-and-white cardboard box that had once held Christmas wrapping. In it my mother had stored all the letters I'd written home from the year I spent as governess for the Robert Kennedy family. She'd typed them out in duplicate so she could share them with the neighbors and friends. The Beaverton High newspaper, yellow and brittle, carried a letter I'd sent to the student body describing my duties and encouraging them to "someday take a wild step into the unknown, as I did the day I began campaigning for Robert Kennedy. You never know where that first step will lead you. I'm sure that you will find your own adventure. Believe me, it's worth the effort."

Pictures of the kids taken those first weeks on Cape Cod in August 1968 and later throughout the year at Hickory Hill filled two photo albums. My mom had stored in a plastic bag the little three-inch reel-to-reel audiotapes that we'd sent back and forth because long-distance phone calls seemed too expensive. I counted twenty-five. *Will they still play?* I wondered. There were a ski race bib from Sun Valley and some cards and drawings from the kids, Mass cards, and the program from Rory's baptism in January 1969. The trove had been roasting and freezing up in the attic for over forty years. *Who even has a tape player anymore?*

When you're over seventy-five, you've got a lot of stories to tell and not that much time left to tell them. You've made choices and followed paths that maybe you'd like to explore again or to explain—to yourself perhaps or to your children, your grandchildren, your curious students who asked so long ago.

Get busy, I advise. No time to waste.

Chapter 1

THE KENNEDY CONNECTION
SPRING 1968

INSIDE SUNSET HIGH SCHOOL'S GYM, FAMILIAR ODORS OF FLOOR wax, hot lights, and sweat mixed with excited voices, rapid and high-pitched, punctuated with explosive bursts of boy shouts. Everyone was waiting for the arrival of the dignitaries, especially the keynote speaker who would open the 1968 Beaverton School District's mock Democratic convention. Throughout the bleachers, delegates sat behind long-handled signs bearing their state's name, while down on the floor boys in dark suits, white shirts, and ties mingled with girls in straight skirts or shirtwaists, as if dressed for National Honor Society initiation or Sunday school.

Portland news mid-May was all about Eugene McCarthy, Hubert Humphrey, and Robert Kennedy, competitors in the Democratic primary for the presidential nomination. Kennedy would be the keynote speaker at the mock convention, and my friend Gretchen, who taught seniors at Sunset, had extra passes for four of us—all University of Oregon English majors, sorority sisters, and now high school teachers. Linda Moore and I both taught juniors at Beaverton High, where we collaborated and commiserated regularly. Ann taught seniors at a new school in Portland and shared an apartment with Gretchen. Tonight we sat together on the hard wooden bleachers, feeling almost like adults among the kids, and waited.

Oregon Congresswoman Edith Green, a family friend from our church and Kennedy's campaign cochair, stepped up to the podium to introduce the senator, and the crowd hushed. When Robert Kennedy came into view, the delegates forgot the state candidates they were intended to support and rose to cheer as they might for a school basketball team. Kennedy had that kind of effect. He waved the crowd quiet and began telling them that Congresswoman Green had told him that if he entered the Oregon primary, he'd get to visit...Sunset High. "That's why I ended up running for president." The Sunset students clapped and whistled. Then he egged them on: "Don't tell me—you mean I'm the only candidate who knows the difference between Beaverton and Sunset High School?" Kids from both schools stomped the bleachers and cheered. The *Oregonian* reported that he treated the audience like younger brothers and sisters and they roared their approval.

The four of us cheered along with them. You couldn't help but be swept up in the excitement. Nothing remains for me of the speech's content that night, only the bright lights of the stage, the energized and moiling crowd of student delegates clapping, cheering, pulsating to the electricity of Kennedy's voice, his presence. A vibration, the kind you might feel at the end of a close game, reverberated inside me. I bought his book that night and read it over the weekend, intrigued by how his ideas and philosophy meshed with what my fellow teachers and I had discussed all year: the need for personal responsibility, the power of one act to make a ripple that, when joined with another, others, millions, could make change happen. It was a message of hope, of the power of each individual action. It reminded me of the feelings I'd had eight years before when I was a sophomore in high school and his brother, John F. Kennedy, was our new president.

THAT JANUARY IN 1961, JOHN KENNEDY's inaugural address had rung through the public address system and into our classrooms, his voice tinny but the rhetoric soaring, the message challenging, "Ask not what your country can do for you—ask what you can do for your country." We all wanted to do something for our country that day.

When he talked about the torch being passed to a new generation, my mind shifted to Rome where I'd watched the runner carrying the Olympic torch into the stadium for the opening ceremony. I'd worn red, white, and blue that day in Rome, proud to represent America. John Kennedy's call made me want to do something more for my country. Even over the lousy loudspeaker, he made you feel excited, as if you could make a difference in the world. He wasn't Ike, that old-man president who'd droned on and on in his radio addresses. John F. Kennedy sounded young and elegant. He had polish. He had an accent. He was handsome.

"A new generation of Americans—born of this century," John Kennedy's voice said over the speakers, talking to us, asking us to do something bold. All his rhetoric, all his admonitions were filled with hope and idealism and belief in doing the right thing. "Civility is not a sign of weakness," he said, and I was sure he meant, *Don't be an Ugly American.* That book, read my freshman year, had illustrated how to behave abroad and how not to. Now his speech advocated for all mankind to work together toward a more peaceful and beneficial world. "Will you join in that historic effort?" he asked the world.

Yes. Yes. Yes, we answered.

"He used lots of parallel-sentence construction," we told Mrs. Ferrin, our sophomore English teacher, when the speech ended, pleased with ourselves for recognizing a rhetorical technique she'd recently taught.

"And he invited a poet to speak," she reminded us.

After class we pondered what we might someday do for our country.

My parents, both registered Republicans, had voted for Richard Nixon, but we all became enamored of the Kennedys, watching them as if they were movie stars or sports heroes, yet feeling close to them in a way, as if they were distant cousins. At home, we didn't talk politics—my parents too busy with work and I with swimming to debate the president's policies. Our liberal friends, avid union organizers and impassioned civil rights advocates, might fire up discussions at potlucks, but mostly we talked about the family.

My mom was fascinated with Jackie's clothes, her pillbox hats and bouffant hairdos. We saw snippets of White House life on the news now and then, photos of Caroline and little John in *Life* and *Look* magazines. We read stories in the *Saturday Evening Post* and *McCall's* and *Ladies' Home Journal*. I'm sure we watched Jackie's tour of the White House and laughed at her breathy speech, but soon we owned A-line skirts and high-collared coats, and my mom wore a pillbox hat to church.

In the three years of JFK's presidency, the whole Kennedy family became known to America. Maybe we'd read *Profiles in Courage* and knew he'd written it while recovering from back surgery to repair an injury from World War II. America knew all about his experiences on *PT-109*, being hit by a Japanese destroyer and thrown into the Pacific, because we'd seen the movie. Maybe we knew that his father had been ambassador to Great Britain before the war, that his older brother, Joe, had been killed in combat, and a sister had died in a plane crash over France. We knew his sister Patricia was married to handsome Peter Lawford, the British actor who ran with Hollywood's Rat Pack—Frank Sinatra, Dean Martin, Sammy Davis Jr. We might even have known that he had three other sisters: Eunice Kennedy Shriver, married to Robert Shriver, who would become the architect of the Peace Corps; Jean Kennedy Smith, his little sister; and Rosemary, the sister who lived in an institution for persons with intellectual disabilities. We knew that Teddy was the baby of the family.

We called the hopeful presidency of John F. Kennedy an American Camelot, and nothing exemplified it more than the summer white house on the Kennedy Compound in Hyannis Port, Massachusetts. The patriarch, Joseph P. Kennedy, known as "the Ambassador," had purchased a "summer cottage" on the shore of Nantucket Sound in 1928. John and Jackie Kennedy bought a house nearby in 1956, Robert and Ethel in 1959. After the 1960 election, this collection of houses that was spread over six acres and protected by the local police and the Secret Service became known as the Kennedy Compound. We knew it because we'd seen photos of the president scooting over the lawns in a golf cart with little John in his lap and Caroline hanging on or of him shoving off the dock with a boatload of tousle-haired children or of Jackie, hidden behind enormous dark glasses with her hair streaming behind her. In the background the huge white clapboard house, the Ambassador's house, stood as the center of the compound.

Camelot lasted until November 22, 1963, my freshman year in college.

At University of Oregon, every girl took Freshman Fundamentals, an introductory physical education class that met three times a week, mine in midmorning. On the first day, each of us had been photographed wearing a saggy cotton leotard in profile alongside a measuring stick. "Slump a little for the first photo so you can show posture improvement. It's the way to get an A," our sophomore sorority sisters had advised.

Over the weeks we hung from rings in the old Gerlinger Hall gym until our arms shook. We hurdled a leather horse—or stumbled over it like toddlers on the big kids' playground. We walked in circles around the floor holding our heads upright. In November, we moved to a dance studio where we stood in lines moving to music, beginning to learn something about modern dance.

About an hour into class on a Friday morning, a girl burst into the studio and hurried toward the instructor, leaned forward, and whispered something. The instructor turned to us, her face a stricken mask. We stopped moving and stared.

It's a fractured memory, shards of images—the silliness of our black baggy leotards, a record playing modern jazz, the pretense that our swaying movement was dance, and then the door opening. The young woman rushing to the instructor. Two white faces and their open mouths.

"The president's been shot. The president is dead."

Outside I hurried along a campus path under low, leaking clouds and followed other students headed toward the dorms. Not far along, a bell began to ring and then another and another. Bells from every tower on campus and from the nearby churches tolling, tolling in a slow, heavy cadence. And no one spoke. The bells pounded against my chest and crowded out thought. I was too numb to cry. How could the president be dead?

In geology that afternoon, the professor came in late, wrote something on the board, began to talk, and broke into tears. "Go home," he told us. "We can't have class. Our president....Go home." I was a freshman, and home seemed far away. Back in Carson Hall, my roommate and I listened to the radio for news reports and then to the classical station where they played requiem after requiem. The next day, University of Oregon hosted the high school swim championships. I met the Beaverton High bus and hugged Mr. Harman, my old coach. I sat with him throughout the preliminaries and the finals. He was the closest thing to home, and I felt safe with him there.

On Sunday morning while my roommate was at Mass, news that Lee Harvey Oswald had been assassinated interrupted the radio concert. I tore out of our room and ran downstairs to the basement where a television was already replaying the scene from the Dallas police garage. On Monday, the national day of mourning for the president, girls crowded around the black-and-white television in Carson Hall's basement to watch the president's funeral and wonder: *What does it mean? What will happen? Are the Russians going to attack?*

I don't remember crying or going home for Thanksgiving later that week or even talking about it at home. After the girl hurrying into the dance studio, after that walk across campus with the bells, after the geology class when the professor cried, only a few images stutter through my memory in black and white: Mr. Harman with his clipboard and stopwatch at Leighton Pool. Carson Hall basement on Sunday morning in disbelief that Oswald had been shot. Jackie Kennedy dressed in black, her two children standing beside her, the long walk from the Capitol rotunda to the church, the sounds of drums and shuffling feet.

Something terrible had happened, something incomprehensible and far away from Eugene, where our first finals rushed toward us. Memorizing German verbs, recopying Western Civ. notes, reading the last Shakespeare plays for the term replaced images of the car cavalcade, the bloody pink suit, the funeral cortege, the fallen president.

Now the president's brother was carrying on the legacy not just in the Senate but hopefully in the presidency too. After the mock convention speech ended Friday night, the four of us—Linda, Gretchen, Ann, and I—stood in the Sunset High parking lot and talked. We already knew Robert Kennedy's background, how he had served as US attorney general for three years before his brother was killed, stood up against organized crime, and fought for desegregation of Southern schools and the end of Jim Crow law. We knew he had marched with Cesar Chavez and the United Farm Workers and advocated ending the Viet Nam War. We'd read how he'd calmed a crowd of African-Americans in Indianapolis the night Martin Luther King Jr. was murdered, speaking impromptu from the bed of a truck. What impressed us was his compassion, how he used the pain from his own experience to convey a belief that together we could make a difference, could better our world.

We finally left for home, Linda to her husband, Ann and Gretchen to their apartment, and I back to my family where I was living almost rent-free. But I couldn't get to sleep. His beliefs, his rhetoric, his voice kept me awake. I'd been swept into the campaign, persuaded to help. Over the weekend I talked about the speech, the crowd, the book. My parents listened as they always did, though I wasn't influencing their votes since they were still registered Republicans. Mom, who'd heard enough, suggested that I call Barbara Fealy, a longtime family friend and avid Democrat. Perhaps I did and she invited us all over for dinner where we would have talked about civil rights, civil disobedience, the Viet Nam War, and Norman Cousins's latest essay on nuclear disarmament.

Chapter 2

SCHOOL YEAR

Several teachers were already in line for the mimeograph machine when I pushed into the workroom Monday morning, my freshly typed masters, strikeovers and all, in hand. An elder social studies teacher wound the ditto crank round and round, his voice loud over the machine racket, as he related events from the weekend convention. He'd also been stirred by Bobby Kennedy's speech and the students' reaction. I piped in that I wanted to participate more, wished I could take a whole day off and work on the campaign.

"Teachers need mental health days now and then," he said. "Days when you rejuvenate your spirit." He caught my eye, his expression suggesting that I might consider my needs.

I hadn't taken a single sick day all year, even when I'd been sick or exhausted. A September cold had caught me three weeks into the school year, as it would for the rest of my career, but I hadn't been sick since then, though I did have increasing spring fever and a persistent sense of dread before my sixth-period class. A small group of four—two girls and two boys—routinely coalesced into an electric buzz of irritation the last period of the day. Had it been a week since the Big Incident?

AT FIRST THE SCHOOL YEAR followed a rhythm familiar since kindergarten when our moms would take us shopping for new school shoes, a box of crayons, round-tipped scissors we'd always lose, yellow pencils with pink erasers, and wide-lined paper. Through the August heat, I now knew that both teachers and students vibrated in anticipation of Labor Day and the beginning of school. After the nerves of opening, the parade of new clothes and introductions, the schedule changes, the subsequent coughs and sneezes of late-September colds, everyone settled in for the long, wet winter.

Dale Harvey, the junior honors English teacher, shared a first-period prep with Linda and me and soon recruited us into daily morning discussions of literature and philosophy and classroom management, the merits of "tracking," the sexual undertones in Emily Dickinson's poetry, the importance of understanding existentialism, the war in Viet Nam. Linda and I downed coffee after coffee, shared cigarettes, and listened to the wise elder. Dale was over thirty. We rehashed *Laugh-In*, reviewed new movies, and came up with ideas "to engage" our students.

In the afternoons, I'd hustle over to the pool for swim practice, glad to escape the classroom. While the team swam warm-up laps, Rod Harman and I munched Fritos from the vending machine, chatted about current events, and gossiped like old friends. After a long day cooped up in school, it felt good to pace alongside the pool and yell at kids to "work hard" or to "quit loafing"—things I felt like yelling in the classroom sometimes but didn't. On Thursdays, we had swim meets that lasted for hours, Rod calling out swimmers' splits in every race while I recorded them. Around us kids chanted cheers and told jokes, did homework, or simply sat leaning into each other in their damp Beaverton sweats. A different aspect of kids emerged in the places they'd chosen to be, on teams or in clubs or activities. For three months, we became an afternoon family with dad, mom, and dozens of siblings.

When daylight savings ended, the school became a lighthouse to guide student travelers into safe harbor. At least that's how it felt to me in the dark mornings when I arrived early and climbed up to my classroom, unlocked the door, and lit the overheads that shone onto the parking lot and street below. On a school record player, I played Chopin etudes and Schubert preludes, music from an appreciation class at Oregon that surely signaled sophistication and invitation. My room was open for anyone who wanted to talk or needed a quiet place to be—at least until the bell, when I'd turn over the space and head down to the teachers' room for the morning confab with Dale and Linda.

The 1967 yearbook photos taken in the fall captured the fashion trends and hairstyles of the times, girls with long smooth flips like Marlo Thomas or slightly shorter bouffant bubbles, boys with Beatles bangs pulled across their foreheads. The principal announced in a faculty meeting that he would suspend any boy whose hair grew so long it touched his collar. We teachers were to monitor and refer long-hairs to the vice principal's office.

"We're English teachers, not hair monitors," Linda and I protested over beers at Ichabod's, the local tavern where we met other teachers on Friday afternoons. Bob Dietche and Dale Harvey railed about the administration. "Fascists," they groused. But they had tenure and did not have to abide by every administrative dictate; Linda and I, the new teachers, did. The next week I stopped beside a quiet boy's desk and leaned down. "I think your hair is almost to your collar," I whispered. "You don't want to get in trouble." In three more years, I'd be whispering things like "Don't ever come to my class stoned. Wait till later."

Weeks dragged after Christmas vacation, those endless days of January, February, and half of March before spring vacation. Teachers and students would listen to weather forecasts hoping for snow days that rarely, if ever, arrived. When the snow finally fell in the Cascades, I drove alone most weekends up the Columbia Gorge, through Hood River, and around the mountain to ski at a new complex. My little Opel Kadett struggled, nose pushing against the east winds, sometimes barely able to reach forty-five miles per hour. All my thoughts focused on the road, my worries on whether or not I'd need to chain up. Classrooms, students, faculty meetings, papers—all vanished into the stark white slopes and bitter winds. On downhill runs, legs pumping, eyes bleary with tears, poles squeaking into the snow, it was all body, all day long. I'd drive home with wobbly legs but awake, revived, and released from the classroom with its adolescent dramas, ready to pick up the piles of papers that needed grading or to design the next assignment or to read the upcoming chapters for a Monday discussion.

Spring break signaled the final leg of the four-term relay. In sports, the strongest swimmer or runner is saved for last, the anchor, but that's hard to manage in the classroom. Time, tradition, and the weather work against finishing hard. Longer, warmer days lured students outdoors. Afternoon lawn mowers sawed back and forth over the playing fields across the street at the elementary school, drowning out discussion and enticing thoughts out and away. Suspicious notes for afternoon absences began to turn up. Prom. Spring Reign. Hookups and breakups dominated conversations. Rumors of senior skip day drifted through the halls every other week. Time developed an unreliable quality. The high wall clock's hands would spin around the face before I could finish a lesson or seemingly seize up two ticks before the freedom bell.

Now in mid-May, each day was beginning to tighten like a drawn bow toward the dreaded last period where Tim, a smart aleck who'd arrived midyear after being expelled from a private school, needled classmates (and me) and instigated three of his friends without ever getting caught. Everything I threw at him from my flimsy bag of tricks—sarcasm, shaming, praise, ignoring—flew past uselessly. Experienced teachers listened to my laments and offered strategies that I might try. Sometimes they'd work for a few days. Class would almost cohere. Almost. Just when Tim seemed to buckle down, one of the girls in the foursome would begin to lip off, not loud enough for me to hear, exactly, but loud enough for me to know I was being mimicked or countered.

They were bringing to life a nightmare I'd had before the first day of school: I am standing in front of a classroom full of unknown students seated in clusters and talking loudly among themselves. A bell rings, but the talking continues. I raise my voice over the din, but no one seems to hear me. "Class! Class!" I repeat from behind my fortress-like podium. "Open your books. Open your books to page..." Some boy might look up, sneer, and turn his back. Or a girl giggles and whispers to a seatmate. Lightning-white awareness strikes me mute. *No one has to do what I say. It's thirty against one in here. I can't make anyone listen. I'm powerless.*

But this wasn't a dream; it was real. And it was more than my powerlessness—it was the injustice of one wily guy pulling down kids not as bright. I knew he'd end up with a passing grade at the end of the term, but his minions were flunking. It wasn't fair.

The Big Incident had happened on a day I'd shown a movie, a serious film, one that ought to have fostered meaningful discussion—at least, it had in my morning classes. After the film ended, leader flapping over the take-up reel, I set up the rewind while students finished notes or wrestled papers back into Pee-Chees or chatted among themselves. Jostling my way back to the front of the room, I asked for someone to put up the blinds, long roller blinds that covered the twelve-foot-tall windows. Tim jumped to duty.

From behind the podium, I posed my first penetrating discussion question. Simultaneously Tim released the first blind from the bottom sill to snap, whip, and flapflap around the roller, drowning out my voice. Everyone turned to the windows to look. A few kids snickered. I began again but not before Tim had released the second blind in a deafening *bang*slapslapslap.

The room went red and silent. I saw nothing but a deep, pulsing carmine. "Get out of here," I must have said with such quiet rage that the room compressed like the inside of a snow globe. I didn't see Tim leave the room, but when my sight returned, he was gone, three blinds were up, two still down, and everyone in the class was staring. Did I re-pose the discussion question? Did I laugh or apologize or lecture? I don't remember. Afterward I told Linda that I thought I could have killed him if he'd been in reach. It frightened me that I could lose control. I wasn't any different than Gene in *A Separate Peace*, a novel we'd studied in the fall, when he jiggled the tree limb that toppled Finny.

THE NEW TEACHER I HAD been when I'd begun the year with excitement and idealism was stumbling toward the finish line, shoes scuffed, crayons broken, Pink Pearl eraser a mere nub that left black smears across tattered papers. Or so it felt in mid-May on sweltering afternoons. Summer vacation could not arrive fast enough. It seemed like an obvious signal that I needed a mental health day.

While I cranked out a hundred or so copies of an e. e. cummings poem, an idea blossomed. I'd read in the paper that on Thursday, Robert Kennedy would be in Portland campaigning again, first over breakfast with a gathering of church leaders before a walking tour of downtown, then on to St. Helens, a river town west of Portland, and back to a rally at Eastport Plaza and a final speech at Madison High School. I could volunteer for the campaign that day. He'd have a full day of events, but maybe he'd stop by campaign headquarters where I might actually meet him. I submitted the paperwork to get a substitute.

I arrived early to the campaign office where volunteers and staffers stapled flyers and stuffed envelopes. Everyone seemed to be from out of town, professional campaigners who traveled from state to state. Sometime midmorning, a phone call came in, and the worker who answered turned to ask if anyone was from Oregon, if anyone knew how to get to St. Helens.

"I'm from Oregon," I answered.

"We've got someone," the phone guy said. The senator would not be stopping by headquarters, but they needed a guide, and before long I was in a car with three campaign workers, out-of-towners, heading west out of Portland on US 30 along the Columbia River. I'm pretty sure I'd never been to St. Helens.

A small crowd clustered together in the town hall square that showery afternoon. It was hard to hear from the back of the crowd, but I recognized Rafer Johnson, who'd been the gold medalist in the decathlon at the 1960 Olympics, up on the platform. He and Roosevelt Grier were working as bodyguards and crowd movers for the senator.

"We were in the same Olympics," I said to the driver of my car as I pointed toward Rafer.

"Really?" he asked, making that quizzical face I recognized as disbelief.

After the rally, the car cavalcade wound its way out of town and up the hillside to the highway before pulling over to a stop on the verge. Several press buses idled behind us. One of the campaign workers knocked on our window and explained that the reporters who had stories to file needed to switch buses. Because we were going right on to the shopping mall and then to the school, we'd take a little break here on the side of the road.

My driver got out of the car and disappeared only to return a few minutes later with Rafer Johnson. He didn't know me, of course, because he'd competed in track and I in swimming, but we shared a few of our experiences of Rome. I told him I remembered the night of his pole vault when it rained so hard the Olympic Village flooded and the event got postponed till after ten o'clock. If he was checking me out, I passed the test. We shook hands before he turned to leave, and he said that the senator might like to meet me. And so he did.

A clear snapshot memory remains of that May afternoon in 1968. I'm on the highway's edge bending down toward an open window. Inside, slumped in the backseat, sits the senator, looking up at me. He looks small, tired, vulnerable.

We talked for over ten minutes, me on the verge and leaning into the car, about the Sunset High convention, the 1960 Olympics, swimming. He knew a lot about the sport, he said, because he had tried it once, but those twelve-month training sports were too much. Football was more his line. He asked about my events, my training, my times. Our conversation ended when one of the loaded buses pulled away from the edge and his driver returned.

We had an easy conversation, the way athletes do, I thought. Jock talk.

Later, when I told my friends about him, I said that he'd been quiet but intense and curious, his face lined deeply with fatigue or exposure to sun and wind and snow. I told my dad that his face reminded me of his, wrinkled, freckled, and sun damaged. "He's a sportsman," I said.

SHORTLY AFTER MY MENTAL HEALTH day, an oral surgeon pulled two wisdom teeth in an operation I believed had been conducted under hypnosis. Obviously I didn't know anything about nitrous or "happy gas," as friends later explained. A nurse had given me what she called a "relax pill" and after a while led me to another room and settled me into a dental chair. The doctor came in and asked how I was feeling; his slow and comforting voice told me to breathe...and then someone woke me up.

"He just told me to relax and talked and talked, and the next thing I heard was someone saying, 'Wake up, Carolyn.' I didn't feel a thing. I was hypnotized," I told my mom in the waiting room afterward. All weekend I glided under the spell of "hypnosis," painkillers, and the roadside encounter with the senator.

Maybe he'd actually be elected and live in the White House with his ten kids, I fantasized. I could be their swim coach or teacher or lifeguard. An idea began to form. I'd volunteer to work with his kids over the summer. The older ones might need training tips, and the younger ones might need lessons. I'd get to see the inside of the White House, never mind that the convention and the election were months away. In my dreamy state, all sorts of plans and scenarios formed. I would write a letter to the senator and offer my services. In between naps, I wrote several drafts until one seemed ready to be typed, signed, and sent.

"I'm going to apply for a summer job with Robert Kennedy," I announced to my mom.

"How are you going to do that?" she challenged, and I gave her the letter to read over. She read it slowly and carefully, not for content but looking for spelling and punctuation errors as she had many a high school essay. At the end she looked up and said that hundreds of people must write to him every day. She was right, but if Congresswoman Green was still in town, my parents would see her on Sunday. She could deliver the letter personally, I reasoned.

"Will you give it to Mrs. Green to give to the senator?" I asked.

When my parents got home on Sunday, they reported that Mrs. Green hadn't been at church so they'd given the letter to other friends who were sure to see her before she returned to Washington, DC. They'd promised to pass the message along, Mom told me.

It's a long shot, but maybe something will come of it, I hoped.

On Tuesday, the senator became the first Kennedy to lose a primary election. Eugene McCarthy took Oregon with 45 percent of the vote. *Oh well*, I thought in a less euphoric state than I'd spent over the post-surgery weekend. *For sure he'll win California.*

Back at Beaverton, the school year inched closer to summer vacation. Final essays came due before Memorial Day, and final exams loomed the following week. Frantic students would be meeting with teachers and trying to make up late assignments. On Friday afternoon at home, a long-distance call came in for me. My mom hurried me to the phone, then stood by eavesdropping.

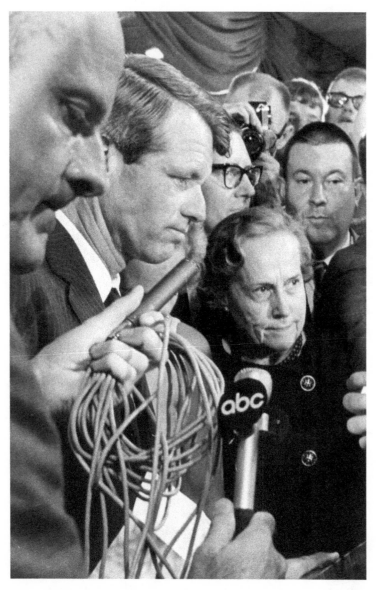

Senator Robert F. Kennedy with Congresswoman Edith Green at a press conference after his loss in Oregon's presidential primary election. Photo courtesy of *The Oregonian.*

"Hello, Carolyn? I'm calling for Senator Robert Kennedy. His kids are flying in to California tomorrow. He wondered if you'd like to come down and go with them to Disneyland? You could get acquainted. We'd fly you down, of course."

"I..." Stacks of papers that had to be read, the test that had to be typed and dittoed for Monday, the term's worth of grades to be tapped into the adding machine and calculated into grade points flashed through my mind. Grades were due in a week—a deadline that could not be postponed.

"I...can't," I stammered. "It's finals. I have papers. Grades."

"Oh, hey. That's okay. We understand. It was just an idea the senator came up with. We'll be in touch. Good luck with those papers."

Oh my God. He'd gotten my letter.

My memory ends with the phone call. I probably screamed and scared my mother half to death and then called Linda to tell her, or the friends who'd delivered the letter to Edith Green. I bet I called Barbara Fealy, who would ask how I could ever have said no. Surely I went over and over the phone call Monday morning in the teachers' room with my first-period buddies. What a lucky chain of circumstances: taking the one day off from school, talking to a fellow Olympian, meeting the senator, sending a hand-delivered letter with a church friend who happened to be the chair of the Kennedy campaign.

How small the world seems when we meet someone on a bus or plane far from home and she happens to be next-door neighbors with your grade-school best friend. Or on back-to-school night when a student's father turns out to be your neighborhood playmate from fifty years ago. Someone you played with introduces you to a coworker who has a friend who knows XYZ.

It's six degrees of separation that, when connected, may lead to a job or a story or an adventure. We build our lives on these connections, a web of roots that support upward and outward growth.

The California primary was on Tuesday, June 4. Just before the ten o'clock news, I came downstairs from correcting papers and joined my parents to watch for the early returns. All indicators pointed toward a Kennedy victory. Senator Kennedy was beating Eugene McCarthy. He'd come back from the Oregon loss stronger than expected, they said. He was gathering momentum for the remaining primaries and the Democratic convention. I gave a quick cheer. Now I needed to convince my mom and dad to vote for him in November. Back upstairs I listened to the radio for a while longer just to be sure he was still ahead, then turned it off, happy and hopeful.

Chapter 3

JOB OFFER

"Minutes after celebrating his California primary victory, Senator Robert Kennedy was shot..."

I jerked out of sleep and reached for the clock radio. The voice went on describing the frantic scene in the hotel kitchen where the shooting happened, naming other wounded victims. I ran down the stairs to the kitchen. "Bobby Kennedy was shot last night."

My father looked up from the morning *Oregonian*. Headlines read, "Bobby Kennedy Shot in LA Hotel" and "New Yorker Gains Edge in Balloting."

"Says here he got shot in the hip."

"In the head," I cried. "It's on the radio."

By the time I got to school, I'd heard more of the unfolding story—Kennedy was in critical condition. The family was gathering at his bedside. The shooter, Sirhan Sirhan, a Christian Palestinian Arab, had been wrestled to the ground by Rafer Johnson and Rosey Grier and was in custody. In the teachers' room, we gathered around a television the librarian had rolled in and listened in shocked disbelief until it was time for class. I went through the day feeling sick, stomach tight, chest constricted, the way I'd felt as a kid when I'd been bad and knew I'd be caught, a feeling of deep dread.

After school I drove to Barbara Fealy's house, and we cried together and then on to a late afternoon Mass at the downtown cathedral. Maybe the ritual and the prayer and the priest's words would ease the ache. Kneeling among the grieving congregation, I tried to imagine God's plan, what possible good another Kennedy's death would serve, but nothing materialized. At home I joined my parents to watch the ongoing news reports.

"You could have been there," my mom said in a kind of TV stupor.

A flare of anger and guilt surprised me. "No, I couldn't. I'd have been back before the election," I said before breaking into tears. I didn't know that grief could contain so many emotions—sadness, anger, guilt, longing, despair.

He was still alive Wednesday night when I went to bed, but we all knew there was no hope. He died shortly after midnight on June 6, and for a second morning the radio came on with shattering news: Bobby Kennedy was dead. It felt like a family member had been murdered. I'd met him, talked to him, been offered a childcare job. He was real. He'd been alive. The violence, the loss felt inexplicable.

No one is left kept running through my mind. No one left to lead us out of Viet Nam. No one who'd climb on the hood of a car in a Black ghetto and articulate the anger and anguish of Martin Luther King Jr.'s murder. No one left to offer more than words because he himself had suffered, suffered losing siblings to violent ends. He had known loss and felt it in others. What was the saying Daniel Patrick Moynihan had quoted at the president's funeral? "To be Irish is to know that, in the end, the world will break your heart."

Each death that year, those years, stunned and paralyzed. In April, Martin Luther King Jr. had been assassinated. In the 1960s it had become so easy to shoot a political figure—John F. Kennedy, Medgar Evers, Malcolm X, Fred Hampton—as easy as it has become over the years to shoot a classroom of students or a crowd of concertgoers or a congregation. In Portland, the senator had talked about gun control.

School went on regardless. We sat in the teachers' room hunched over coffee and repeating what we'd heard, echoing each other's disbelief, each other's shock, talking in the way that holds back emotion—repeating and repeating our questions, our thoughts. Someone may have suggested a poem to bring to class—W. H. Auden's "Funeral Blues," "Stop all the clocks, cut off the telephone... / Silence the pianos and with muffled drum / Bring out the coffin, let the mourners come" or e. e. cummings's "Buffalo Bill's." My feelings that sunny June morning in Portland ran more toward Percy Bysshe Shelley's "A Dirge": "Rough wind that moanest loud / Grief too sad for song." Perhaps I found some excerpts from the senator's book or his eulogy for his own brother and typed them out. Perhaps I brought back the quote from *A Farewell to Arms* that we'd read and discussed in the fall when we studied *A Separate Peace*, the one where Frederick says, "If people bring so much courage to this world the world has to kill them to break them."

Saturday the television networks broadcast another Kennedy funeral, this time from St. Patrick's Cathedral in New York and then from the train and along the roadside as the senator's body was returned to Washington, DC, and to Arlington National Cemetery. My father stayed home from the store where he worked, and my brother came over from his house, and together our whole family sat watching, numbed by the images that recalled those from five years before—the stark, black-clad congregants, the stunned and stoic family, the shuffling feet, the heartbeat cadence: Why? Why? Why? The long, elegant goodbye to an agent of light and hope.

SCHOOL FINALLY ENDED, AND THE kids disappeared to summer jobs or American Heritage tours or lazy days of sleeping late, listening to records, watching TV, or aimlessly driving around, but a few teachers stayed behind to work on curriculum. In the English department, Dale Harvey, Linda, and I had been given an extra week of paid time in June for coursework, a chance to revitalize and coordinate the entire junior curriculum.

The school felt abandoned early Monday morning, lights off, halls dim and silent. Maggie, the school secretary, greeted me in the office with a time sheet and a smile and told me that Dale was already in and waiting in his room. My tennis shoes sent echoey squeaks bouncing off the lockers. Dale sat behind his desk flipping through a file cabinet but spun around on a wheeled chair when I said hi, his hands aflutter with papers. The room smelled of chalk dust and coffee. Before I could sit, Linda's heels clicked down the empty hall and she entered with her Rose Festival smile. We were ready to dig in.

We wanted an organized, progressive program that we called the Philosophy and Spirit of American Literature, an historical survey of significant American writers. That had been in our funding proposal. By Tuesday, we had decided to focus our teaching lens on how literature can be both an expression of its time and a guide to finding meaning and purpose in life. Our classes needed a core based on hope, we agreed, on the importance of individual responsibility and action. Dale suggested we begin the year with Viktor Frankl's *Man's Search for Meaning* in order to introduce the idea of spiritual survival in a violent or threatening world. Linda and I didn't know the book, but when I read it at night it felt like a guide, like a soothing balm. We were all still mourning Kennedy's death, but working together brought comfort; selecting works that offered insight and optimism renewed our sense of hope. It was hard to believe that less than a year had passed since I'd started teaching.

IN AUGUST 1967, SOME TEN months before, I'd joined a dozen or more new teachers for a Welcome to Beaverton orientation where we sat in the library wearing our modest shirtwaist dresses or blazers and ties and listened. Listened to a reading and explanation of page 37 of the school handbook. Page 72. Page 86. By ten o'clock, late-summer heat seeped into the open windows and through the propped-open door. "On page 110 is the attendance form you'll fill out..." Outside the window behind Mr. Boyce, the activity director, maple leaves hung like limp laundry from the trees lining 2nd Street. My eyes flicked between him and outdoors. We dutifully made notes of important information: fire drill schedules, Stanford-Binet testing, the first pep assembly.

After lunch, Margaret Knispel, English department chair, met with all the new English teachers. She had advocated for us to have only four academic classes in order to assign and respond to more writing from the students. In addition, we'd have a prep period and a study hall or independent reading class. First-year teachers would all teach junior English because juniors were more teachable, past puberty and pre-senior graduation worries, she told us, before adding that we were also most likely more familiar with American writers. She smiled and handed each of us our schedule and room assignments.

Our text was an old clothbound anthology, one whose checkout sticker bore names of kids from even before my graduating class. I thumbed through the index looking at the short story options. John Steinbeck's "The Chrysanthemums," Shirley Jackson's "The Lottery," and Ray Bradbury's "The Flying Machine." She told us to start with short stories because kids would be transferring in and out the first weeks of school. It would be pointless to start with a novel.

My first-period prep was followed by back-to-back classes held in the old library annex, a cavernous second-floor room divided by a flesh-colored, plastic folding wall through which voices, scooting desks, music, and laughter permeated in a muffled roar. The south side was windowless, suffocating, and perpetually dark, but for some unknown reason, I got the side with a row of east-facing windows. It was still hot but not claustrophobic.

Longtime teachers become property owners of sorts, settled in "their rooms" where they fill the bookshelves with paperbacks from old college classes or sample textbooks from subject matter conferences. They cover the walls and bulletin boards with artwork and posters, keep lesson plans in four-drawer file cabinets that they've scrounged from retiring teachers' classrooms. New teachers are always itinerants, and I was no exception.

After my mornings in the noise factory, I moved to another classroom for one period and then on to Mrs. Ferrin's room for the last period of the day. Leota Ferrin, an institution at Beaverton, her reputation bigger than her closet full of high-heeled shoes,

Me as "Miss Wood," twenty-one years old, addressing my junior English class for the 1968 Beaverton High yearbook.

taught advanced sophomore English, advised the literary magazine, and coached the dance team. She'd been the demanding teacher who'd taught me to write.

In our first English department meeting "Leota," as I was instructed to call her, sat across from me as a colleague. She looked the same as she had my sophomore year back in 1960, the year I'd returned from the Olympics rather self-conscious and uncertain, a bit like I felt now. The thought triggered a memory of her strutting into class, a pile of papers cradled in one arm, cigarette smoke teasing from her sweater dress. She'd sauntered to her podium, unfolded her arm as if to place the papers and then swept them back to her bosom, looked out at the class with a sneer, and marched to the windows, unlatched one, reached out her laden arm, and dropped the stack to the parking lot below. Turning back to the class, she commanded, "Don't waste my time again."

Did she really say that? I wasn't sure. But the entrance, the parade, the gesture was always dramatic: Mrs. Ferrin, with her bleached-blonde pixie cut, her five-inch heels—a different pair every day—her long Shirley MacLaine dancer's legs and golfer's tan, her massive white Pontiac convertible that roared into Beaverton every morning, top down, cigarette smoke trailing. At sixty or sixty-five, she'd exuded East Coast liberal arts temperament. "I went to Columbia, dahlings. You've got to read and write to get into Columbia. *Read and write.*"

We sat in long, straight rows diagraming sentences, cutting out "dead wood," correcting for parallel sentence constructions. We read *Night Flight, Silas Marner, A Tale of Two Cities, Lord Jim, Jane Eyre.* We might talk about the books in small groups, but she did not foster large class discussions. She preferred performance, her own, which often began with a trick question.

"Who likes Jane Eyre? Not the book, but Jane?" she asked midway through the book.

A few hands raised, and she called on the most vulnerable among us, a girl who blushed blood red under her black bangs. "You do, sweetie? You like Jane Eyre?" Suddenly Mrs. Ferrin hunched over and emerged from behind the podium lifting her knees like an egret. "The simpering little priss?" She mimicked a line from the book in a high, tremulous voice: "Oh—the poor little dead bird..." And then she uncoiled, the trap snapping: "I hate that Jane Eyre. I hate how she is such a mouse. A *mouse*! How can you like her?"

We stared, as shocked as the day she had thrown our essays out the window.

I wondered if Mrs. Ferrin did her performances to enliven her own dull days after years in the classroom. Or did she intend to entertain, terrify, humiliate, or motivate? *She was a great teacher. Now she's my colleague.* The thought scared and excited me.

After thirty-five years of teaching, I now know that a teacher is first a performer, sometimes scripted, sometimes improvisational, with a captive yet rotating audience four or five times a day, five days a week, over 170 days a year. A teacher is writer, director, stage manager, and actor. We ought to have spent a year or two in theater for training.

If a great teacher is first a performer, she's also a cop: detective, warden, sentry, and guard. I started off with well-trained lifeguard eyes. Tualatin Hills Park & Recreation District instructed new employees to see the whole pool, to scan the decks and sidelines, the diving boards and pool bottoms for anything amiss. "When you're up in the chair, don't converse. Keep your eyes moving," trainers told us. It's easy to get focused on the flashy star doing flips off the diving board or on the timid toddler lurching along the deck and never notice the kid who's stepped in over his head or the bully dunking someone in an obscure corner or the runner racing behind the guard tower. School can be like a pool with hidey-holes where kids get in trouble.

I took my wraparound vision and big ears into the classroom. Plus, I already knew many of their names and families. My goal every year was to learn every name by Friday of the first week. When you can see and hear what's going on even as you engage with a single student, when you can call someone by name, you are connected in ways that enhance control, a school version of neighborhood policing. Even so, the nightmare of powerlessness haunted me that night after orientation, and it would recur many Septembers over the years.

On the first day of school, I woke before the alarm sounded into dull, gray, predawn light and the promise of afternoon heat, my outfit carefully chosen the night before, a dress from The Dark Horse or a plaid skirt and crisp white blouse with a sweater over my shoulders, something Sandy Dennis might have worn in *Up the Down Staircase*. I had a purse that matched my shoes packed with an almost empty wallet ("Don't bring cash to school," we'd been warned), lip gloss, blush, cigarettes and matches, and wads of receipts and gum wrappers and broken combs and ballpoint pens and stubby pencils with broken lead. All the junk that accumulates in purses. Into one of my mom's knitting bags, a large woven basket-like bag, I'd stuffed the student handbook, the American lit text, a couple of paperbacks, a lesson plan book and grade book, along with my lunch and after-school coaching clothes, and hauled both basket and purse to my car.

On the short drive to school that morning, I tallied my power points in an effort to reassure myself: I was the grown-up; I had the grade book; I knew names, or some of them, from the Beaverton pool and the Portland Golf Club where I'd lifeguarded, taught swim lessons, and coached. The bad dream drifted out the Kadett's window with the smoke from my first cigarette of the day. Still, by noon, sweat stains dripped down to my waist, and during lunch I drove home to change hoping no one would notice.

THANK GOODNESS THAT FIRST YEAR was over. Now at the end of June, I was beginning to imagine my second year. Instead of scrambling from story to story, book to book as they became available, I'd be part of a team that actually had a vision and a sense of purpose.

In our mission statement, we quoted from William Faulkner's Nobel Prize acceptance speech: "The poet's, the writer's, duty is to write about these things. It is his privilege to help man endure by lifting his heart, by reminding him of the courage and honor and hope and pride and compassion and pity and sacrifice which have been the glory of his past. The poet's voice need not merely be the record of man, it can be one of the props, the pillars to help him endure and prevail." We quoted Robert Kennedy: "Each time a [person] stands up for an ideal, or acts to improve the lot of others, or strikes out against injustice, he sends forth a tiny ripple of hope, and crossing each other from a million different centers of energy and daring those ripples build a current which can sweep down the mightiest walls of oppression and resistance." We were determined to introduce our students to authors who uplifted their spirits and encouraged them to stand up and act.

On Thursday morning I squeaked down the hall and Linda click-clacked her way to Dale's room where he had the coffee pot ready for us. We spent the early morning going through the stories, books, and films we'd teach. We were setting up a rotation schedule when the intercom buzzed and the principal's secretary's voice rattled through.

"Carolyn? Carolyn? You've got a call on hold in the office." I'd been dreading the call for a week, ever since grades had been mailed. The sixth-period smart-mouthed girl's grade, one of the fearsome four, had dropped to a C. She'd been furious when I handed out the report in class. This would be a parent demanding a conference. The morning's idealism quickly dissipated, and I felt slightly nauseated walking the empty hall to the office.

"Hello, Carolyn?" a pleasant voice began. "This is Blanche Whittaker, a family friend of Ethel Kennedy." She told me she was from Seattle, that we were almost neighbors. Her husband was Jim Whittaker, the Mount Everest climber. Did I know him? she asked. He'd led Bobby on the expedition up Mount Kennedy. They were close friends.

I listened and mumbled while she talked on.

"Mrs. Kennedy is trying to fulfill all of Bobby's wishes as best she can. He wanted his children to work with you. She wonders if you can come back here for a year? As governess."

If this were a film, I'd fall back onto a chair dumbstruck. Maybe I did. A little window had opened, and excitement, hope, the promise of adventure rushed in a moment before obligation and duty slammed it shut.

"Oh no. I just signed a contract with the district to teach an-other year."

Mrs. Whittaker persisted. "Well, maybe you can check on that. Ask for a leave of absence. You wouldn't be starting until August." And she gave me a number to call after I'd talked with my principal. "Ask for Blanche when you call."

What does a governess do? I wondered. Julie Andrews as Maria running over green hills with little kids in tow came to mind. Or Mary Poppins floating over London. Or Jane Eyre! I'm sure I ran back to the classroom and shouted the news. I'd been asked to be a governess for Robert Kennedy's kids. I had the Kennedys' phone number! If a parent wanted to complain about a student's grade, I didn't care. I'd been inoculated with celebrity power.

"You don't want to miss this opportunity," the principal told me when I asked if it was possible to break my contract. A long summer of waiting began. They wanted me in Hyannis Port on August 15.

Chapter 4

SUMMER

I LAY AWAKE UPSTAIRS, TOO EXCITED TO SLEEP, LISTENING TO THE night sounds—the lift and fall of fir boughs outside the window, whispers through the poplar stand up the road, cats yowling from somewhere beyond the garage. The room felt hot and stuffy while my mind jostled between disbelief and anticipation the way it had after I'd made the Olympic team or before my first day of teaching. *Is this really happening?* I wondered. I tried to imagine myself working in Hyannis Port on the Kennedy Compound. Had it only been a year since I'd visited the East Coast and toured by Hyannis? My thoughts returned to the previous spring, 1967.

THANKS TO FIFTEEN HOURS OF Advanced Placement credit, I'd graduated a term early, and what money was left from my summer and campus jobs paid for a week of ski lessons in Sun Valley and a plane ticket to New York. I lived with Bob and Helen Burke who were like second parents to me, as mine had been for their daughter, Lynn, when she came to Portland in 1959 to train for swimming. They'd always welcomed me—after the 1960 Olympics, after the 1961 European tour, and again over spring break my senior year in high school. When I wrote to ask if I could come for a visit, Bob had answered that my room was ready and he'd get discount tickets to *Mame*.

All spring I'd ridden the bus from the Burkes' house to downtown Flushing, then hopped onto the number 7 subway to Midtown. Bob got me tickets to Broadway matinees where I watched Mary Martin and Robert Preston and Angela Lansbury perform in plays reviewed in the *New Yorker*. I'd almost saved enough *New Yorker* covers to wallpaper one side of my bedroom. A tour of the United Nations and another at Lincoln Center filled other days. I window-shopped at Saks Fifth Avenue and Bergdorf Goodman's, wandered through the lobby of the Plaza hotel, had a drink at the Sherry-Netherland. *Barbara Fealy would order a martini*, I thought when I sat down.

Of all my mother's friends, only one had a career outside the home. Barbara Fealy, smart, witty, and passionate, was one of the most noted landscape architects in the Northwest. At her house we talked politics, literature, art, and philosophy, and I idolized her. She'd given me books by Eleanor Roosevelt and Margaret Bourke-White and subscriptions to the *New Yorker* and the *Saturday Review*. She told me that she knew what it was like to grow up in a backwater. You have to fight as a woman to get recognition. She fostered my ambition to be more than an athlete. *Here's to you, Barbara*, I thought as I sipped my drink, pretending that she was with me.

A friend from college traveled with me for a while. We met up in her sister's below-ground-floor Manhattan apartment, not much bigger than a dormitory room, where we planned our adventures while smoking cigarettes that her stewardess sister had filched from a plane. We bused to Washington, DC, first, then headed north and east on our way to the Montreal World's Fair, taking a long detour out to Cape Cod in Massachusetts.

I can't remember what fantasy brought us hours out of the way. Had we expected to glimpse Jackie and Caroline strolling down the street? When we stepped off the Peter Pan bus, Hyannis was just a wet, gray seaside town like any along the Oregon or Washington coast. A bit rundown. No magic, no beauty. We walked along the streets and poked around a gift shop. Maybe I thought we'd see something special there, something beyond a *Life* magazine photograph, but like many real things, Hyannis had been quite ordinary. The whole experience had left me with a vague sense of searching for something but forgetting what exactly.

Looking back on that time now, some memories are photographic, bright images surrounded by black. Maybe the image animates briefly and then returns to a still. Here's one: I'm riding back to Flushing one late afternoon on a steamy overcrowded subway hanging on to a ceiling strap, my bicep beside my cheek. A black soot line edges the cuff crease of the orange silk dress I'd put on fresh that morning. Incinerators burned on every rooftop, and cinders rained on the city day and night back then.

Other images arise from New York in 1967 and flicker past with no connecting details. It's as if you're riding the subway and the lights in the car flicker and dim and come on again so brightly you see the person across from you, her face sagging toward sleep. Or while you are looking out the window at the black walls and reflected images of riders, the train jostling along, an unexpected light bursts into the car, the brakes squeal, and you see the white tiles, the graffiti scrawls, and a man bending toward a bundle before you are past and back into the darkness.

You might remember the action, the look on a face, the gesture, but nothing else. Or the image may grow into a scene, dialogue pouring forth in a familiar exchange from a story you've told repeatedly over the years. Sometimes the memory is obscure, like a low place in a far field where fog gathers over an ancient streambed. It evokes emotion as sensate as mist on your cheek without reference to any specific event.

It's three hundred and seventy-five miles from Hyannis to Montreal, eleven hours by bus, but not a single memory of that long ride remains. All I remember of the Expo is an American exhibit comprised of a wall of hats designating professions: a baseball cap, a chef hat, a football helmet, and a mortarboard. Police hats, sailor caps, engineer caps, nurse caps. Billed, peaked, hard, flat, fedoras, berets, and boaters. The wall of hats and a short film of hopscotch patterns from different American cities and jump-rope girls from different sections of New York each with a unique version of skipping rhymes. For someone who grew up in semirural suburbia, a place without sidewalks, the exhibit seemed as foreign as one from France or Thailand. The memory subway rattles away from Montreal, another seven hours back to New York City, and all that's left of Expo '67 are two USA exhibits: hats and a jump-rope movie.

More memories of that time back East, sudden well-lit images, materialize from the darkened passages: My friend and I have finished a tour of West Point. We're on a double date that Lynn Burke has arranged for us. After two martinis in a restaurant overlooking the Hudson River, my cadet offers a light to the cigarette I've pulled from its pack. When I reach to roll the ash, I see another cigarette burning in the ashtray. I'm now smoking two at once, but still sober enough to pretend not to notice. Later in the hotel, we laugh and laugh about it.

Or at intermission of a Broadway matinee, women crowd in the balcony lobby, everyone lighting up cigarettes, the space filling with perfume, voices, and smoke. A woman in front of me backs into my lit cigarette, and when she steps away, a black singed circle brands her rump. In another year, I'll do the same to myself while flying between Washington, DC, and New York on the Eastern shuttle. My hand drops, and suddenly a black hole appears in the gray wool of an I. Magnin mini-legged pantsuit. *Damn it,* I think. *Damn it.*

Or on the long bus ride from New York, I light one cigarette from another, my throat dry and aching, the bus blue with smoke. *Why am I having another one? Why am I even smoking?* Hadn't the health teacher at Oregon told us that smoking wouldn't kill us, at least not right away? The first effect of smoking would be appetite suppression and weight loss, he'd said. A good reason to begin. The girls in the sorority house who smoked were thin. So was Mrs. Ferrin, my high school English teacher, and Mrs. Malagon, my student teacher supervisor. We smoked everywhere back then, back in the 1960s. In college classrooms, every desk hosted a butt-filled tin can. The sociology professor lectured for fifty minutes, never smoke-free. "Gotta match?" served as introduction to seatmates in lecture halls.

It had taken only a couple of weeks my senior year in college to become an accomplished smoker, a grown-up, an intellectual with my coffee and cig and *Oedipus Rex* critical essays. I was a twenty-year-old student teacher when I stood in front of those juniors and seniors at North Eugene High who were sixteen and seventeen. Smoking seemed the hallmark of adulthood. My brother smoked unfiltered Pall Malls, my father Tareytons. I chose Camel straights. *It's what Hemingway probably smoked,* I thought. I'd arrive at North each morning with the car windows down, radio blaring, and cigarette smoke trailing. I wanted to convey a new image—not a swimmer or jock but an English teacher, like Mrs. Ferrin. Like Mrs. Malagon, who never seemed to watch me teach but spent her free period smoking, drinking coffee, and chatting in the teachers' room while I struggled through *Oedipus* with the Advanced Placement class.

I STAYED IN NEW YORK another month after my friend left, not ready to go back home but out of money. With no summer job lined up, I wouldn't have a paycheck until the end of September. *How do people get jobs in New York?* I wondered. Placards in windows offered "job placement," but the buildings looked sooty and the signs tattered. What could I do for a month or so without any city skills? Lynn, who was a second-year teacher, dropped by her parents' house after school one day and suggested we look through the want ads. We sat in the kitchen, the paper spread out on the table, and she turned right to the section labeled "Mother's Helpers."

"These are perfect," she said. "If it's terrible, at least it won't last long."

I'd been a lifeguard but never a babysitter. A mother's helper lived in, basically a short-term nanny. We found one listed for two kids, two weeks, in Jericho, Long Island. Not too long, not too far away—perfect, Lynn thought.

In my application letter, I listed my qualifications: college degree, guaranteed high school teaching job, lifeguarding. Within a week I had a phone interview, and Lynn sat with me in the kitchen while I called. The mother questioned my experience with children, and I told her I'd been a swim instructor and lifeguard for several years.

"Tell her about the Olympics," Lynn elbowed me and whispered while the woman described the situation: the kids were five and two, a girl and a boy. The dad was going away on a business trip, and she wanted a companion, a house helper, a babysitter, someone who would be good with the kids. She had a private audiology practice in her home, and the job would be to keep the kids busy and quiet while she worked.

Lynn whispered again, "Tell her..." and I worked it in. Being an Olympic swim champion pretty much sealed the deal. I didn't yet know the value of playing that particular card beyond the swimming world. It had gotten me jobs lifeguarding, and I knew that certain parents paid extra for me to give their kids private lessons. Using it to get a babysitting job was new to me though. I had no idea that it may have influenced my hiring as an English teacher or that it would cement a job with the Kennedys.

There's a big difference between being a lifeguard and a nanny. A lifeguard can whistle down any kid large or small and have backup for compliance. An in-house nanny has to handle both child and parent twenty-four hours a day. I'd never been a babysitter, never had a younger brother or sister, never taken an early childhood psychology class or given much thought to managing preschoolers. The five-year-old girl figured out pretty quickly how much fun a power struggle could be. I worked on wearing her out by playing outdoors nonstop. Several afternoons the mom arranged for us to go to the community pool so I could give her swim lessons.

In the pool, there were no power struggles, but at home, she took control of the backyard, a cookie-cutter square exactly the same as the next-door neighbor's, and the next and the next, with a minuscule cement patio and a red-and-green swing set. She would stand at her yard's edge and yell into the neighbor's yard, "This is my prah-pah-dee. You can't step on it."

The little boy pumping away on his swing would look over and yell back, "I can too."

"It's *my* prah-pah-dee!'" She exercised her power struggle with him.

Sometime during the second week, the Arab-Israeli War broke out. In Jericho, a predominately Jewish neighborhood, the war dominated every conversation. Over one weekend, a fundraising campaign raised hundreds of thousands of dollars to support Israel. The mother talked about it constantly, and we kept the TV on nonstop, listening to speeches and discussion from the United Nations. After one speech, I called home. "I think we're going to war," I told my mom. "I'm kind of scared."

"What are you talking about?" she asked.

The affairs of Israel and Egypt or Jordan didn't mean much back in Portland. It reminded me of a friend saying her brother had called from New Haven in 1962 to say goodbye and he loved them. He was sure that the East Coast would be bombed by Russia during the Cuban Missile Crisis. We had snickered riding home from swim practice. *What on earth is he worried about?* we'd wondered. But everything seemed more serious and consequential in the East. Life was more immediate, more important. People knew things in New York that they didn't in Portland.

As a mother's helper, I earned enough to stay extra weeks in New York and to buy a matinee ticket to see Lauren Bacall in *Cactus Flower* and an evening performance of the New York Philharmonic, where Andre Kostelanetz conducted the world premiere of a piece that included Anne Draper and E. G. Marshall reading from correspondence between Emily Dickinson and T. W. Higginson.

I'D BEEN PRETTY SURE THAT summer that I would begin teaching at Beaverton High School somewhat worldly and sophisticated. Now I wondered if any of those experiences would matter inside the Kennedy Compound.

Everyone wanted to help me get ready for the Kennedys'. Two married friends whose husbands had National Guard duty and didn't want to be home alone invited me to stay with them, each with young children. *How lucky*, I thought. *A chance to get some childcare training.* For two weeks, I lived in Northeast Portland with a six-month-old and his mom. Then I moved up to Wauna Lake, a tiny cabin community of summer dwellers above the Columbia River. My friend had a two-year-old who she kept on a strict schedule. I practiced feeding and cleanups, potty time and nap time, story time and play time. In the afternoons, we strapped a life jacket on the toddler, launched the boat, and puttered over to the swim dock. There, the running, splashing, crying, flirting, pouting teens and preteens reminded me of the behaviors one gets with older kids. Other moms who hung out on the dock lounging and tanning and talking wondered if the Secret Service had interviewed me yet—or the FBI? Had anyone talked to my principal?

"Not that I know of," I'd answer, wondering if they had or when they would or if they might be watching me.

In late July, Linda and her husband, Craig, and I drove together up to Hood River for a sorority sister's wedding. After the reception, we stopped along the Columbia at a new resort and sat outside by the river drinking and talking. Linda and I gossiped about everyone at the wedding the way you do after an event: Who was there and who wasn't. What so-and-so said after a couple of drinks. We told endless remember-when stories. Craig nursed his beer and listened. Then we moved on to horror stories from our first year of teaching and then to tales of other teachers. After the sun went down, late light reflected rosy off the river, and we watched as the sailboats drifted back to dock. Linda wondered if I'd go sailing in Hyannis.

"I don't know how to sail," I said, wondering if I'd be asked to help on a boat and what I'd do then. That began a deluge of questions: What would be my duties? Would I be responsible for all the kids? Who else lived on the compound? Where would I sleep? Who would I meet? What were the names again?

"You have to write everything down. Everything," she said.

After a few drinks in the late-July twilight beside the Columbia River, it seemed a bit unreal that I'd ever be anywhere else. *Maybe it's all a joke*, I thought. *A hoax.*

"Has anybody talked to you about me?" I asked.

"Yes," she said. "I told them you smoke and drink and carry on. I bet they're here now watching."

We looked around at the riverside tables full of sunburned families and Saturday-night dates. No one seemed interested in us. Linda bobbed her head toward a nearby table where a guy with a crew cut and a half-empty pint leaned into his bleached-blonde date.

"What about him?" Linda nodded, and we giggled while Craig got up to order another round of drinks.

Edith Green's word and the senator's California invitation were all the background checks that occurred. They were enough, apparently, although for the rest of the summer I half expected someone to say they'd been contacted for a reference. Sometimes, when trying to imagine myself just outside the frame of the magazine photos I studied daily, I'd get a sudden sensation of being watched, but I was reading a lot of mysteries that summer.

Look magazine had arrived at the end of June, with a photo of Mrs. Kennedy and all her children smiling on the cover, unaware of the tragedy that was crashing toward them, had already happened by the time the photo was published. For weeks I studied the picture, memorizing names, ages, hair color and style, imagining what each child would be like. At night, I'd run down the list:

Kathleen was oldest at sixteen, named after the senator's sister who had died in a plane crash in 1948. Her dark hair, side parted, looked to be growing toward folk singer length.

Next came Joseph, fifteen, named for the senator's father and his oldest brother who'd died in the war. He looked like a football player, tall and heavyset. *Maybe a lineman with his toothy grin*, I thought.

Bobby Junior, fourteen, looked slightly bewildered and a little geeky, like many a freshman boy. According to the article, he had two falcons he flew regularly and a terrarium housing a giant turtle and various reptiles.

Those three would be easy to recognize, and then they'd be gone, off to boarding schools.

The middle four kids would be my main responsibility.

David Anthony, thirteen, looked like an angel in the picture, his blonde hair cut with bangs, his eyes squinting against the sun.

Mary Courtney, her face covered with freckles and her dark hair pulled into ponytails tied with pink ribbons, looked friendly.

She sat clutching a little brother, holding him still, I imagined. She'd turn twelve in early September.

Next in line was Michael LeMoyne, ten, named for the president's lifelong friend LeMoyne (Lem) Billings. He was the only one out of uniform. The older boys wore blue oxford shirts, the little ones white polos, but Michael wore brown paisley. *He's the independent*, I thought.

Tucked in close behind Mrs. Kennedy was little blonde Mary Kerry, eight. Do they call the girls by both names? I wondered. Mary Kerry? Mary Courtney? Could I tell them apart? Yes! Freckles = Courtney. Blondie = Kerry.

It's not until you see a large family together that you notice how very different siblings can look. The three "babies"—Christopher, Matthew, and Douglas—could have been from different families.

Christopher, five, had Courtney's freckles and Joe's smile but his own Charlie Brown round head.

Matthew Maxwell Taylor, three (*What do they call him?* I wondered), with his chocolate-brown eyes and a soft, wistful air, seemed a cuddle bunny on Mary Courtney's lap.

The real baby, Douglas Harriman, struggled in Mrs. Kennedy's arms and waved to someone off camera, unaware of the photographer.

Here was the clan: Kathleen, Joseph, Bobby, David, Courtney, Michael, Kerry, Christopher, Matthew, Douglas. I recited their names like a nightly prayer. Another baby was due before Christmas.

I must have filled two suitcases with clothes for every occasion I could imagine. Shorts and bathing suits, tennis shoes, jackets—all for outdoor activities I'd read about in the magazines. I thought I'd be teaching swimming for sure. I didn't know what

Gretchen and I sunbathe at Wauna Lake in the late summer before we each leave on new adventures.

else. Touch football? Yes. Sunday Mass? Yes. Dinners? It would be hot and humid I assumed, the way it had been in Detroit at the Olympic Trials and in New York the previous August. In went all my spring school clothes. My mom would ship out the cold weather wardrobe later to the Kennedy house in Virginia, an estate called Hickory Hill.

The summer oozed along, and I felt both excited and reluctant, the way you do sometimes before setting off into the unknown. I spent one last afternoon at Wauna Lake with my friend Gretchen, lying out on the back dock talking about books and teaching and our uncertain futures. She was leaving her teaching job at Sunset for graduate school at Stanford and I was going East, unlike our other friends who would soon be returning to the classroom. After the sun fell behind the foothills and shadows greened the lakes, we took out the canoe and paddled along the shoreline in and out of channels and dead ends. Startled turtles slid off their logs, and froggy choruses silenced as we paddled past. We didn't know when we'd see each other again. She'd be home for Christmas, but would I? We talked about our friend since grade school, Gretchen R., whose husband was going to Viet Nam, and then about a grade school classmate who'd been killed that year over there. I felt thoughtful and uncertain in ways I hadn't been the year before. Lights from the cabins glimmered from behind trees, and the first stars appeared in that blue-gray twilight that lingers so long in August.

Chapter 5

ARRIVAL IN HYANNIS PORT
AUGUST 1968

AT THE PORTLAND AIRPORT, I FELT LIKE AMELIA EARHART LEAVING her entourage and flying off into the vast unknown. Linda and another friend joined my parents and aunt to see me off. My father carried a long, heavy box that held an ice-packed Chinook salmon, his gift for Mrs. Kennedy. He'd slipped a jar of Columbia River sturgeon caviar—a specialty made from my grandfather's secret recipe—into my shoulder bag and reminded me that his rich patrons at the fish market told him it was better than any Russian caviar. He patted my back as my mother fussed with a corsage her sister had given me.

When the flight began to board, we lined up for two quick snapshots that captured my grinning attempt at poise. Before I picked up the salmon box, Auntie Mildred hooked my elbow and took me aside. She had something special for me, she said. From her handbag, she took an amber pill bottle and shook it. Two or three pills clinked inside. "These are just in case you get overexcited," she said. "Or if you can't get to sleep. Put them in your pocket till you need one."

The seven- or eight-hour flight shuddered across the country with a stopover in Chicago before continuing on to Boston. About an hour before landing, excitement and fear built like a storm. *Who'll be at the airport? What if it's Mrs. Kennedy? What will we talk about?* I fumbled in my pocket and pulled out the bottle. "Valium," it said. Within a few minutes, I experienced myself lift up off my seat and float close to the luggage rack to peer down at my seated body. *How strange*, I mused calmly.

At baggage claim I could barely lift my suitcases. Thankfully, Bob, "the temporary governess," he told me, carried them to the car. I'm not sure what I'd expected exactly, but it wasn't Bob, who was happy I'd finally arrived to take over duties. He was really a boatman, he told me. I'd see him tomorrow on the *Marlin*, he said, but his comment didn't mean anything, and besides I was lost in self-doubt: Had I really thought that Mrs. Kennedy would be meeting me at the airport?

The drive from Boston to Hyannis took almost an hour and a half, enough time to ask questions and hear stories. We drove south and then east out the Massachusetts peninsula that hooks into the Atlantic Ocean, Cape Cod Bay to the north, Nantucket Sound, where Hyannis sits, to the south.

"What are my duties exactly?" I asked.

He rattled off a list: first off I'd get the kids up for Mass, around seven thirty, get them dressed, cleaned, and into the car with Mrs. Kennedy—or Mrs. K, as he referred to her. Then I'd have to get them to meals on time. I'd be eating with them unless it was too crowded. *How will I know?*

He answered before I spoke, "You'll figure it out. Just stay out of Mrs. Kennedy's way."

"What do you mean?" I asked, feeling a slightly sedated chill.

He rambled on and on about what he meant. I'd have plenty to do because the kids were all on schedules, and it would be my job to get them everyplace on time: Mass, breakfast, lessons—swimming, tennis, riding—on different days. At twelve thirty we'd sail out to the island for a picnic lunch. He assured me that Mrs. K would have someone with her. He advised that I stick with the kids. When the boat returned, it would be playtime until five. That's when the kids were supposed to read.

"Good luck with that," Bob said. Dinner was at five fifteen for the little ones, and I'd need to clean them up...clothes, nails, hair, everything.

"But why would I have to stay out of her way?"

"Stay away or you'll get more work to do." Bob laughed. "You'll figure it out."

We drove into Hyannis, that little beach town I'd visited the year before, around eleven thirty at night, winding through dark streets beyond the shops and past hulking houses with a few lights on or none. Bob pulled the car to a stop before a wooden booth, like a ticket seller's at high school football games, and a man leaned out to look. Bob flicked a wave and pointed at me. "New governess—coming in." And the man motioned us through. I felt a little thrill at my title, not yet aware of all the privilege it would provide.

We rolled slowly along a dark drive, the air heavy with salt and the remainder of the day's heat, until a lit house appeared—a big, white, barn-shaped house. As we drove through the covered carport, someone stepped out the side door, and when we pulled in beside another car, Bob said that the crew had waited up to meet me. "We'll go in for a minute, but you're sleeping at Mrs. John's, not here." I stared at him, thinking how impossible it seemed that I would be sleeping in Jackie Kennedy's house. *Is this a joke?* I wondered.

I grabbed the salmon box from the trunk and lugged it in. Inside the Robert Kennedy house, in a sort of entry room with a desk and a sofa and a couple of comfortable-looking chairs, Bob introduced me to two other employees: Tim-the-Tennis-Teacher and Joe-the-Butler. Both looked young. Tim was tall, handsome in a gangly sort of way, with a sharp, straight nose. He was a college student who'd taught tennis and run errands for the Kennedys the past few summers. Joe, on the other hand, was short with enormous, expressive brown eyes, curly black hair, and a British accent. I handed the salmon to him when he told me he worked in the kitchen.

They welcomed me with smiles, a catalogue of who would be visiting over the weekend, and the threatening information that in one year they had gone through fourteen governesses. "Hope you're up for a challenge." Joe laughed.

I survived my first year of teaching, didn't I? How hard could this be? The Valium had worn off, and my nerves were a little shaky, but I laughed with them and followed Bob out into the dark, through a gap in the hedge, and across a wide lawn to where I'd be staying for a couple of weeks—the John F. Kennedy house. Light from an upstairs window cast a path over the grass. Bob carried my little white hatbox suitcase and the big Samsonite I'd taken to Rome. I followed him upstairs to a small bedroom wallpapered in a blue-green print and simply furnished with wood, antiques I was sure. A drop-leaf table with two stacks of books and a little reading lamp sat next to the double bed, which had been turned down for me. The room had a warm and cozy feel with its low, slant-roofed ceiling. I wondered how much time I'd have for reading until Bob told me to take my time in the morning. It would be my last time off in quite a while, he warned.

Postcard from the corner tourist shop sent home to identify my room and where we played softball in the afternoons.

Even though it was after one in the morning, I sat on my bed and wrote my first letter home beginning with flight details, Bob's warnings, a weather report (it was seventy-eight degrees when I arrived), and a detailed description of my room in "Jacqueline's house." Original oil paintings hung on the wallpapered walls, and antique tables, chests, and chairs gave it a cozy feel. A huge walk-in closet off the bathroom had empty hangers and shelves for my clothes. The linens, towels, and even a bathrobe for me came from France, I scribbled breathlessly before collapsing into bed.

MORNINGS ON THE OREGON COAST emerge from forest shadows and gray mist. It almost felt like home when light whispered me awake the next morning. My eyes blinked to sea-green light, a salt-scented breeze ruffling the sheer white curtains. The oil painting

View from my bedroom in President John Kennedy's house overlooking the Robert Kennedy house, Ambassador Joseph Kennedy's house, and Nantucket Sound.

caught my eye. *Had the driver last night really told me that this was the president's room, that he'd painted this picture?*

"You'll be staying here in Mrs. John's house until she gets back from Europe," Bob had said.

Just thinking that made my heart speed and my stomach clench. *Don't get excited, Carolyn. Get up and get moving.*

As soon as I looked out the window and saw the sunlight glaring off the sound, where already a few sailboats skimmed across the blue, I knew I was in a foreign land. From somewhere below, out of sight, children's voices piped high and indistinct. It was time to get out and meet the Kennedys. I took a deep breath and turned away from the window.

Downstairs I retraced the path Bob and I had taken at midnight, following a tall, unruly boxwood hedge along the lawn, aiming for the gap I knew opened into the Robert Kennedy driveway.

About halfway across the yard, jitters struck, like they had my first day of teaching. *Keep walking,* I ordered myself. Overhead a few gulls hung on the updrafts, white against the clear, blue sky. *Is anyone watching from the silent house behind me?*

Ahead the house stood still and quiet, the side-door entrance closed. *Should I knock?* I wondered. Through its window I could see Joe, plates in hand, in a far-off room. The entry room, which I'd learn was also the secretaries' office (there were two working up on the cape that summer), was empty. I knocked and turned the knob at the same time, and Joe looked up, smiled, and put out his hand to wait. He disappeared and quickly returned, empty-handed.

"Good morning. Ready to get with it, kid?" he asked in a greeting I'd come to know as all Mrs. Kennedy.

I followed him past the desks and worn-out sofa, past a carpeted staircase, and into the far room. At one end of the dining-room table, Ethel Skakel Kennedy sat talking on the phone. She looked smaller than I'd expected, but solid, her thick sun-bleached hair tangled and wild as if she'd come in from a windstorm, and that leathery brown skin of women who've spent too much time outdoors playing tennis, sailing, skiing, lying out in the sun. Her eyes roved the room while she talked, catching everything momentarily in her foxy gaze. She'd be on the phone or talking with friends almost every time I saw her those first weeks. Even when she stopped talking, you could *hear* her.

Joe-the-Butler pointed me to a seat at the other end of the table, not at the end but next to it. "Would you care for eggs or cereal this morning for breakfast?" Joe asked in his proper English accent. I was afraid I might break out laughing.

"Wheaties?" I said.

Mrs. Kennedy glanced up, made eye contact, and talked on.

If anyone else was at the table that morning, I've forgotten them. All my senses focused on her. Perched on the edge of my chair, I slurped at my Wheaties, waiting for the opportunity to introduce myself and present my father's gift. When she finally ended her call, I stood, identified myself, and handed her the little jar of caviar.

"Terrific, kid. We'll serve it tomorrow night when the Whittakers and Glenns are here."

Did she know about the fresh Chinook delivered to Joe the night before? Before I could ask, another call came in, and her focus shifted. I pushed on into my first day with no real instructions. *What next?* I wondered.

In the bright entry, a young woman now sat at a desk by the front door: Lee Geisen, Mrs. Kennedy's secretary, who would become my touchstone as the weeks unfolded. This morning she looked up from the cluttered desk, a cigarette smoldering in an ashtray, and commented, "You must be Carolyn. Welcome to the monkey house."

Lee was older than the boys I'd met the night before, in her late twenties. She'd served in the Peace Corps in Tanzania for two and a half years, had met Robert and Ethel at the regional school where she taught when they were touring Peace Corps sites. She told me Ethel remembered her when she returned and applied for a job at Hickory Hill as business secretary for the family. Lee had a solemn look, her long dark hair side-parted and drawn back, her profile like a Modigliani, but her wit was sharp. She reminded me of the smart girls in college who looked pensive but made wisecracks from the back of the room.

While I was talking with Lee, a little person burst in from outside, all brown eyes and shivers, under a wet towel. I recognized him without Lee's help—Matthew Maxwell Taylor Kennedy, aged three.

"Come on," I said. "Let's get you dressed."

"Max, this is Carolyn, the new governess. Show her where your room is and introduce her to Ena." He chattered out an "okay," and I followed his lead up the stairs, down a short hall, and into a sunny room just above the office.

Someone with an accented voice called a greeting from the bathroom. It had to be Ena, the nanny or nurse—I wasn't sure of her title—who'd been with the family since Kathleen's birth sixteen years before. She'd come from Costa Rica, where her own daughter was being raised by family there. Ena wasn't generous with her stories, but I'd hear some of them over the year. She'd mothered every child, waking for night feedings after the baby nurse left, helping the toddlers to walk, toilet training them, breaking up fights, and keeping them in line when necessary. Once they got to school age, the governess was supposed to take over. But all this I'd deduce over time.

Max pulled his summer uniform from a shelf: faded-blue turtleneck and navy-blue cotton knit shorts. The little kids wore shorts and turtlenecks or shorts and Izods every day, but the older boys lived in surfer shorts and the girls alternated between bathing suits, riding clothes, and pastel-print pullover shifts.

Ena came into the room nudging Dougie in front of her as Max pulled on his shorts. She wore a white uniform dress, slightly wet from bath splashes, and I introduced myself. She seemed shy, her English accented. I hoped she would be a help to me, but when she turned away, toweling off Dougie and murmuring to him, I felt dismissed.

Max and I headed back down the stairs just as Christopher,

his year-older brother and roommate, streaked out of the dining room and through the office to the yard.

"Meet Christopher George," Lee said. "He turned five on the Fourth of July and thinks he's boss of the world." I'd already recognized him from my photo studies, with his round head and alert blue eyes under wispy blondish bangs. Lee suggested that Max might show me the beach and maybe we'd find Christopher and bring him along. Off we went to play in the sand, where we dug holes and threw rocks and Max told me stories and climbed on my back and took my hand to pull me through beach grass and to wade in the sound. But no Christopher George. By eleven we were through with the beach and returned to the house.

Bob sat sprawled on the sofa. "We're going out today," he said, sounding bored. He told me to be down at the dock early because the *Marlin* sailed at twelve thirty and to wear a bathing suit under my clothes because they might make me swim. It sounded like both a threat and a tease.

Lee looked up from her desk, where now a Chihuahua sat curled on her lap, a little dog's safe haven from the Kennedys' menagerie. She introduced Rocky, a stray found in the Grand Canyon on last year's raft trip, now Lee's constant companion on the cape.

"You want to be on the boat today," Lee advised, a chance for me to meet most of the kids. "They're curious, you know."

But I didn't know. So far, only Max had shown any interest in me. I ran through the list of who might be aboard: David, Courtney, Michael, Kerry, Christopher, and Max. Dougie would be home taking a nap. The oldest three, Kathleen, Joe, and Bobby, hadn't yet returned from summer travels, and the youngest three I'd at least seen.

Bob ran through the routine again. Every day he waited for a signal from the Ambassador's house that the boat would be available for a lunch cruise. Mrs. Kennedy and Pat Lawford usually sailed at noon, but the kids, both sets of Kennedys, the Shrivers, the Lawfords, and the Smiths plus the guests motored over to the island on the *Marlin*. Images I'd seen in *Time* and *Look* and *Life* of the Kennedy clan rolled through my mind. The adults would be recognizable for sure, but the kids? How many would be on board?

Bob liked to talk and was happy to answer: if everyone showed up, there could be fifteen or more. Then he went on about the boat, a fifty-foot, mahogany-paneled, wide-hulled "rum runner" that had been in the Kennedy family since the early 1950s. It belonged to the Ambassador, but he rarely went out anymore since his stroke. It was for the families, mostly the women and the little kids, who liked to motor out and picnic on an island and then go for a swim. The bigger boys, I'd learn, were too cool to go picnicking with the moms.

BECAUSE IT WAS TOO EARLY to change, Max and I went back outside to find Dougie and Ena. He led me out to the paved area behind the house where the cars were parked and the kitchen wing extended. A lazy-looking sheepdog lay stretched in the sun. "That's Panda," Max said in his high three-year-old voice.

"And that's Freckles," Christopher shouted, stepping out from behind some shrubs, his cousin Willie Smith tagging along. I'd recognized Freckles, the black-and-white springer spaniel, as the senator's dog who'd come campaigning with him in Oregon. An iconic photo taken on the Oregon coast—the senator, his pant

Max, three years old, and Christopher, five years old, in front of the big boys' clubhouse/band room.

legs rolled, running barefoot through the water at surf's edge, Freckles jogging behind—had been *Life* magazine's heartbreaking cover the week after he was killed.

Across from the kitchen and parking area, close to the hedge separating the RFK property from the JFK was a garage, a converted clubhouse. We peeked inside where I could see a drum set and a couple of guitars leaning against a rumpled sofa.

"David and Bobby and Chris Lawford have a band, and they practice in there," Christopher announced with authority. "And over there's Grandpa Joe's house," he continued with his tour-guide voice, pointing to the big white house set apart from the two brothers' houses. "That's where we see movies." Lee told me later that yes, indeed, there was a movie theater in the basement and every Saturday night the clan gathered to watch a film.

All this time, Ena had been standing outside the kitchen door watching, Dougie playing in a flowerbed with a shovel and bucket. She might have been relaxing in the sun. She might have been assessing my engagement with *her* kids. Probably both. She'd have an opinion. I suspected that her evaluation of me would determine my success. I don't remember thinking that explicitly, but I knew the importance of hierarchy and respect among women. I'd watched it with my mom and her friends whenever they organized a fundraiser or a church dinner. You didn't want to la-di-da into their domain with your twenty-year-old's bright ideas. I hoped Ena liked what she saw and that she'd be an ally.

Around noon I returned to the JFK house to change into a bathing suit and a bright pink-and-orange-striped shift. Walking across the lawn, I reflected on the morning. It had gone pretty well. Mrs. Kennedy seemed pleasant, Lee was funny, and I'd fallen in love with Max. I was feeling rather jaunty in my boating attire striding across the lawn. Beyond the hedge gap, I could see Christopher and Willie standing in front of the clubhouse where a Coke machine dispensed free Cokes to anyone who punched the buttons. They were punching away and soon had Cokes in hand.

I called out a howdy and waved, my smile as generous as Julie Andrews's. Which boy began to shake his bottle first, I couldn't say, but both shook and shook the bottles before taking aim and lifting their thumbs. Coke erupted, spraying my face, arms, dress.

I lunged, grabbing Christopher's arm just above the elbow at the lifeguard's nerve that releases a victim's grip, yanked him toward me, and hoarsely whispered in his ear, "Don't ever do that to me again." His face turned bright red. I let go, turned, and strode back to Mrs. John's house, my back rigid. Silence followed. I stripped the dress, rinsed my arms and legs, pulled on a clean shift, and ran back to join the armada.

On board, Max plunked onto my lap, but Chris and Willie kept their distance. Four preteen girls clambered aboard, their voices a bit too loud, their laughs little explosions. They conspicuously ignored Max and me and disappeared into the cabin.

"Who're they?" I asked Max, my interpretive guide.

"Courtney, Caroline, Sydney, and Maria."

Of course, I'd recognized Caroline Kennedy, and Courtney had to be the freckle-faced one leading the pack. They disappeared into the cabin before I could distinguish the other two, a blonde and a brunette.

"Is that your sister Kerry?" I asked Max, nodding toward the blonde at the center of a gang of eight- and nine-year-olds. We watched her riffle through the picnic basket and pull out a bag of potato chips, which she held up and out of reach as the other girls grabbed at her arm, laughing. Off they scrambled to the foredeck, Kerry chased by her cousins. She'd be a handful, I suspected, vying for center of attention.

As we motored out to sea, the grown-ups—Mrs. Kennedy, Pat Lawford, and guests—had chilled daiquiris made by Joe-the-Butler followed by a fancy picnic of soufflé and Sancerre. I was not invited to join them—and hadn't expected to be—and instead shared peanut butter and jelly with Max. I don't think there were any demands for me to swim that first day, or at least I didn't write home about it. What I remember is feeling the warm mass of Max on my lap and the bubble of isolation created by the noisy and rambunctious kids, performing for someone new but not ready to break the fourth wall and talk to the audience. If I was smart I might have thought, *All in good time.* More likely I felt slightly overwhelmed by the sheer number of children and continuous erupting energy. I clung to Max as if he were a stuffed animal meant to keep me calm.

The boat returned to the compound around three, a routine followed most days for the rest of the summer unless the weather or the Ambassador canceled. The boys who hadn't gone on the picnic—Michael, Stevie Smith, and Tim-the-Tennis-Teacher—were waiting for us when we landed, and they snagged everyone for a softball game. Two kids called, "Captain!" and teams began to form made from cousins and neighbors, brothers and sisters, governesses and other employees all amid shouts and jostles.

"Are you playing?" someone asked, but no one seemed to listen, and I ended up last picked. Now I wonder whose team I played on. What I wrote home that night was that on my first at bat, I hit a double. In between innings the girl I'd picked out as Courtney announced to her cousins, "Our new governess went to the Olympics." They squinted their eyes and asked, "Where?"

Kennedy cousins, or "The Teen Posse" (left to right): Maria Shriver, twelve years old; Courtney Kennedy, twelve; Caroline Kennedy, eleven; and Sydney Lawford, twelve.

"Rome," I said, happy to finally be acknowledged.

"And you won a gold medal, didn't you?" Courtney asked again as if reconfirming what she already knew even though she'd ignored me throughout the whole boat trip.

"How old were you?" the tall brunette asked, sounding a bit accusatory.

"Fourteen," I answered. And whatever had held them back dissipated.

"What?" they said in unison. "Fourteen?!"

In between innings we talked, and soon I had four names matched to faces. Sydney Lawford was the slender blonde, and the brunette interrogator was Maria Shriver. Along with Caroline Kennedy, they composed a preteen posse that roved the grounds together. I'd get to know them better.

I got four more hits, and our team won 10 to 5. Suddenly, I was *in*. Or it felt like it after that game. Kerry, the eight-year-old blonde, linked arms with me and asked if I'd take her into the village to get a bike lock. Christopher wanted to go too, having forgotten or forgiven our noon encounter. With cash from Lee, we pedaled past the Secret Service station and the police posts on into town. By the time we returned, it was almost dinnertime. We weren't going to eat at home, Lee informed me. Instead, I was to accompany the children to the Lawfords' where every Wednesday they hosted the kid dinner. Thursday nights would be a regular cookout at West Beach Club, the swim center.

There was no time to ask about Friday. I dashed across the lawn again and up to my room to change, the fourth or fifth change of the day.

So this is what it's like, I thought. A blur.

Chapter 6

THE FIRST WEEKS

IF THE FIRST DAY FELT LIKE A BLUR, SO DID THE FIRST WEEK. ONE day slid into the next like slides in an out-of-control projector, like fish across a deck. The alarm blasted off at seven, and I'd clamor out of bed, check the weather from the window, and pull on Bermudas and a T-shirt or a summer shift with a sweater. Downstairs, the JFK kids' summer nanny, an Irish girl about my age who looked after the kids and did the cooking while the real governess was on vacation, would be putting on a kettle, and I'd skitter out and across the lawn, in the back door of the RFK house, and up the stairs to Courtney and Kerry's room for a gentle shake and a whisper to rouse them. Some days I drove them to Mass in Mrs. Kennedy's white Pontiac convertible with the red leather interior or in the yellow, wood-paneled Mercury, Detroit-made specially for the senator. Sometimes Caroline or Sydney Lawford joined us. On Sunday the whole family went together.

The first Mass I attended, the girls led the way to "their" pew and I followed, kneeling by the aisle, aware of whispers and nodding heads around us: "There they are, those poor little things." Beside me, Kerry fidgeted, and I reached out to put my hand on her knee. She looked up and smiled. When it came time for

Communion, I stepped into the aisle and waited for them to file out of the pew. On the way to the altar, Courtney and Kerry looked back at me expectantly, and I fell into line behind them. I hadn't had time for impure thoughts or deeds.

We were back for breakfast around nine, and then the action began. It might be playing with Max and Christopher or taking them to swim lessons at the Beach Club. It could be hitting tennis balls around with Kerry or heading out to the pier to fish. At first, I joined the kids on the *Marlin* and motored over to the island for a picnic lunch and a swim every day. On Wednesdays I took them to the Lawfords' for dinner and on Thursdays to the swim club.

On the weekend the guests arrived. Guests were always arriving, and Mrs. K had rented several old houses near the compound where they all stayed. Lee told me that when Mrs. John returned from Greece, I'd be staying in a room in one of the big rented houses several blocks away. "How big?" I asked.

"Big!" She might have added, "Like the House of the Seven Gables."

UNCLE TEDDY, AS THE KIDS called him (or Senator Ted as the employees did), returned after more than a month sailing up the Massachusetts coast and around its offshore islands. He'd chartered a sixty-foot yawl with a small crew after his brother's death and withdrawn to the sea to grieve. He was thirty-six years old, the youngest of four brothers, now the only one alive. When he came to the house, the little kids and the girls pulled at his arms, trying to tug him into play, but he'd usually rub their heads, muss their hair, and disappear inside to find Mrs. Kennedy or whoever was currently visiting.

The boat, available for another ten days, was big enough to carry the whole clan: Pat Kennedy Lawford and her three girls, Jean Kennedy Smith and her two boys, three Shriver kids, Caroline and John, and most of the children I'd begun to think of as "my kids." Most of the guests, identified for me only by name and a few stories sketched out by Lee, piled onboard: Blanche (who'd called me in June) and Jim Whittaker, the Seattle mountaineering friends. Ann and Colonel John Glenn, the first American astronaut to orbit earth. Liz and George Stevens Jr., filmmaker and producer who was working on a documentary about the senator. Bill vanden Heuvel, the senator's assistant attorney general during his brother's presidency. LeMoyne (Lem) Billings, an old family friend who'd just returned with Bobby Jr. after traveling in Africa. The only guests who didn't board were Art Buchwald and his wife, Ann, who were in town but chose not to sail—wisely, I would think later.

I'd been excited about sailing on a big boat out onto Nantucket Sound where Ishmael had begun his journey with Ahab. But the summer day we sailed had some of drizzly November about it. The two masts pierced into a fog that leaked mist on us as we came onboard. Some of the adults found a place helping the crew on deck; others stood looking out to the cloud-shrouded sea or hurried below to chat and lunch in a fancy cabin.

The children were crammed into a different below-deck cabin and I with them, where my stomach sloshed with the waves. In fact, almost as soon as we set sail I felt nauseous, and when one of boys threw up, I almost lost my breakfast. Max sat on my lap, moaning and crying until he fell asleep, and I didn't move for hours as we banged on the Nantucket waves. That foggy afternoon voyage shattered any fantasy of learning to sail or setting off for Typee.

On Monday I happily volunteered to drive the girls—Courtney, Kerry, Sydney Lawford, Maria Shriver, and Caroline—to what they called the farm each day for riding practice. It was possible to delay enough out at the farm or in stopping for treats on the way home to miss the *Marlin*'s launch. Eight ponies were stabled there, with names like Macaroni and Leprechaun, Atlas and Geronimo, Blarney and Bambino. The instructor and stableman, Freddy Bacon, a jolly young man who might have been a jockey but for the weight he carried, was prepping the girls for the end-of-summer events: the Osterville Pony Show, a serious equestrian competition with dressage and jumps, followed by the Grandpa Joe's Birthday Pony Show. Interspersed would be a dress-up day and a wilderness ride through the woods to a pond for bareback swimming with the horses. The corral and woods and pond, the practice for coming competitions, felt much more familiar to me than sailing or motorboating.

Driving the girls with the eight-track tape blaring out the Doors' "Alabama Song (Whiskey Bar)" while we all sang along made for a raucous start to the mornings. I'd lean against the fence under mostly sunny skies and watch the girls as they practiced their jumps and stops and sidesteps. Freddy would call out instructions, which I could tell the girls sometimes ignored. If anyone got too independent, he'd walk into the ring and turn the rider around to redo a jump. But mostly they seemed serious about practice, especially with the end-of-summer competitions coming up.

When the lesson ended and the girls had free riding time before cooldown and tack removal, Freddy would join me at the fence to talk and trade stories.

"She's the best of the bunch." He nodded toward Caroline. "She listens, and she practices. When her mother's here, she rides

Girl cousins ride into the pond on a day off from horse show training.

with her. It makes a difference." I wondered if he was suggesting that the other girls weren't serious or self-disciplined. Or was he implying that their mothers didn't pay enough attention? But I didn't ask what he meant. Out in the dusty ring, the girls chattered and laughed while the ponies cooled down. Maybe I'd share Freddy's observation with Lee or Joe to see what they thought.

We all traded stories and passed along rumors—who came in late, who didn't come home, when Mrs. John would return, who would go to the Democratic National Convention in Chicago August 26 to 29.

"Richard Burton called yesterday" was my tidbit one morning. He was narrating a documentary about the senator for the convention.

Another day it was "Frank Sinatra's flying Joe-the-Butler's brother out to his yacht to chef a dinner."

"I heard Eunice Shriver smokes Cuban cigars. She buys them in Paris and smoked one in the car all the way from the airport to the compound."

Joe was a wonderful source of information, and Freddy, who bunked out at the stables, was a ready listener.

Experiences came faster in this new world, and I worked hard to keep up with the gossip. I wanted to know the who's who of the rotating guests so I wouldn't seem ignorant. I recognized astronaut John Glenn and movie star names but needed briefings for politicians, artists, and journalists. Besides competently herding kids all day, I needed to keep my eyes and ears open for "news" in order to catch up with everybody else. Out on the farm, I could relax. I didn't need to impress Freddy. On Friday I asked him, "What's the Davis Cup? Someone's coming for lunch, and I don't know who he is. Arthur Ashe?"

The workers who had been on the cape all summer taking care of lessons and play, bedtimes and Mass, playing miniature golf or going to town for ice cream were as ready for summer to end as I'd been for the school year to end. For them my arrival meant escape, but for the kids, it made everything new again. I was game for driving into town for a cone or up to a challenge on the putt-putt course. Sure, I'd love to take a carload of girls to see the musical *The Fantasticks* and out afterwards to Howard Johnson's. Every time we drove past the Secret Service post, I could hear them call ahead to the police, "The governess is taking out a carload," and when we returned, they called back, "All are in with the governess."

One night after an early movie at the Ambassador's, the grown-ups disappeared somewhere for a late dinner, and the kids scattered across the compound. Courtney had a sleepover at the Lawfords' and Michael at the Smiths'. David had disappeared before the movie, out chasing trouble beyond the compound perhaps, leaving Kerry, Christopher, Max, and me to wander home through the dark and misty night. Ena took the boys upstairs for bed, but it was too early for Kerry, and she hung around me like those little gnats that hover just in front of your eyes. I was the only playmate available.

"Let's do the jigsaw," she said, referring to a barely begun puzzle that had been sitting beside the sofa ever since I'd arrived. That was the last thing I wanted to do—too tedious, too frustrating, too boring.

"Nah. Do you know any card games, like gin?" I asked, already realizing that there weren't many two-person card games to play with a nine-year-old.

But there was a two-person game that I'd learned and played when I was ten, a game to pass the time on long car rides to swimming meets. "Ever play Battleship?" I asked.

She shook her head.

"No? Geez, it's fun but I haven't played for years."

When I lifeguarded on rainy days, a few of the pool rats would hang out in the snack bar bored but unwilling to go home. I'd taught them to play then, and we'd sit in pairs with our secrets, sending out shots. Battleship would be a good game to introduce here as the weather became more unsettled and we more housebound.

"We need two sheets of paper each, and pencils," I said.

Kerry ransacked the secretary's desk for the necessary supplies and brought them back to the sofa. We sat side by side, each with a magazine on our laps for a makeshift desk, and I began to explain the instructions: first, we'd make a grid with one hundred squares.

A to J across the top, 1 to 10 down the side. I showed her how to make the grid and then a mockup of how to place the boats—five carriers, four battleships, three cruisers, three destroyers, and two submarines—all aligned in contiguous vertical, horizontal, or slant lines, not intersecting and strategically separated. The second grid was the shot record. We each had five guesses per turn, and a hit had to be announced when it occurred.

Kerry was a quick study, and we played a practice round before a real game. She studied her sheets and made hopeful guesses, her brown eyes bright, expecting to blast my battleships. Her intensity reminded me of my old swim team partner from years before. I'm not sure I'd ever seen her sit still for so long. We called it quits after two games, and I promised to play with her again in the morning. I'd won both games, but she'd made strategic guesses and gotten her hits. She had a competitive spirit, and we were well into our rematch on Sunday morning when Courtney came home.

"We're playing Battleship," Kerry announced, relishing her new status; she knew something Courtney didn't...yet.

By afternoon, the entire preteen posse wanted in. Courtney and Caroline picked it up right away, then Sydney and Maria. Michael cozied in next to me for a few games and then challenged the winner of Maria and Sydney. Even David stopped to watch before slouching out to the boys' music garage. After everyone was in bed one night and the Irish nanny and I sat down in the kitchen for a beer and a chat, she told me that Caroline was practicing to beat me, developing a strategy.

Maybe it was all my years at swim meets finding ways to pass the time or my work as a lifeguard where the pool was filled with mostly kids, or maybe it was that year of teaching under my belt, but I had no trouble shifting from playmate to shepherd, from

Christopher and I watch awards night at the swimming pool.

teacher to pupil, always alert to what was going on around me, who was watching, who was veering off play and into trouble. I could be both participant and observer, playmate and adult, although I admitted in a letter home that my title should be "official playmate," not governess.

I loved being recognized with the title. It had literary connotations and seemed to evoke authority even though I wasn't sure yet how much authority I actually had, let alone what my duties entailed because they seemed to shift daily as if I were in an improv show. The entire staff could have been a troupe of actors, each with his or her role to play for the audience of Mrs. K and her family and friends.

We were the cast who carried the family, each known by role: the secretary, the butler, the cook, the upstairs maid, the downstairs maid, the tennis teacher, the laundress, the governess. A name might be attached, like Joe-the-Butler or Tim-the-Tennis-Teacher. Ena, however, was Ena, no work identifier. She had become part of the family and would continue with them until the unborn baby, Rory, went off to school. Even then, the family would support her in a Florida retirement community where she would live to be 105.

Thinking back now, I see similarities between how I felt in the classroom my first year and that year at the Kennedys'. In both I'd felt like a performer, onstage with a captive audience that had to be managed and entertained. At the same time, I knew that at any moment a superior might appear to observe and evaluate, but I would never know how or when. In school at least I knew the curriculum, knew my hours and duties. School was a system I'd known my whole life—being governess was not.

I could be in the midst of a tickle fight rolling around on the floor with Christopher, Max, and Kerry and look up to see Ena standing, her hand on her hip, watching, her face inscrutable. *What does that stance mean? Disapproval?* I wondered. I'd smile, wait an instant, then resume playing, still unsure.

Once at bedtime Mrs. K appeared in the doorway while I was reading *Stuart Little* to Max and Chris. She lingered, leaning against the door frame. *Does she have something to tell me? Should I stop?* I wondered. When I reached the end of the chapter, she was gone. It would be several days before she mentioned that the boys liked to be read to. I wasn't sure if it was a compliment. I was used to a bit more feedback from supervisors, and I felt hungry for approval. I wanted to perform well, to please my audience.

I wanted to be worthy of the position, of the trust, to prove myself good enough, that age-old endeavor for many women, for anyone stepping out of their known role into a real or imagined "better place"—college, sorority, job, marriage, social class.

As a first-year teacher, I'd struggled to be good enough. Good enough to keep a class engaged and moving forward, good enough to understand what I was reading, and good enough to lead a discussion or encourage a slacker or critique a paper. Good enough to be as inspirational as the teachers I'd loved in fourth grade, in sixth, and again in tenth- and eleventh-grade English. I didn't think these things in the evenings after I'd read to Christopher and Max before bed or tucked Kerry in or scooted Courtney and Michael up the stairs and dimmed the lights in the office. I'd simply trudge back across the night-lit lawns to the JFK house, where the Irish nanny would greet me in the kitchen with the question, "How'd it go today?" and I'd answer, "Fine, I guess. She never tells me what to do or how I'm doing."

"Sure, don't worry. If you're doing anything wrong, you'll be told!"

And so I would be, but not right away, not during the grace period.

Chapter 7

COMINGS AND GOINGS

T<small>OWARD THE END OF</small> A<small>UGUST AND AS THE</small> D<small>EMOCRATIC</small> N<small>ATIONAL</small> Convention approached, the atmosphere shifted on the compound. One by one, the older kids returned from their summer travels. Bobby Jr. and Lem Billings had arrived first from Africa, followed by Kathleen, who'd spent the summer working on a Navajo reservation in the Southwest. Joe was last to return, back from his time with a friend in Spain. They brought fresh energy to the breakfast table, when they got up in time to eat. They were well beyond tennis lessons or island picnics and often disappeared for the day with friends to who knows where. When I could, I'd eavesdrop as they entertained their mother with stories or when the discussion veered toward the Chicago convention.

Joe-the-Butler or Lee told me when I first arrived that if I could last out Hyannis, I could make it all year. The dark and ominous warnings didn't stop my fun, but they did give pause. Lee, who'd seen a lot over the past year and a half, issued a new warning: "When Bobby Jr. is home, watch out for trouble." She wasn't specific, just that things happened when he was home. I'd heard rumors about David too, who so far had kept his distance from me. Lee warned that I'd need to keep close tabs on him during the school year to be sure he got in on time, studied, and stayed out of trouble. There had been some incidents of vandalism in the past.

So far, none of the big boys had been a problem because they spent most of their time in the music garage with the older cousins Chris Lawford and Bobby Shriver or off-compound with friends. When we returned to Virginia, David would be my eldest charge, and I figured I'd really get to know him then. For now, I'd keep my focus on the preteens and the little boys.

Out on the cape, several worlds operated in occasionally intersecting orbits, all with Mrs. Kennedy at the center. The children's world revolved in a stable and predictable circle of lessons and play, picnics and beach barbecues; the servants went round and round with repetitive daily duties. The adults' sphere was more obscured from me. I had thought it was about distraction and play when I first arrived, the flow of guests and boat rides, tennis challenges, late-night dinners. I'd written home that it felt more like Hawthorne's "The May-Pole of Merry Mount" than Dickinson's Amherst. But after a few weeks, I realized that the adults were channeling their loss and grief into extending the senator's life and legacy into the future, first at the convention and later in some lasting memorial.

On Thursdays, people arrived who were working on the RFK memorial film to be shown at the convention. Arthur Schlesinger Jr. sent manuscripts for a book he was writing. Richard Burton, who was narrating the film, talked with Mrs. Kennedy from his yacht. One morning in the sunroom, Robert Berks was refining his Bobby Kennedy bust. The Kennedy sisters Pat and Jean, Lem Billings, and Dave Hackett—the senator's best friend—watched silently as he worked among three clay pieces—a tiny one, another about eight inches tall, and a life-sized one—the face emerging, rugged and vulnerable in the rough-chunked clay.

During the time I spent on the cape, photographs and albums, manuscripts and movies arrived, were perused, discussed, evaluated, accepted, rejected—projects hatched, plans made. But it all happened behind closed doors or in other places, not where I and the children romped.

"START PACKING YOUR THINGS," LEE told me one morning. "Mrs. John is coming home." The next day Bob-the-Boatman loaded up the station wagon and drove with Lee and me to a big old rented house about a half mile from the compound. It was a huge echoing place with ten or twelve rooms on the first floor, several staircases, and long, uncarpeted wooden floors. We followed Bob up the creaky stairs, pushing open bedroom doors all along the hallway. In a room with two twins and access to a bathroom that separated it from the bedroom next door, Lee stopped.

"This is your room. Like it?"

It certainly didn't have the cozy feel of John Kennedy's room. Instead of antiques and French linens, it had worn-out furniture, thin cotton bedspreads, a too-bright ceiling light, and a too-dim bedside lamp. Between the two beds lay a small, round, fraying rag rug.

"Don't you want to stay here with me?" I asked, gazing around the semi-barren room.

"Are you kidding? You're going to love it here, away from the compound."

I wasn't so sure. It meant getting up a little earlier, walking a little farther, and giving up my late-night beer and debrief with the JFK Irish nanny. And let's face it, the house was a little scary and I'd be coming in alone, at night, in the dark.

Lee and I poked through the rest of the house and found a narrow stairway at the end of the hall leading up to an attic with a row of tiny rooms set under a slanted roof, one bed each, with hooks on the doors.

"For the servants," Lee told me.

The same staircase, barely wide enough for us to pass single file, wound down and into the kitchen.

The first night I walked home with a flashlight through a dark and strangely empty neighborhood of hulking, silent houses set on a gently rising hill. I sped up the stairs and into my room feeling like a character in a Mary Stewart mystery or a scary movie. It was too dark, too quiet, too empty. In bed I willed myself to quick sleep.

Around midnight, voices wakened me. *Guests must be coming in*, I thought before falling back to sleep.

In the morning, Lee shook her head—no, nobody else was staying there. She suggested that maybe the voices had drifted from next door, but I had definitely heard voices, and they came from downstairs. The third night Lee agreed to sleep over with me.

It might have been that sleepover night while we sat down in the kitchen before bed with our last cigarettes that Lee began telling me what to expect at Hickory Hill, the Kennedy home in Virginia. The previous year, as governesses came and went, she'd had to do double duty as secretary and governess. She itemized some of her responsibilities: make doctor appointments for school, take part in a carpool, buy clothes, sew in name tags, pack, drive places, sort out personal mail to the kids and supervise their writing, get them to meals and school on time, get them to bed on schedule. She explained that I'd get a day off one week and two off the next—so six free days per month. She did not mention that the day off would be canceled if any of the kids were sick. With ten kids, what were my chances of days off once school began?

She told me it was a gift that Bobby, Joe, and Kathleen would be away at boarding schools. I vaguely remembered her earlier warnings. I didn't ask for specifics but assumed it would be easier because there would be three fewer people to wake up and get going every morning. Four seemed like enough. Depending when the baby was born, I'd be going to Sun Valley for Christmas, she told me. She'd gone with the family the year before.

What fantastic luck! I knew Sun Valley, knew how to ski. The fact that Lee was telling me all this suggested that she thought I was going to make it, at least until Christmas. And so did I. Every letter home those first weeks ended with "I love the kids," "I love the job," or "I think I'm going to stay."

But Lee had more to say. She warned that I'd get my fill of Christmas. The first wave of greenery had to be fixed on all the banisters and windows and cars. For some reason, all the presents were opened on December 13. There'd be a whole room full of packages and presents. "And guess who'll be wrapping them all," Lee asked. She gave her wicked laugh and continued listing the duties: returns and exchanges, shopping and packing for every child going to Sun Valley.

"It's not over even then." Lee leaned back and dragged on a cigarette. "You replace all the greens when you get back and start planning for Easter."

Though she implied that the holiday would be a horror, I thought it sounded sort of fun, like Truman Capote's "A Christmas Memory," except in a mansion instead of a country house.

"You'll help me, won't you?" I wheedled.

She laughed. "I'll be long gone by then. But you can call me."

I would call her. She might have seemed cool and aloof and so much more experienced, but it felt like she could be my friend, someone to count on for advice.

That night Lee brought along Rocky, the little Chihuahua, who barked off and on all night long, her yips echoing through the cavernous haunted house, but each time we woke, neither Lee nor I heard a sound. She left me on my own the next night.

A crash, laughter, and voices awakened me around midnight, and I crept to the narrow servant staircase that led to the back kitchen where the ruckus was coming from. I recognized some of the voices and then party sounds of bottles and girls' laughter. What teenager could pass up an unlocked, empty house when the grown-ups were gone—or when they thought they were gone? They must not have known someone was living in the house full-time now. I retreated to my room and reported to Lee in the morning. The big kids weren't my charge. I don't know who she told or who warned them off, but nights became quiet and undisturbed.

ONE MORNING LEE ANNOUNCED THAT a girl had finally been hired to learn her job. I'd have a roommate up in the haunted house, and Lee could go on vacation. Lee wasn't the only one leaving as summer wound down. Tim-the-Tennis-Teacher had left for some time off before college would resume. The JFK Irish nanny would soon be replaced by the Swiss governess who'd been off all summer. I wouldn't be the newbie anymore. A couple of weeks' experience was an enormous advantage. The kids knew and liked me: *big*. I could drive all the cars and not get lost: *big*. I recognized many of the returning guests and could confidently greet them: *big*. When Mrs. Kennedy sat down at the table, I didn't get so nervous that my spoon shook or I babbled incoherently: *huge.* I'd even weathered a couple of blowups without dissolving into tears.

Before she left for Washington, Lee had to train the new hire. Penny was short and perky, seemingly a little too peppy and desperate to please. Her quick wit matched Lee's, but she could not replicate unflappable Lee, who for more than a year had absorbed Mrs. Kennedy's every mood from mania to fury, who'd managed the staff, the kids, the grown-ups, and the pets and had handled every crisis with an aura of calm. Penny was stepping into shoes impossible to fill. Nobody had written out a job description. As far as I knew, nobody had ever detailed job descriptions at the Kennedys'. You were expected to do whatever needed doing. If you were around when it was needed, it was your job. At least Penny had a few days with Lee, who would explain some of the duties, all of which began with the Red Book.

The Red Book, a massive red leather daily appointment tome, set the agenda for each day. In the evening, Mrs. Kennedy filled it with thoughts, orders, assignments, phone calls to be made, people to be contacted, questions, observations, plans, more (possibly contradictory) orders. Every morning Lee would go through it, create order, and proceed to fulfill the requests, make the calls, convey displeasure or subtly suggest changes. Lee could interpret Mrs. Kennedy's wishes and often soften the blows or clarify requests without raising hackles. But sometimes Mrs. K had the conversations herself.

"Mrs. Kennedy wants to talk some business with you today," Lee informed me when I came in from Mass a couple of days after Penny arrived.

Finally, I thought, with a stab of fear, a plink of adrenalin. *Have I done something wrong?*

So far, Mrs. Kennedy had only addressed me a few times if you counted the eye contact of the first day. On the yacht one afternoon, she'd asked me—ordered, really—to swim, to show her and Pat Lawford my stroke. I'd obliged with some butterfly and then crawl. "Marvelous," they shouted from the boat and turned back to their daiquiris. I'd felt a bit like a trained dolphin. She always seemed too busy to pay any attention to me, and requests or orders came through Lee, as if I were only slightly visible.

Mrs. Kennedy was upstairs bathing Dougie, and Penny was already up there taking notes, Lee told me. She reached down and picked up Rocky, who circled once and settled in her lap. Her expression gave no hints of trouble. But it would be Penny's first time with the Red Book, and I imagined how nervous she'd be up there alone with Mrs. Kennedy. She could use a buddy.

As I turned to go, I remembered Blanche Whittaker bursting through the dining room doors one day at lunchtime. Mrs. K had introduced me and laughed, "Here's our marvelous governess, Caroline. This is about the longest I've seen her." Later, Mrs. Whittaker—the person who'd called me in June to offer the job and suggested I check on breaking my teacher's contract—pulled me aside near the entry. "You wrote such a touching and heartfelt letter. I'm so happy for the kids that you decided to come." Her open and sincere friendliness felt familiar even though this was the first time I'd met her in person. Maybe it was a West Coast thing. She'd been a booster, like Congresswoman Green, who'd helped me get to Hyannis Port.

Lee gave me an encouraging smile, and I started up the stairs, glad I wouldn't be alone, but wondering what the business could be. At the top of the stairs, I turned down the hall toward the bathroom. When I stepped in the door, Mrs. Kennedy looked up from the edge of the tub, where she sat dictating. Penny was inside, against a wall, her pen racing across the Red Book. In the tub, Douglas splashed with a plastic cup in one hand, a little bucket in the other. I could hear Max and Christopher down the hall, yammering with Ena as she dressed them for the day.

"Caroline." Mrs. Kennedy drew her attention away from Penny to address me. "Now that all the boys are home, I want you—" she began but then glanced at the tub, where Dougie had become very silent.

"Gawd! What's that?" she shrieked and jumped up from the edge.

Dougie looked at her quizzically while a few bits of crap fluttered in the water and a fat turd floated toward his feet.

"God Almighty, get it out of there!" she screamed.

Penny, Red Book tucked under one arm, grabbed a Kleenex and bent to dip it out while Mrs. Kennedy watched in horror.

"In all my years, not one baby has done anything like this."

The tissue dissolved in the water while Dougie splashed and laughed.

"I'll never take a bath in here again."

I backed out of the room and turned toward Max and Chris's room, afraid I'd be seized with laughter, that hysterical kind that can quickly turn to tears if you don't grab on to it. I was trying to maintain control when I caught Ena's eye. She'd poked her head from the bedroom and withdrawn it as quickly as a turtle pulls into its shell. Was she smiling?

Mrs. Kennedy rushed down the hall toward her bedroom muttering, "I'm going to be sick if I don't get out of here."

The morning business I'd been waiting for had been canceled.

Ena, towel in hand, swept in to rescue Dougie, leaving Penny and me to sanitize the tub. We knelt on the tiles and scrubbed. I'm sure we whispered our alarm, our eyes igniting laughter that we desperately tried to choke. We became bonded buddies of the bathtub.

That night on my way back to the haunted house, I stopped in Mrs. John's kitchen to visit the Irish nanny and regale her with the tale. We hooted with laughter over the absurdity of it all. When I said that Mrs. K had never told me the business, she said with a laugh and an Irish brogue, "You'll be told. Ach, sure, you'll be told."

I might have felt more empathy for Mrs. Kennedy those days if I hadn't been so young, inexperienced, self-absorbed. Those were tense days. The Democratic National Convention loomed, a reminder of all the hope that had been lost. There had been a movement to draft Teddy to run with George McGovern, but he'd disappeared on the boat all July. Decisions needed to be made on the RFK memorial film. Books, sculptures, movies, articles. All the guests arriving and leaving, all the friends and comrades of John Kennedy and Robert who'd spent time in the administration, who'd planned and worked through two campaigns, who'd been through one assassination and now another, who must also have been reeling or stunned or suffering with personal pains while trying to support a grieving wife.

All that pain and loss and grief swirled over the cape waters and swept onto the lawns and through the houses like fog. But I was oblivious to everything except the sunburned, freckled kids, their wild and wind-tousled hair, and my own sun-bleached eyebrows, which I wrote home about. I practiced dropping the *r* at the end of *watah* and broadening the *a* in *Nahvahdah*, aping the Boston accent to signal my fitting in, heedless of the ache around me masked by busyness and activity.

Foremost in my mind then was to please Mrs. Kennedy, to discover what I was supposed to do, do it, and not be noticed—or be noticed only when I was doing it right. The world there, like many places, had a right and a wrong way to do things: to dress, to eat, to launch a boat, to serve a tennis ball, to call a play, to ride a pony, to treat a worker. The rules had been set long before I'd ever been born, set in two wealthy households, one where servants were servants and another where they were considered part of the household...or so I was told.

A few days later, Mrs. Kennedy's voice echoed down the stairs into the sun-flooded entry, and I climbed upstairs. In the older boys' room, Bobby and David—or Joe and Bobby—or all three—stood along the windows watching while Mrs. Kennedy screamed as she yanked at one corner of the rug, unable to lift it because beds and chairs were set on it.

"Get this dirty thing out of here," she shrieked. "What were you thinking coming in here filthy?"

Were they smirking? Grimacing? I caught only the briefest glimpse before I ducked into Max and Christopher's room.

"Ready for your lesson?" I asked, hoping they were so we could get out of the house. I wasn't used to parents yelling. I felt scared, my heart racing, as if I were the one who'd sullied the rug.

I must have looked stricken when I came downstairs, trailing Christopher and holding on to Max's hand. Lee looked up from her desk where Penny sat beside her.

"Don't worry. It's not your fault. Just an explosion. If you take it to heart, you'll have a nervous breakdown...like the last governess." She laughed her little chuckle, petted Rocky's head, and looked back at the papers on her desk.

Chapter 8

RECOGNITION

A FLASHBULB POPPED, AND LIGHT EXPLODED ACROSS THE AISLE AS heads turned toward our arrival: Mrs. Kennedy, Courtney, Kerry, Michael, David, Caroline. We hurried past the woman, camera in hand, who leaned out from her pew. This wasn't the first time someone had intruded. Another morning an old woman had rushed toward Courtney and kissed her cheek before I could hurry her outside. Today after Mass a semicircle waited near the door—parishioners? tourists? who? We made a quick escape in tight formation with long strides, moving as a herd among jackals.

All day long sightseeing boats motored past the compound, the tour guides' voices drifting over the water: "And here's where Ambassador Joseph Kennedy built his family's compound. Next door, that barn-shaped house, is the Robert Kennedy home. And beyond them—see the old airplane on the grass?—is the president's house." Sometimes one of the little kids would look up and shout, "Go away." But mostly they ignored the intrusions as they might ignore seagulls or sand fleas: disruptive, annoying, but not worth much attention.

When someone in the News Shoppe, a little grocery about two blocks from the compound and a place Christopher or Kerry begged to go in the afternoons, stepped too close, I'd elbow between them and the kids. When a middle-aged woman seemed to stalk the girls one day in the grocery, I hustled them out and into the car, calling over my shoulder, "Charge it to the account, please." Nobody had told me what to do. I'd not been briefed on protocols. It just seemed natural to intervene, to protect a five-year-old's or a ten- or twelve-year-old's space. Who were these people who wanted to grab a photo or hug a child or tell them, "I'm so sorry," or "You poor thing"? These people who felt they knew Caroline and John and now Courtney and Kerry? These people who mistook familiarity with personal connection. When we went into town, strangers crowded around like friends at a tailgate party, as if they were part of the family, distant cousins come for the reunion. They recognized faces from photos and called out names in the ice-cream shop, the market, Howard Johnson's. *I know you*, they seemed to think.

I remembered the night I'd taken the girls to see *The Fantasticks*. After we'd finished eating, the manager and the waitress stopped by the table and wanted to introduce themselves and talk to the kids. The girls had glanced up briefly and then sat at the table in silence. "Thanks for stopping by," I might have said. Afterward on the way to the car, Courtney whispered to Caroline, "I don't know how you'll make it. If they're like this here, I don't think you can make it in New York." I assumed she meant people gawking, people wanting to make a connection, to be acknowledged by someone famous.

Well. Weren't they me too? Hadn't I been to Hyannis just a year before, a tourist looking for traces of Kennedy lore? Wasn't I taking photos now from inside the compound?

Yes, I was. And writing letters home with details—edited, to be sure—that I asked my mother to share with my best friends? She

A family gathering at the farm after riding practice. Caroline, Jackie, and John Kennedy are in the foreground. Ethel Kennedy and friends lean on the Pontiac listening to Ted Kennedy. Freckles wanders in the background.

typed my letters with carbon copies, editing out sections I thought too private to share. "Don't tell anyone the parts I put between * and *," I instructed her. I sent home color slides and later prints that she collected in a shoebox, numbering each envelope as it arrived, keeping them all together with her typed copies and all the memorabilia I sent home from that year with the Kennedys. She was my archivist.

I didn't want to think of myself as "one of those people," attracted to celebrity. But I knew that if the Kennedys had walked through Portland six months before and I'd recognized them, I'd probably have stopped and gawked even though I had some insight into the helplessness you feel as an object for admirers. When I'd returned from the Olympics with my small-town fame, I developed a kind of fan radar that quickly detected intruders, found ways to outmaneuver them. Now I was using that skill to protect my kids from outsiders.

Of the insiders who visited the compound, many I'd never heard of before: General Maxwell Taylor? Rowland Evans? Art Buchwald? Lee and Joe knew every guest, could capsulize each of them in a phrase or two and then follow up with an anecdote. When Mrs. K was trying to beat Art Buchwald finishing the Sunday *Times* crossword, she'd call Art Schlesinger for answers, Lee told me. I was both impressed and unimpressed with almost everyone who wandered through the house that summer and fall. Those whose names or faces I recognized from magazines or television became quite ordinary sitting down for lunch or gingerly stepping off the dock and onto a boat or running a bit too slowly in a touch game and dropping the ball.

AFTER MASS ONE MORNING, PENNY had the Red Book ready to give me my assignments for the day, which meant another "business chat," hopefully not in the bathroom with Douglas:

- gifts for Courtney's birthday
- party favors for thirty guests (mostly cousins)
- school clothes for Bobby (see Mrs. K for details)

"By the way, are you ready for this?" Penny paused dramatically. "Christopher yelled for 'Carolyn' from the john this morning instead of 'Ena.' He wanted you to come wipe him. Isn't that great news! I thought you should know."

"Thanks, Penny. I'm really *in* now."

Secretly, it did please me because it meant he accepted me.

Just like it had pleased me when Mrs. Lawford called me by name when she said goodbye and when Mrs. Smith greeted me by name outside in the morning. *It only took them three weeks.* And Mrs. Kennedy hadn't yelled at me recently, although her parting words yesterday were, "See that the children clean their toenails." *Why do orders always sound like reprimands?* I wondered.

Commands could come directly at the breakfast table or from the Red Book, and the priorities changed daily:

Clean up the lawn.

Dirty fingernails.

Drink more milk.

Messy hair. *Whose hair?*

Shirts too big. Whose shirts does that mean? What am I supposed to do, buy new ones? Dress the teenagers?

Kerry's dinner. *Hmmm?*

I'd complained to Lee before she left, "One day she tells me the boys have to get up for Mass; the next she asks me why I woke them up. 'They need their sleep.'"

"Don't worry. Just go along. It's not personal. She likes you."

I knew I wouldn't get any sympathy from Lee—she'd been through it all—but I couldn't resist grousing, "She makes me the bad guy. She doesn't listen, she just nods yes when the kids ask to do things they *know* they shouldn't. Then I get in trouble the next day."

Lee shrugged a whadda ya gonna do?

THANK GOODNESS I'D BEEN IN a college sorority and learned proper table manners. I began to channel Mrs. McCready, our housemother: "Napkin on lap, Kerry." "Wipe your mouth, Michael."

"Mummy is coming soon, better wash your hands again and comb your hair, Bobby." "Here comes Mummy. Stand up," and up we'd rise when she or she and Pat Lawford or some guest entered. We were jumping jacks in the dining room and anywhere else when an adult entered a room. The grown-ups didn't usually eat with us, but Mrs. K would sit awhile and question the kids about their day.

"At home you'll be expected to lead the table conversation—history questions, current events. It's what we do at dinner there," she told me. Her offhand comment sent a zing through me. It affirmed that I was doing okay. I'd be going on to Hickory Hill.

The morning that Jackie Kennedy entered the dining room, we instantly pushed back our chairs and jumped to attention. The room felt airless. I tried not to gape. My Mrs. K introduced me as she always did, "This is our marvelous governess, Caroline." I'm positive that I said, "How do you do?"—it felt that formal.

Then Mrs. John said, "I hear you've been driving the girls to the farm. Is everyone ready for the horse show?"

"Yes." The Osterville Pony Show was scheduled for Sunday morning, and she'd returned in time to watch Caroline compete.

The two women moved on to the sunroom, and we all finished breakfast. I feigned nonchalance. As soon as everyone boarded the *Marlin* for the daily picnic, I headed to town on shopping errands. From an exclusive shop where they carried baby and children's clothes, women's lingerie, and fancy bed linens, I had orders to bring back to the house baby gowns and linens for Mrs. K to choose from. She'd make her selections, I'd take everything back to the store, and they would hold them until the baby arrived, so the gender-appropriate color could be sent.

No one paid any attention to me when I stepped into the store. I pawed through the embroidered silk gowns and set a few aside.

The little crib sheets, linen so sheer it felt like silk, were embroidered with flowers or ducks or ponies. If only I could afford them to send to my friends who had new babies.

I'd also been instructed to bring home every cute dress in Courtney's and Kerry's sizes. "Only from Florence Eiseman" was the decree. Mrs. K would make her choices, and I'd return the rejects later. Imagine an unlimited budget, a bottomless credit card, and the most beautiful linens and fabrics you'd ever seen. I was in heaven, although seemingly invisible to the two clerks in the store. An overdressed shopper—one I instantly labeled as nouveau riche, a term from my sociology class—strutted in with two bratty children and gave me "the once-over before dismissing me like dirt," I wrote home. A clerk stepped from behind the counter to assist her at the same moment that Jackie Kennedy poked her head through the door.

The room went to freeze-frame. She looked around, caught my eye, and I smiled and raised my hand in a shy, semi-sophisticated wave, like one Audrey Hepburn might have given in a movie I'd seen. Her eyebrows raised as she glanced past the gaping nouveau riche lady, smiled, and voiced a hushed "Hello, Caroline" before disappearing out the door. That recognition was better than Pat Lawford, Jean Smith, and Teddy Kennedy remembering my name. *She only met me this morning*, I swooned, my feet momentarily floating off the floor.

I was the waitress and the manager at the Howard Johnson's. I was the tourist in the sightseeing boat.

But I was also the girl doing her job buying birthday presents and baby clothes for a stay-at-home mother. The film rolled on, a clerk hurried over to assist me, and off I sped to buy shirts, ties, shoes, handkerchiefs, socks, and jeans for Bobby before heading home in time to remind everyone to wash hands and comb hair before dinner and then to take Kerry and Michael to the club for sailing class awards. I brought along my camera and took photos of them getting their ribbons, feeling almost like a proud parent.

Chapter 9

TROUBLES

EVERY DAY ON THE CAPE SEEMED EPIC. SO MANY EVENTS FILLED THE days that each seemed longer than a week. Lee had been going to go on vacation for months. I'd been going to have a day off for years. But really, I'd been there barely three weeks, and Lee was still training Penny. The compound buzzed with activity day and night.

Anything could happen while I was off on an errand or overnight while I slept in the haunted house. One afternoon Courtney broke a toe playing football while I was in town picking up laundry. The same day Andy Williams, a pop singer and family friend, broke one of his, and they sat together after dinner singing songs while someone from the Kingston Trio played guitar. Max, who was deathly allergic to horse hair (after riding, everyone had to change clothes in the laundry building and leave their gear outside), had a frightening asthma attack that confined him to bed for a few days at the same time that Christopher broke out in boils. The notion that I'd get days off if no one was sick began to seem like a pipe dream. Toes. Asthma. Boils.

Now David and Bobby were sick with colds. And no wonder. The haunted house wasn't the only hangout in town. After hours the boys found lots to do without supervision. Every morning Joe or Lee passed along rumors they'd heard—a police chase across the golf course one night, a party in some house another.

One morning Lee told me they'd been up half the night—Bobby and David had tried to hire a skydiving plane. The details were fuzzy then, and almost forgotten now. Bobby had forged Ethel's signature for permission, and he had fake ID for his age. Did they complete the jump? Or did the pilot call and check? I only remember understanding that Lee wasn't kidding when she'd warned, "Things happen when Bobby's home," and realizing that there was no way on earth I could control him. Who was I to stop his midnight prowls? My situation wasn't unlike that pre-teaching nightmare when I asked the students to open their texts and they continued to talk or looked at me with contempt.

One night before dinner when I asked to check the kids' fingernails, Michael and Kerry held out their hands with smiles, but Bobby looked at me as if I'd spoken gibberish, his face frozen in a heavy-lidded stare. He seemed to sweat with rage. I smiled and shrugged. "Your mom likes them clean." Maybe he left to wash up, I don't remember, but I thought, *Thank goodness he'll be off to boarding school soon.* The next day he offered me a mahogany-carved hippopotamus he'd brought back from Kenya. Was it appeasement? Apology? Or had he simply found an extra souvenir and I happened by at the right time?

What could that summer have felt like to the children? How does a five-, an eleven-, a thirteen-, or a sixteen-year-old process a parent's murder? Maybe the older three had talked about their father, their feelings, their loss and grief, on their summer trips with their friends.

But there were no counselors, no grief groups.

Kathleen, who'd returned with her sixteen-year-old girlfriend, mingled easily with the adults, adding ideas as they discussed various projects. At lunch one day she and her friend told me about their summer and the work they'd done on a Navajo reservation in Arizona. Talking with them was like being back at school with my students, throwing around books we'd read or should read, talking about songs that captured summer. I asked what they were thinking about college, and they each rattled off a list of possibilities. I loved being part of a real and familiar conversation, if only for one lunch. Joe, the fifteen-year-old sophomore-to-be, disappeared from the compound to hang out with friends he knew in town. But Bobby and his age-mate cousins tumbled into teenage trouble and brought David along. Was alcohol involved? Dope? 1968. It must have been available.

WHILE LEE WAS PREPARING TO leave, it dawned on me that I hadn't had a day off since I'd arrived. If a day off wasn't possible, at least I would get a morning to sleep in. Or so I thought. At ten on my sleep-in day, Penny shook me awake.

"Carolyn! Get up! Get up! Everybody's going to Chicago today with Senator Ted!" Mrs. Kennedy had been calling for me to get the kids outfitted and ready. Penny filled me in on the plans as we raced back to the compound. Bobby needed a new suit. He'd left his someplace in Africa. Joe's suit pants were too short. Somebody yelled to check their room to see if I could find some dress shirts.

I plowed through the boys' closet, a filthy tangle of turtlenecks and muddy pants, underwear, mismatched socks, khaki pants, and moldy wet bathing suits. But no dress shirts. No suits.

Why would they have suits at the cape anyway? When I came downstairs, Kathleen pulled me aside. She needed a pair of navy-blue kid gloves and nylons.

I poked my head into the little boys' room and asked Ena where I'd be able to find all that stuff, and she told me there was a Brooks Brothers in Osterville and to get some fresh shirts and socks for all the boys while I was there. "And cuff links too," someone hollered from the office door as I fired up the yellow woody convertible and blasted off to Osterville, leaving Ena and Penny and Lee and probably Joe-the-Butler to track down dress-up outfits for the rest of the clan.

Brooks Brothers was only selling Bermuda shorts and pastel polos, no suits. "Are you the governess?" the salesman asked. He had a telephone message for me to call the compound immediately.

"I don't have the number," I said helplessly. Information wasn't going to give me the Kennedys' phone number. My only option was to drive the seven miles back to Hyannis Port. I wound my way through tourists and traffic, cursing the amblers and pokey drivers all the way to the compound, where Penny looked up from her desk. "They're not going to Chicago now."

Instead, Mrs. Kennedy wanted me to take the little kids to Otis Air Force Base for bowling and swimming. I did, and by the time we returned, the plans had changed again.

Now I was to round up all the kids because Senator Ted would be making an announcement on television from the front lawn. Mrs. K wanted all the family to be together.

Like a bloodhound, I tracked them down one by one: Kerry was out playing softball; Joe had gone to town; Courtney was over at Caroline's. I found Bobby at the golf club with Christopher Lawford. David remained lost. As it turned out, no one was going to be on television with Uncle Teddy. When we were all back on the compound and milling around in the office, Penny delivered the news that Mrs. K wanted everyone to have a haircut while the hairdresser was there. She thought that someone might take a photo while Teddy was being interviewed, and she wanted everyone to look sharp.

Days often had that quality of intensity, of frenzied activity that came to nothing, a frantic buildup that quickly overflowed and fizzled out, like the soda pop shaken and sprayed. It was a rush for the shaker but a mess to be cleaned up by someone else.

OTHER THAN THE LITTLE BOYS, who cried as any two- or three- or barely five-year-old is likely to do, I didn't witness anyone crying on the cape. Tears might spring with the sting of a ball on bare legs or an accidental tackle in touch football, but no one wept, not even the night of the convention when the thirty-minute documentary *Robert Kennedy Remembered* played. We sat around the TV scrunched together—all the kids, Lee, Penny, Joe-the-Butler, and Angie Novello, the senator's longtime secretary. How could it be that none of them cried?

"Listen to them clapping," Courtney said when it ended. "They clapped on and on, didn't they?"

Maybe all the tears had been shed long before I'd arrived. Maybe, in that magical thinking of children, they still believed that he'd come back. I had no idea how I might respond to my own father's death or my mother's. Other than my grandmother, I hadn't yet lost a close relative. The classmate killed in Viet Nam seemed remote. I really didn't know death personally or how it made you feel or act other than the shock that came with the

1960s assassinations and the numbness that followed. Maybe the kids felt numb.

The Kennedys gave Americans a template for public grief: Jackie Kennedy walking behind the president's cortege, Caroline and John at each hand. Ethel Kennedy with a line of children beside her filling a pew in St. Patrick's Cathedral, the slow train from New York to Washington, DC. Faces masked behind lace. They handled grief like a business. The work memorializing, the albums, the photos, the statues, the films, the foundation, the dedications created Dickinson's "formal feeling." And in the off-hours, every minute filled with sports and noise, hilarity, friends, and family kept the senator's energy, his laughter and competitiveness and physicality, beside them.

JACKIE KENNEDY HAD BEEN BACK for less than a week when a fresh batch of guests arrived the weekend of the convention: Roosevelt Grier ("Rosey-Baby," Mrs. Kennedy called him); Rafer Johnson, the Olympian I'd met on that overcast Oregon roadside; and Bill Barry, a former FBI agent who had provided security for the senator during the campaign. Dave Hackett and his family, George and Liz Stevens, and Lem Billings all returned.

After early Mass on Sunday, I drove the girls—Courtney, Maria, Sydney, and Kerry—to the farm for the Osterville Pony Show. The constant announcements of events and the milling, nervous participants reminded me of swim meets. Now I was the mother hen holding ribbons, giving pep talks, keeping track of riding jackets, crops, numbers, and hats. At some point I found lunch for us all and carrots for the ponies and then settled back to watch class after class perform—walk, trot, canter, jump—while the judge watched with her clipboard from the center of the ring.

For one event they asked me to present the awards, making a big deal of the introduction: "1960 Olympic gold medalist Carolyn Wood, presenting..." The grown-ups and parents watched part of the show, but the girls and I stayed until the end. It was past two thirty when I drove everyone, even Caroline, first to the ice-cream shop and then back to the compound.

I eased the car into the drive and up under the carport, the 8-track tape deck blasting the Doors' "Hello, I Love You" and the girls singing along full throttle. I cut the motor, and we could hear shouting and bursts of cheers from beyond the hedge.

The grown-ups were battling in a full-on competitive touch game—all the older Kennedy boys and their cousins, Rosey Grier, Rafer Johnson, Bill Barry, Dave Hackett, Steve Smith, and...Jackie Kennedy! On the sidelines, cheering like high school sophomores, were Jean Smith, Pat Lawford, and Ethel Kennedy.

Down the field a bit, a clump of longtime governesses—the Smiths', the Lawfords', and Ena—stood together like chaperones watching a school dance, laughing, clapping, and tittering among themselves. The girls wiggled in next to their mothers, but I headed down to the elders and stood just a little apart, close enough to feel included, but not so close I was intruding. It was a riot to watch them play, all the strategizing, the elaborate plays, the fancy footwork, and the arguing. "Tagger's word," echoed across the lawn.

"This is the first time Mrs. Kennedy play at our house since her husband died," Ena told me, shaking her head as if disbelieving what she was watching. But I was watching the men, the three who had been with the senator the night when he was shot, who had been his bodyguards. I wondered if they felt him beside them that afternoon running on the long, wide lawn, stretching out to make an impossible catch.

When the grown-ups quit, the kids took over, and I played for a while with Maria and Sydney, Courtney, Michael, and Stevie Smith. After dinner we piled back in the car and headed for town to play a final game of miniature golf with Caroline and John. They would not be returning to the cape after the commissioning ceremonies for a new aircraft carrier, the *John F. Kennedy*. Rumors had circulated daily about who from our family would attend, and for two seconds I thought I might get to go. But no. Ena had more experience with these kinds of things, Lee told me. She knew what they should wear and how to keep Bobby in line. "Besides, trust me, you don't want to be there." It might have been fun, something new, but I was glad I wasn't going. It would be quieter on the compound. Maybe I'd finally get a day off.

BEFORE I GOT A FOOT in the door the next morning, Penny pushed me back outside into the carport with a *shhhhh*. In a low voice, she told me that Mrs. Kennedy had had an *emergency* the night before. She'd been sick and had cramps that felt like contractions. Two doctors came in to check on her, and a nurse had spent the night. Penny said she was doing okay now but needed to rest. My job was to keep the kids quiet all day. We went back inside where Senator Ted, Pat Lawford, Jean Smith, and Lem Billings murmured together in the sunroom. No one else was around. The house seemed muffled, as if the walls had been felted.

Penny warned me not to alarm the children, but the unusual hush alone was unnerving. Of course, everyone worried that she might lose the baby. What they said was that she needed to slow down a bit, rest. No more tennis or sideline cheerleading. What they didn't say was that no one could bear another loss that summer.

I didn't know whether she spent the day in bed or not because I had the kids out of the house and down on the beach as soon as I could that morning. In the afternoon, Bob-the-Boatman took a boatload of us out to waterski and putter around Nantucket Sound. Later we filled up the station wagon and went into town to play pitch-and-putt. Everything seemed almost back to normal when I came in for breakfast the next morning, but Mrs. Kennedy's vulnerability had been exposed, and the house seemed a little quieter.

Chapter 10

TIME OFF

The Saturday morning of the USS *John F. Kennedy* aircraft carrier commissioning felt warm enough for shorts, and because I was staying home and having a "sort of day off," that's what I pulled on. Outside the haunted house, the clear, blue September sky, as blue as Crater Lake, reflected off the sound. I waved at the policeman inside the guard booth and walked onto the compound. Freckles trotted toward me from the front lawn as usual. Panda would be stretched somewhere in a sun spot. Inside, Chris and Max, who weren't going on the trip, sat slurping cereal at one end of the dining table, Kerry at the other, her hair a tangled mess. Joe-the-Butler poked his head out of the swinging kitchen door to say good morning and report that so far no one else had come down. Kathleen and Courtney were probably getting ready, but I needed to be sure the boys were awake.

We weren't going to have the get-ready-at-the-last-minute scene I could imagine. The Chicago fiasco had taught me important lessons about preparations. The night before, I'd gathered all the boys' suits with clean white shirts, four sets of cuff links, four appropriate ties, four PT-boat tie clips, and four pairs of black socks and stowed them in Chris and Max's room.

Downstairs, their loafers lay hidden under a secretary's desk so they wouldn't take a hike through mud in the night. A Navy plane scheduled to depart at ten forty-five Saturday morning would fly everyone to Newport News, Virginia: Jackie, Caroline, and John; Pat Lawford and her four; Jean and Steve Smith and their boys; Bobby and Maria Shriver; Senator Ted, Joan, and their children; and Ena with seven from our family. My kids would be on time and ready when the car cavalcade left the compound!

When the last car pulled down the drive and disappeared, I had a whole day ahead with not much to do. One of the maids had been assigned to look after Douglas. Chris and Max were spending the day at the Smiths' with cousins too young to attend the ceremony. For the first time since I'd been on the cape, I had time alone to relax. At first, I felt at loose ends, as my mother might have said. It seemed too quiet, too empty. Was there something I hadn't done? If I hung around the house, I knew that Mrs. Kennedy would think up a job that had to be completed or some errand that just couldn't wait.

What do other employees do on their days off? I wondered. At home on a Saturday, I might sleep until noon, call a friend, make plans to go out for a beer or to a movie. But here in Hyannis, I didn't have any friends to call. By the time I got back to the haunted house, I felt desperate to talk to someone, someone who knew me for myself. It was too expensive to call anyone in Portland, but I could call the Burkes in New York. Collect.

Bob answered, accepted the charges, and started off with "Where the hell are you? I thought you were coming here for a week before you started that job."

I explained that he'd never written back when I'd told him I was coming east.

"What the hell, brat. You're family. Show up when you can." I loved his brash New York accent scolding me for not staying with him and Helen on my way to the Kennedys'. I should visit Lynn, he added, who was living in North Carolina where her husband was stationed, just a half-hour flight from DC. He had a few stories about the Olympic Trials and swimmers I knew on the team headed for Mexico City. It must have cost a fortune to talk on and on, but it felt so good to hear him, I wasn't going to sign off. When he told me that he might snag a ride up to Hyannis with a friend who had a plane, I got nervous and told him I didn't have much time off and wouldn't be able to see him. I didn't say that even he wouldn't be able to talk his way past the police stands and Secret Service if he did show up or that I wouldn't dare ask for time off to meet up with him. But what a relief to know that I had a home away from home waiting for me any time. The Eastern shuttle that flew between Washington and New York was cheap and easy. When my real schedule began with regular days off after our return to Virginia, I'd be able to visit Bob and Helen. The longing to get away, to be somewhere I felt like myself instead of either invisible or subservient, overcame me for the first time since I'd arrived.

Don't linger there, Carolyn, I thought, reminding myself that last year at this time, I'd just finished my first week of school. On this clear September day on the cape, it seemed impossible to imagine being trapped in a classroom again, a new wave of overdressed juniors sweating out Indian summer trapped behind too-small desks and being coaxed into reading stories that made no sense to them. My kids, the four who'd be my responsibility in Virginia, wouldn't be starting classes until late September. Instead of lesson planning, my duties for the next couple of weeks included doctor appointments for physicals and sorting out clothes and yes, coaxing them to read stories they didn't want to. They each had a summer reading list, one that had been lost before the summer began and that now I was responsible for finding and for encouraging, forcing them to read. Reading time had been added to the daily schedule between tennis, softball, and dinner.

I stretched out on my bed in the upstairs room of the haunted house—silent in the afternoon, a sea breeze blowing in through the open windows—and thought about books. Last year, class sets of paperbacks had rotated among the junior teachers: *Adventures of Huckleberry Finn*, *Ethan Frome*, *A Farewell to Arms*, *The Red Badge of Courage*, *The Catcher in the Rye*, *The Crucible*. I'd read them all when I was a junior at Beaverton too, all except the new novel, *A Separate Peace* by John Knowles. Now here I was in New England near where that book had been set.

On my first read-through before teaching it, the story had swept me into its grasp. I had experienced Gene's jealousy. And his love, unexpressed, for Finny—that repressed and angry desire for what was denied had felt familiar. I loved Finny for his play, his exuberance, his irresponsible and irrepressible energy, his athletic gifts. I identified with both boys, as I was well practiced in doing, since we read only of male heroes. Who else was there to emulate? Even the one female-authored novel, *Ethan Frome*, provided only a silly girl and horrid Zeena as the female characters.

When I first read *A Separate Peace* in my room at home curled in an armchair under yellow light, I wept for Finny and for Gene, for all the damaged boys. For wars. For the boys I was teaching who too soon would be going off to Viet Nam. During prep period, Dale and Linda and I discussed the book. Dale brought us a copy of Hemingway's *In Our Time* and read aloud the passage when

Nick, the wounded soldier, makes his "separate peace." We talked of *A Farewell to Arms* and read the passage where Frederic Henry ruminates about Catherine's death. "The world breaks every one and afterward many are strong at the broken places. But those that will not break it kills. It kills the very good and the very gentle and the very brave impartially. If you are none of these you can be sure it will kill you too but there will be no special hurry."

He could have been speaking of Finny or the president, I'd thought then. Now I thought he could have also been talking about Robert Kennedy. They were all too good to live in this world. I remembered how last year it had seemed so deep that one piece of literature might speak to another just as a character might speak directly to a reader. Even if I didn't miss the anxiety of the first days of school, I did miss the daily conversations with colleagues on books, art, philosophy, the Friday afternoon gripe sessions about administrators or students.

In fact, I sort of missed the students I'd had the year before who were now seniors: The identical twins, so innocent looking, who had switched classes a couple of times. The drama student who had created an undulating psychedelic backdrop for his group's project by placing a glass cake pan filled with water, oil, and food coloring on an overhead projector. *So groovy,* I'd thought. Groovy immediately brought to mind a girl, not a particularly good student but an interesting one. She'd approached my desk after class one afternoon to ask if I smoked the Winstons she'd seen in my bag. She informed me that they were very dangerous because they used spun glass in the filters.

"You shouldn't be looking in my things," I'd told her.

She blinked behind her thick-lensed glasses and then asked for a ride home. Before I dropped her off at a driveway that led toward a little house down in the woods off Canyon Road, I told her I'd consider changing brands. What a curious exchange we'd had. *How would her senior year go?* I wondered.

The breeze ruffled the curtains, and another episode drifted into memory: I'd spotted a boy lighting a match during free-read time and demanded to know if he had just lit a match. He readily admitted that he had, and I ordered him out of the room to see the vice principal. He wasn't a troublesome student. It was just such a stupid thing to do in an English class. *Why wasn't he reading?* I'd thought. When he returned at the end of the period to pick up his things I asked if he'd seen the vice principal and he said yes, he had. But at the end of the year, he told me that it was so funny me asking if he'd seen the vice principal the day I kicked him out—all he'd done was walk past his office, look at him, and then hang out until the period ended. That was a rookie mistake I wouldn't make again.

The Kennedy clan returned exhausted late Saturday night. Ena scooted everyone off to bed while I sat in the haunted house kitchen with Penny and listened to the first tape that had come from my friends back home.

"I'm so glad I am a Kappa Kappa Gamma, rooty-toot for KKG," my friends belted out before they dissolved into giggles and snorts, tried to start another song, and the tape ran out. They'd gathered together, five or six of them, to record news from Portland. Ann was back teaching seniors at her high school after a summer in Europe. Meredith was pregnant. Gretchen, the Sunset teacher who'd provided passes to the mock convention, was packing for graduate school at Stanford, and Linda had finished the first week of school back at Beaverton High.

I opened a bottle of beer, rewound the tape, and pressed record: "Hello, loyal friends. Here's the scumpty: It's 10:37 Eastern

Daylight Time at the kitchen table of the haunted house. In front of me is a bottle of Heineken, two jars of grape jelly, a jar of peanut butter, and a Coca-Cola. Oh. And beside me one of the secretaries, Penny."

The scene set, I launched into a methodical presentation of my life in Hyannis, starting with a description of the cars: the yellow Mercury convertible that looked like a wood-sided station wagon and Mrs. Kennedy's white Bonneville convertible with the fabulous tape deck.

"I'm spending more time as chauffer," I told them, "especially for Maria Shriver and Sydney Lawford." Penny guffawed beside me. I laughed too, amused by the innuendo that these girls were manipulating, while aware that any reason to get away from the house felt like a welcome escape. I was a willing victim to the imperious twelve-year-olds.

I stopped the tape, lit a cigarette, and clicked it back on. "Oh. Oh! Here's a story of a typical day. Let's call it 'The Day I Slept In, or the Day We Went to Chicago." On and on I prattled, egged along by Penny, almost as if I were back in the sorority house sharing news of the day before dinner or in the teachers' room embellishing stories from the classroom. But unlike a sorority confab, taping was basically monologue. With Penny beside me in the kitchen, I could imagine my friends sitting beside us gabbing away.

I had stories to tell of press boats chased away by the Secret Service, of trotting bareback with the girls out at the farm and the consequences on my body, of finally enjoying a conversation with the big kids—Kathleen, Joe, and Bobby—one night when the younger ones were off to a cousin's birthday.

"I really miss swearing. I just want to yell '*Damn it!*' sometimes." The tape rolled on.

"I do," Penny mumbled at my side.

"But I have to be good in front of the little kids. I'm not super tired, but I get kind of angry. I suppose when you're around little kids, you can get fed up."

My voice petered out, and I dragged on a cigarette and then laughed. "But I'm such an ideal governess"—laughter—"I don't even know what I'm doing half the time."

Like the reading list, the clothes list for boarding school had disappeared long before I arrived at the compound. Now I needed to outfit three kids and get them packed and off to Putney and Milton and Millbrook before I could start on everyone else. But the school shopping had to wait for the birthday shopping.

The cigarette made me think of one last story to tell before the tape ended. Most days I was too busy to sit down and have a cigarette, but in the evenings after the kids had gone to bed and I was in the kitchen or back at the haunted house or somewhere with the other staff, we'd puff away like we did in the Kappa house. One night, long after the little kids had been tucked in, while Penny and I were still in the office at Mrs. K's house and the grown-ups were finishing dinner, Jackie Kennedy slipped out of the dining room and tiptoed over. In a breathless whisper, she said, "Oh, Caroline, could I borrow another cigarette, please?"

I told my friends that I didn't know why I got so nervous when she was around because she was always nice, but I had popped up and fumbled in my black bag for the cigarettes mumbling something. My hand was so shaky when she bent toward the match, I could see the flame fluttering. Even though I was a complete klutz, she smiled and thanked me like I'd done her a big favor. I laughed into the tape. A few minutes later the dining room door opened again and Mrs. Smith crept through. "Do you mind if I borrow one too?" she asked. I told my friends that this was the Kennedy trick to cut down on smoking and save money—bum "OPCs, other people's cigarettes." Penny thought it was a riot.

The tape reel neared its end, and I hurried to finish. "Oh. Oh. I loved your singing. It brought tears to my eyes, a lump in my throat, and all that crap. Congratulations, Meredith. Good luck, Gretchen. Send me addresses and photos of Craig's new store, Linda. And say hello to Dale and all the philosophy gang at school."

I even mentioned my student who'd warned me about the dangers of Winston cigarette filters. I told Linda to tell her I couldn't wait to hear if she was going to go to college or Haight-Ashbury. Later that year I'd learn that she'd be doing neither. She'd been arrested at a motel near the Memorial Coliseum along with an underage girlfriend. She'd developed a scheme: She pimped her friend and then broke into the room to accuse the john of statutory rape. They used their extortion money to buy drugs in California, which they brought back and offered to bands and groupies in exchange for free concert tickets. She wrote to me from jail to say she was learning a lot of new ways to make money in juvie.

ONE BY ONE, EVENTS WOUND down at the cape after the commissioning. On Sunday, the children performed skits and songs, poems and dances for their grandfather's eightieth birthday. Monday, Courtney celebrated her twelfth birthday with a party of cousins and friends, complete with a treasure hunt on the beach that Joe-the-Butler and I devised. Two days later Kerry turned nine, and we partied again. The back-to-school party for Kathleen, Joe, and Bobby came on Thursday. Good thing I'd had Saturday off

Courtney and Joe-the-Butler plan her birthday party while Michael, aged ten, contemplates badminton on the front lawn.

because I'd been on a tear for presents for all of them, not just the birthday girls. Mrs. Kennedy made lists daily of items for me to find for school: calendars, stationery and envelopes, hairbrushes, crucifixes, rosaries, cuff links and ribbons, picture frames, and a flag for someone. If "We're Going to Chicago" had been a governess's preliminary test for organizing and improvising, prepping for the aircraft commissioning qualified as the semifinals. Now the final test was packing for boarding school and the return to Hickory Hill. *A competition I will master*, I persuaded myself.

Chapter 11

HICKORY HILL

My God, it looks like the Kappa House, I thought when we turned off Chain Bridge Road and crept up the curved drive and under wide-spreading oaks and hickories toward the three-floor white Georgian (brick, not wood) mansion. Twenty-two tall windows, flanked with pale-green shutters, stared blankly at our approach, but inside I imagined everyone braced for the onslaught of kids, dogs, and Mrs. Kennedy.

Here we were at Hickory Hill, the house where John Kennedy had written *Profiles in Courage,* where he and Jackie had lived while he was a congressman, before selling it to Robert and Ethel because they needed more space for their growing family. Where Robert and Ethel had lived together with their ten children until June 1968. Robert Kennedy had been dead only three months; the president had been gone for five years. Because I couldn't reconcile the magnificent house, the tree-shaded hillside, the sunny lawn wending down toward a tennis court, and the terrible fate of these two men and their families, I focused only on the house and our journey there.

We'd left Cape Cod that morning aboard one of the Skakel Great Lakes Carbon Corporation planes, not the turbo jet that would fly us to Sun Valley in December but a slow, old prop plane, the kids complained. It was my first flight in a private plane and seemed pretty special...walking out on the tarmac among the crowd of seven kids, four or five adults, Freckles and Rocky, being greeted by the pilot who climbed in behind us and disappeared into the cockpit. Lee had told me to stay clear of Mrs. K and keep the kids in line. She was a nervous flier for good reason: both her parents had died in a plane crash when she was in her twenties and her brother in another crash just two years before.

Freddy Bacon and Joe-the-Butler were driving the cars back to Virginia with the suitcases, supplies, Panda—the English sheepdog too big for the plane—and a trailer with the horses. Had they left over the weekend? Would they be at the airport to greet us? I don't remember the landing or the drive from the DC airport over historic Chain Bridge and along old Chain Bridge Road to McLean. Someone may have pointed out Uncle Teddy's house along the way. Clear memory begins with the turn onto the property, the drive up under the trees, and the big white house with its red door. Only later I'd notice the eight-by-ten photo of Brumus, their great, lazy Newfoundland, his chin resting on his outstretched paws, his eyes at half-mast, and the sign: "Attention au Chien."

The kids burst into the house in full holler. Kerry linked her arm through mine. "Come on. Your room is right next to mine." We scurried across the white tiled entry hall toward a flight of red carpeted stairs, but not before I spotted the Hickory Hill secretary, Sally Irish, coming out from behind her desk in a room off the entry. Kerry tugged me along before I could officially meet Sally, but I knew a few things about her already. She had also been a Peace Corps volunteer and served as Mrs. Kennedy's personal secretary. She was a few years older than Lee, maybe thirty, but everything else about her could wait.

Courtney, David, and Michael streaked past us up the stairs, and we followed them to the second floor, where they each disappeared into separate rooms while we climbed on up another flight to the third floor. Kerry pushed open the door at the top of the stairs.

"This is your room," she told me before dragging me down the hall to the next door. "And this is mine."

"What about the little boys?" I asked.

Their room was down the hall toward a bathroom. Kerry led me to the first door opposite hers and into a big nursery with two twin beds, low bookshelves, tables, and toys. Next to it, a small room directly across from Ena's held a low toddler's bed where Dougie slept. Windows looked out toward an enormous tree growing atop a broad hillside that sloped down to a swimming pool and a long, high-roofed, modern-looking pool house that held more than showers and dressing rooms. Like the Ambassador's home on the cape, it housed a movie theater where every weekend we would watch recently released or golden-oldie movies selected for kid-appropriate content by Sally Irish.

Kerry pointed down to a platform in the big tree that shaded a patio where wrought-iron chairs surrounded a glass-topped table. "Bobby set up a zip line from that tree fort down to the pool once," she told me before running out of the room.

I followed her back down the hall to the top of the stairs where I paused and looked again into my room. It was about as big as our rooms in the sorority house had been, with a twin bed against one wall, a big closet, and a high window situated almost directly above the front door. Fitted into the window, a large box fan whirred, one that would run day and night for all the time I lived there, at first to cool the room from Virginia's Indian summer heat and humidity, later as white noise to screen out little kids' natters and whines and in December a new baby's cries. Bold, pink-poppy-flowered wallpaper covered the walls, and a gorgeous bedspread—creamy white with pink-black-and-green-patterned flowers—matched the walls. I'd write home that all the linens, like at Jackie's, had labels from France. A dresser, one chair upholstered in the bedspread fabric, and a bedside table with a fabric lampshade completed the décor. Someone had already put my suitcase in the room, but this was no time to unpack. From the second floor, the children's voices reminded me that I was on duty.

BEFORE EVERYONE SCATTERED TO PLACES I didn't yet know, I rounded them up one by one and suggested they change into play clothes and begin unpacking. Courtney and Michael were the easiest to motivate. Courtney began to empty her case, placing shorts and shirts in drawers, while I helped hang a few shifts in her closet. Through the shared bathroom, I could see David fiddling at his desk. The bathroom would be a point of ongoing conflict between them, one or the other always locked out and banging on the door.

"Bet we can beat you unpacking," I called to David. He probably sneered a *Hah* back at me followed by a sly smile. I'd help him later or do it myself just to get it done.

Courtney's and David's rooms were at the south end of the second floor across the hall from each other with windows to the south and the east. Courtney's room, directly below the nursery, looked out toward the pool. The room next to hers had been transformed into Mrs. Kennedy's dressing room and walk-through closet. Beyond a small bathroom, the master bedroom—Mrs. Kennedy's room—occupied half of the new wing and looked out toward the pool. David's room, below Ena's, had windows looking out toward the front of the house. A closet separated his room from Michael's, which was below Kerry's room. When I'd mastered the third- and second-floor layouts and felt satisfied that the first bags had been unpacked enough, I asked who would show me the downstairs and the pool house.

This time Courtney took my wrist and led me down to the first floor. The stairs stopped at a little foyer in front of a powder room, the last stop for handwashing before entering the dining room. We turned left through a door into a big airy room where floor-to-ceiling sheer pink-white-and-green-flowered drapes covered the windows and huge pastel paintings of Kathleen, Joe, and Bobby Jr. as toddlers hung in ornate gold frames on the walls. The elegant dining table was long enough to seat twenty. Antique gold French chairs upholstered in pink leather seemed over-the-top after the simplicity of the compound and out of sync with the comfortable, down-cushioned furniture in the television room and the secretaries' office. The windows looked out to the patio that I'd seen from Courtney's room, and I asked if we'd ever eat outdoors. She told me probably not but that sometimes the little kids, Dougie, Max, and Christopher, would, at least until the weather turned.

Before going outside, we wound our way through the ground floor. From the dining room, we entered the new wing where a massive drawing room and parlor that had been added to the original house held multiple desks, bureaus, sofas, tables, and chairs that looked to me like samples from the Metropolitan Museum of Art's furniture collection, every flat surface crowded with silver-framed photographs of the children, the senator, the president, the Kennedy family members, famous people—some I'd already met. An American flag from the Oval Office stood beside a desk against one wall, its droopy folds heavy and still. To complete the full circle of the downstairs, we left the parlor and entered a cozy, green-carpeted room with a fireplace and overflowing bookshelves, sofas and overstuffed club chairs, where we'd spend evenings after homework watching television or playing games. Across the entry hall was a matching room with two desks, sofa, and chairs that was the secretaries' domain during the day. Those first weeks back, we actually had three secretaries working: Sally, Lee, and Penny.

We returned to the dining room, where Courtney pulled me out the patio door to present the view down to the pool. I can almost guarantee that a couple of kids had changed into suits and were already splashing around, Michael shouting, "Marco," and David, Kerry, and Christopher hollering back, "Polo." I can't be sure, but I'm guessing that I checked in with Mrs. Kennedy or Sally Irish that first day to see what needed to be completed before I joined the kids in the pool. The Washington humidity felt warm and thick compared to the winds off Nantucket Sound, but we could pop out of the pool, pick up a football, and run a few plays without getting cold. For the little home games that we played after school, we'd usually line up boys against girls. Courtney would quarterback us, I'd try to block out David, and Kerry would dash and dart like an Irish hare. On defense, Courtney was ferocious chasing after Michael or David full throttle. After a couple of plays, someone would bail out and run to jump in the pool, the rest right behind.

Christopher, Max, and Douglas ate a half hour before the rest of us. Usually Ena fed them, although sometimes Mrs. Kennedy came down early and sat with them before the rest of us entered for the later meal. Otherwise, we five waited in the foyer for her to arrive and enter the dining room. She sat at the head of the table with Kerry on one side, Courtney on the other, and David, as eldest son home, opposite her at the other end. Michael and I took the chairs left over.

In Hyannis, I'd not eaten dinner with Mrs. Kennedy except a few nights when the older kids came home and everybody ate together. Those I considered the grown-ups, the Kennedy clan and guests, had always eaten much later than the kids, so I felt a little nervous with the six of us alone at the table. She'd told me once that I would lead dinner table discussions and pose questions to the kids about history when we got back to Hickory Hill, but really, I had no idea what she expected. I was worrying about this when in through the swinging door to the kitchen Joe-the-Butler appeared in his white jacket and black bow tie with dinner plates in hand, the way house boys had done in my sorority. So this was what the sorority had been training us for, I thought, although I doubted that anyone I knew in Portland had butlers serving dinners prepared in unseen kitchens. The conversation that first night was probably about getting ready for school and who was coming for dinner on Friday and what movie everyone wanted to see. There were no suggestions that I lead a discussion.

By the time school started for "my four kids" (David, Courtney, Michael, Kerry) and Christopher later that week, I'd scouted out the house a few more times to be sure of everyone's room, including the empty ones on the third floor of the new wing, rooms for Kathleen and Joe when they were home or for guests when they weren't. The second-floor new wing was divided between the senator's office, dressing room, and bath and the master bedroom with its southeastern wall of sliding glass that opened to a balcony and looked toward the pool through the huge hilltop tree—Mrs. Kennedy's domain. No snooping in there. It was a room to which you were summoned.

Every kid needed to be prepared for the opening day of school. David and Michael wore the uniform blue blazer, blue oxford button-down shirt, tan khakis, cordovan loafers, and a tie with the *PT-109* Kennedy tie clip. Always a narrow navy or black tie for David and a wide, crazy-patterned or psychedelic-colored, sloppily knotted one for Michael. It didn't take long to notice that both boys had outgrown their school clothes over the summer. Shopping for uniform clothes would be in my future. For now, I frantically sewed name tags into every article of clothing, from underpants to T-shirts, reassigning Bobby's somewhat tattered shirts to David and David's to Michael. Christopher, starting kindergarten at the Potomac School, didn't need to worry about a uniform, but both Courtney and Kerry, in seventh and fourth grades at Stone Ridge School of the Sacred Heart, wore the traditional plaid skirt and white blouse of every Catholic middle schooler. Like their brothers, last year's uniforms no longer fit, so I'd be sent into Georgetown to shop ASAP.

Just as for the JFK commissioning, I laid out the boys' clothes the night before the first day of school and set my alarm for six thirty. The bathroom door was closed when I looked down the hall in the morning, water running inside. Kerry's bed was empty, and I assumed she was up, excited for her first day. Or maybe Ena had wakened her. I hurried down the stairs to Michael's room. Rap rap rap. "Time to get up. School!" I chirped and moved on to David's door next. I could hear Michael pushing the dogs off the bed, but David lay like a hump when I looked in. It would take a week to figure out a routine that worked with him. Knock and enter. Pull back the drapes. Turn off the fan. Gently shake a shoulder and return and return. But I didn't have that dance down yet.

Next came Courtney's room. Her bed was empty, like Kerry's. But the bathroom was empty too. I turned on the light and pulled back the curtains. Her clothes lay over the chair. Back upstairs I looked for Kerry again. Not in her room. Not in the bathroom. Not in the nursery either. Ena's door was closed, and I knocked.

"I can't find the girls," I said, slightly panicked that they'd be late for breakfast and carpool on the very first day.

Ena look pleased with her hypothesis: "They probably in with Mrs. Kennedy. You have to go in there and get them up."

"In her bedroom?" I asked incredulous. I couldn't go into Mrs. Kennedy's bedroom while she was asleep—or any other time. It was like contemplating walking in on—I don't know—the pope. I could tolerate being part of her audience, could observe a tennis game or perform a swim exhibit, dive for a catch or sit at a luncheon and politely listen to Washington gossip, but I couldn't go into her bedroom while she was sleeping!

Ena poked a finger through her hair and scratched while she eyed me. "She won't be asleep. You gotta get them up."

I looked at her in her white nursemaid dress, her sturdy shoes. She'd been with the family since before Kathleen was born and lived in this tiny third-floor room, cradling, carrying, feeding, comforting one baby after another, then turning them over to some educated outsider, a governess, who got to eat at the table, meet the guests, drive the cars, and then—after a year or a few months (or a few days according to rumor)—return to their comfortable lives somewhere else.

She wasn't going to help me.

I turned to the long hall and hurried down the stairs, looked in on Michael, shook David again. "Get up. You don't want to be late." One more scan of Courtney's room. Empty. I took a deep breath and then tiptoed through the dressing room, through the bathroom, and tapped on the closed bedroom door. The fan whirled inside. *Did someone say something?* I tapped again and listened.

The whir.

Slowly I turned the doorknob and looked into the semidark room: Mrs. Kennedy a long lump closest to the door with two smaller bumps beside her. I started into the room, and her head popped up.

"Courtney. Kerry. It's time for school," I stammered.

"I'll wake them. Thanks, kid."

I wasn't prepared for the intimacy of my position. *Geez.* I thought as I pulled the door shut. *I can't believe I just did that.*

The girls scampered out in the next few minutes, and soon we were all at the breakfast table, even David, discussing the morning headlines, ready for school to start. Sometime later Mrs. K informed me that in the future I was to come in the door from the senator's office and to waken anyone sleeping with her without knocking first. I think she was joking when she told me that she didn't need to be up for school.

Even on my days off that year, I made the wake-up rounds in this order: Michael and the dogs; David, blinds up, fan off, a gentle shake and a whisper; Courtney and Kerry in Mrs. K's bedroom, where she also kept the fan blowing every night from September until June, through heat, rain, and blizzard. One winter morning I had to thaw her water glass because it had frozen over. By then Christopher had joined the nightly migration to the big bed in the windy room. Little kids seeking animal heat, maternal warmth, family comfort.

Within two weeks of arriving in McLean, Virginia, I wrote home that things were under control again. Finally my duties seemed clear: I was on the carpool schedule for the Potomac School and for Stone Ridge. I would represent Mrs. K at all school events and conferences since she was making no public appearances for the year of mourning. I was to organize the after-school lessons in tennis, riding, and swimming as long as the weather held. Sally Irish would let me know when to make dentist and doctor appointments, and I'd be the driver. Then there was the shopping for school clothes and play clothes and later for ski trips and Christmas.

Mrs. K called me into her room one morning after I'd returned from driving. She sat at her desk, the Red Book open as she made notes. She wondered if it was "beneath" me to teach Max something each morning while Chris was away at kindergarten. "You can do so many creative things with him," she said.

Is she being critical? I wondered. Does she think I slough off when the kids are in school? Does she think a high school teacher wouldn't want to work with a three-year-old?

"I'll try, Mrs. Kennedy," I answered. "We'll have home school." But what did she actually mean? What did "teach him something" mean to her? A word a day? The alphabet one week and numbers the next? He already knew all the words to "On Top of Spaghetti." Maybe we would have song time every day. What I remember doing is bundling him into the car and driving off to Great Falls to wander along the paths and look at the river or out to Manassas. A few times we visited the Smithsonian once I got the hang of driving in DC. And everywhere, we looked at things and talked about them: snails, mushrooms, leaves, clouds, ants, rainbows. We drew pictures, told stories, read books, sang songs.

When it got rainy, we did jigsaw puzzles and art projects with construction paper. I must have taught him something every morning we spent together.

Teaching Max wasn't the only job she had on the list, though. She wanted me to arrange the bookshelves, organize the ski clothes, select classical music to be played at dinner from their record collection. And I'd be responsible for initiating dinner conversations. This time she was more explicit. She wanted me to bring up explorers, inventors, sportsmen, artists, statesmen to share what I knew and to quiz them.

The quizzes, throwing out some clues and getting them to guess who, started a nightly game that might end in "Guess who's coming to dinner this weekend" or "How many gold medals will the US win in Mexico City?" or "How will poor Hubert Humphrey ever beat Nixon?" If Mrs. K was present, I might start the conversation and get the kids to jump in, but soon she'd take over. I never minded yielding the floor because she usually had interesting news to report or behind-the-scenes stories to tell and she could be very funny.

One night she had *big news*, she excitedly told us. It was not to be discussed outside yet, but the senator's book, *Thirteen Days*, had sold for the highest price in publishing history: one million dollars! *McCall's* magazine would print excerpts around Thanksgiving, and the hardbound copy would come out for Christmas. It would reveal details of the Cuban Missile Crisis never before made public, she told us.

That explained what had been going on since we returned to Virginia. Robert McNamara, the secretary of defense during John Kennedy's administration, had been an ongoing visitor recently and meeting with Mrs. Kennedy for hours at a time. Now Ted

Sorensen, who had been the president's main speechwriter, would be coming the next day to help her prepare the announcement.

You could tell that she was remembering those days back in 1962 when the United States and Russia seemed to be on the brink of war over Russia's placement of missiles in Cuba. "You can't imagine the pressure," she said. "Khrushchev and Jack were sending letters back and forth. The military wanted to use the atom bomb. It was Bob [McNamara] who kept us from using it. Bobby was in the room for all the discussions," she said and paused for a while. Then she added forcefully, "It's much safer to have a civilian run the Defense Department than a military man." We all nodded in agreement.

I'd been in high school during the crisis and remembered hearing that someone's brother at Yale had called home frightened. But it hadn't seemed a big deal. Now I had so many questions. She talked on through dinner, answering the questions I asked until finally she offered to let me read the manuscript when she finished. This felt like the first real adult conversation we'd had, talking together while the kids sat listening, as if I'd been moved to the grown-up's table. But the next day I babbled onto a tape like a teenager: "She went berserk calling people all over the world. And at dinner she told us all sorts of things she remembered about that time."

The night I selected "The Pines of Rome" for our dinner music, Mrs. Kennedy complimented the choice. She'd never heard it before, she said, so I dredged up what I could remember from program notes at the symphony in Portland (and probably from the album cover as well). I could have talked about how the piece evoked images of Rome for me—the long, soft evening light and how warm the air had felt when I was fourteen. But I'm sure I didn't. In my weekly letter home, I relayed Mrs. K's compliment and thanked Mom for making me go to the symphony with her, then pronounced the Kennedy record collection sketchy. I'd be asking Sally Irish for an allowance to buy some new ones, I wrote. Those concerts and the music appreciation class my senior year at Oregon had given me a mini-cultural edge. Holding my own at the dinner table now felt about as important as keeping my classes under control had felt the previous year.

Chapter 12

ON THE TEAM
SEPTEMBER–OCTOBER 1968

AFTER DROPPING COURTNEY, KERRY, AND THEIR CLASSMATES AT Stone Ridge in Bethesda on my first carpool day, I drove on into DC along Wisconsin Avenue first to pick up the new uniforms and then on to Saks to buy essentials. The stores weren't open yet, so I found a phone booth and called home to tell them where I was, then wandered around window shopping. At the car later with the uniforms I fumbled in my pockets but found — no keys. A desperate dash to the shop ensued and then on to the phone booth, where they sat waiting inside on the little ledge.

My search for Saks that day became a lost cause. I wound up and down the streets of DC and finally asked a taxi driver, who somehow sent me whipping along the beltway and back into Virginia. That night after I'd tucked in all the kids and laid out the morning clothes and Joe-the-Butler had finished cleaning the kitchen and set up the breakfast table, he spread out a city map and patiently drew the route to Saks for me. I confessed to him that I'd lost the keys too, but to no one else. At least not to anyone in the house; it was a good story to write home, but Sally Irish and Mrs. K did not need to know.

Lee Geisen and Joe-the-Butler became my best friends at Hickory Hill, additions to my friends back home. At nineteen, Joe was closest to me in age, and we shared a similar sense of humor. He lived somewhere in DC and arrived for work each morning shortly after breakfast. He ran errands, helped Ruby with dishes and meal prep, served both lunch and dinner, and stayed after to do kitchen cleanup. On weekends he might work until midnight if there was a dinner party.

The youngest of an Italian immigrant family, he'd grown up somewhere near London and followed his brother to the States, where he hoped to be naturalized. In his role, he always wore black slacks, a fresh white shirt, black suspenders—which he called "braces"—and a black bow tie with a starched white jacket. He cut quite a figure in black and white with his black hair and thick eyebrows, chocolate brown eyes, and fabulous British accent. We loved talking, debriefing, passing along what we'd heard each day and laughing. We were simpatico.

Sometimes on weekends we'd share a cold beer or an unfinished bottle of wine (Pouilly-Fuissé always) that he'd sneak from the kitchen, but not often. His older brother lived in New York, a live-in chef for the man who owned Avon, and a couple of times when his boss was traveling, he came down to cook for Mrs. K so that Ruby, the longtime live-in cook, could have time off. He was a master Italian chef who offered dishes I couldn't pronounce. Mrs. Kennedy swooned over his cooking but the kids preferred Ruby's; they were always glad when she returned.

The day after getting lost in Washington, DC, I headed back to the world where what you look like determines your treatment. My daily "uniform" at the Kennedys' now consisted of powder-blue Levi's cord jeans, a polo shirt, and someone's wool pullover I'd found in my closet, along with a pair of grass-stained sneakers. I did not look like the ladies shopping in the Saks children's department. As on the cape, no clerk seemed interested in helping me. I lingered. I loitered. I fingered through underwear until finally someone sidled over and I pulled a list from my pocket:

Five pairs size 4 boys' underpants

Five pairs size 5 underpants

Three pairs size 10 girls' undies

On and on ran the order for underpants and undershirts, boys' socks, knee socks, turtlenecks, and jeans. When we'd finished, I handed over the credit card: Robert F. Kennedy, 1147 Chain Bridge Road. A month or so later when I returned to buy clothes for the Sun Valley ski trip, two smiling clerks spotted me and instantly hurried to help.

Shopping in exclusive stores reminded me of an experience I'd had as a college senior, when I'd felt as out of place as I looked in Saks. By the time I turned twenty-one, I had learned lifestyle essentials: to buy Cutty Sark for a house-dance date, to drink Fumé Blanc with freshly caught trout grilled streamside, and to serve adults sherry before dinner. At Christmas that year, I shopped for sherry glasses to give my parents (my effort to sophisticate them). Sorority sister Linda, who worked holidays in a downtown store, told me who carried them—a chic boutique, the kind of store that sold Christian Dior silks and long gowns I couldn't imagine anyone wearing, where a blouse cost more than a month of lifeguarding wages, where glassware was part of the holiday merchandise. As soon as I stepped in from the rain-soaked Portland pavement, I knew this wasn't the Dark Horse, the purveyor of cozy Pendleton skirts and Villager sweaters. An elegant saleswoman, tall and slender, with rings and bracelets and polished red nails, approached and I felt like an imposter asking for sherry glasses, but she smiled and pointed out two types. She lifted one tiny tinted glass, waved her hand over the others, and said these were ten dollars.

I can manage that, I'd thought, surprised, until she asked if I would want eight or ten in the set. *Oh!* My cheeks pulsed red. *Apiece!* I turned away, pretending to look at something else. *How could I be so stupid?*

I'd been so ignorant then and felt so humiliated. What was the difference now, I wondered as I cruised along in the big white convertible. Feeling the Kennedy power, of course. Being one of the "chosen." With a store credit card representing the Kennedys, I never felt embarrassed or an outsider no matter what I was wearing. I was a "somebody" on their team, and I knew it.

SEPTEMBER PASSED INTO OCTOBER, AND Hickory Hill mellowed from green to gold. Most days Ena fed the boys their lunch, or Mrs. Kennedy would feed Douglas then chat a bit with Chris and Max before her luncheon guests arrived. Sometimes they would be old friends who came over to help with the correspondence and we'd eat in the dining room served by Joe or Katherine, the downstairs maid. Mrs. K was still receiving condolence letters, and each was answered, not by her but by the secretaries and the fleet of volunteers. I'd received a Mass card and formal thank-you from Mrs. K in June after I'd sent a condolence card for the senator, but I realized now it had probably been signed by Lee Geisen or Leora Mora or any one of the many helpers. My mom had been right when she'd said that they must get scores of letters a day.

When other friends like Kay Evans, wife of *Washington Post* columnist Rowland Evans, or Liz Stevens, who I'd met on the cape, or Mrs. McNamara came, luncheon felt more formal. Mrs. Kennedy would invite me to eat with them, while I knew the secretaries would be gossiping over their sack lunches. I learned how to demur. Once when she had special guests that fall, Jomo Kenyatta's brother and friend from Kenya, they were served down by the pool. She called me over and introduced me, "Our wonderful governess…an Olympic gold medalist…" Then she invited me to sit with them even though there was no place for me.

"Oh, I'm on a diet," I laughed. "No lunch for me today." But really, I wanted to escape, to sit with the secretaries, to find out who was who and what the visit might be about. I could write home about "the personages" I'd met without sitting through a fancy luncheon.

After the kids returned home from school, I'd dog them to their rooms to change before going out to play. The boys would go out for a tennis game, and the girls often headed to the stable, where Freddy would help them saddle up. They'd do some circuits in the ring or ride up and around the trails in the woods surrounding the house. I tagged along with them sometimes for the chance to talk to Freddy and watch the lesson. But one day Courtney said she wanted me to try out her pony, Atlas, a big, strong, white gelding she'd ridden up on the cape. He looked twice as big as Kerry's little spotted pony. I told her I'd only ridden a few times, having flunked out of riding school after two lessons. All the way to the stable, she teased and coaxed, dared and begged, demonstrating her many dramatic skills. A regular little Sarah Bernhardt. At the stable Kerry, outfitted in helmet and boots and a big smile, asked if I was going to ride with them today, and Freddy held out a riding hat. It seemed everybody was of one mind.

I told Courtney to ride a few circuits to warm up Atlas so I could see where to go. When my turn came, she held the reins with a big grin, looking so innocent with little side pigtails poking out of her helmet. Freddy went over a few basic instructions, reminding me to use the reins, not my heels. Atlas took a few side steps when I mounted, unaccustomed to the extra weight. Freddy gave him a pat on the rump, and off we started up the track toward a little grove of trees. I tried to remember posting protocol as we trotted along and up into the woods. All was going well until the trail curved and turned back toward home. Something launched Atlas from trot to gallop in a gear shift that almost knocked me off. We were instantly running flat out downhill, my feet out of the stirrups, me clinging to his mane, half on half off, flung around like Raggedy Ann all the way to the barn. When Freddy stepped away from the fence with his arms up, Atlas finally stopped. Courtney practically fell down laughing before she asked if I was okay.

I hadn't fallen off and I was laughing, so I guessed I was okay, though my pride felt bruised. At dinner Courtney must have told the story three times, dissolving in hysterics every time so that Kerry had to finish. Mrs. Kennedy laughed too and reminded Courtney that Atlas did have the tendency to run for the barn. They were all in the know, I realized. Maybe it had been some sort of test.

When Courtney was still telling the story a week later, I admitted that I might have looked pretty ridiculous riding practically sidesaddle and hanging on for my life, but a twelve-year-old could really wear out a joke. Maybe it was time for a swim contest! I hadn't been the butt of a joke for a very long time, not since my brother had teased me in childhood. But Courtney's tease wasn't mean—more like an initiation that welcomed me into her club.

Some afternoons if it was hot and muggy, we'd go for a swim, pull on shorts and run some football plays, and then jump back in the pool until Joe rang the warning bell for dinner.

The little boys ate at six, and afterward Ena took them up for baths and bedtime. The rest of us ate at six thirty, and my duty was to get everyone downstairs and presentable, shirts tucked in, hair combed, face and hands clean, before Mrs. Kennedy came down. She could explode over messy hair and dirty fingernails. Courtney was a neatnik compared to Kerry, who at nine had her own hygiene standards. I kept a brush handy to fix her wild hair five minutes before dinner. Same for Michael. David's long blonde hair always looked good from the front, but his nails! I convinced him to let me scrub them in the downstairs powder room after an explosive encounter neither of us wanted to see repeated. When he broke his wrist playing football one weekend, I became his meticulous hand washer to keep the cast dry. Even so, we made at least three trips to Georgetown University Hospital that fall to get it recast because he destroyed the plaster. Hand washing became our bonding experience.

After dinner Mrs. K usually disappeared upstairs to make phone calls or plans for the next day, to fill up the Red Book, or maybe to read. We "kids" might play a game of Scrabble or watch television. In October we followed the Mexico City Olympics, betting on who'd win races as they came on. Sometimes they'd do their homework while watching, other times up in their rooms. Bedtime for Kerry was at nine, Michael and Courtney at nine thirty, and David, who often found work he'd "forgotten" to do, stayed up until ten or later.

One Sunday night after dinner, we horsed around in the TV room for half an hour, a tangled tickle war that ended as usual: David pinched Kerry, and she stormed off in tears; Courtney needed to study for a test; Michael, whose work was done, he promised, called the dogs into his room and disappeared; and David mumbled that he thought he had some homework and closed his door. Courtney and I were running through questions for a Monday test when David appeared in the doorway, blonde hair dangling over one eye, his blue shirt rumpled and untucked.

"What's an adverb? Do you even know?" he challenged in his surly, sarcastic, not-yet-changed voice.

"Ahhh. Yes. I *was* an English teacher," I responded, with equal sarcasm.

This was the closest David ever came to asking for help, but I heard him. I told Courtney that she was going to ace her test. All she had to do was run through the questions one more time and go to sleep.

In David's room, a beautiful, wide, wooden desk filled one corner, illuminated by a lamp that reminded me of the ones in the New York Public Library. Papers and books lay strewn on top, dirty clothes pushed off toward the wall.

"So, what's the assignment?" I asked. A traditional grammar book lay open to a page of sentences.

"We're supposed to find the adverbs in these." His hand brushed across the page.

I hadn't studied grammar since Mrs. Ferrin's sophomore English class. It had gone out of fashion, first replaced by trans-formational grammar, which nobody understood (although that's what the nuns taught at Stone Ridge, I'd learn when Courtney needed help later that year), and then by nothing. High school

English classes focused on literature and composition, not sentence parsing.

"Look for words ending in -*ly*," I told him first. "They *add* on to the verb—get it?"

We went through the first sentences, and it seemed too easy—we found too few. There had to be more than -*ly* adverbs. Working with the exercise sentences and a dictionary, we looked up the words that were placed close to the verbs (or I did) and suddenly found gobs more adverbs: *a lot, lots, always, every, never, so, upstairs, nowhere.*

Later that week David told me that he'd gotten a 95 percent on the assignment and his teacher asked him who he'd had for English the year before.

"She said, 'That figures,' when I told her." He smirked. We shared a secret now.

"What did you get last year in English?" I asked.

"A D, I think. Or maybe a C-."

"You'll do better this year, for sure."

Sometimes after everyone was in bed and I was downstairs watching TV, David would appear and plunk down nearby. We talked about sports, football or the Olympics, or maybe what was going on with the election coming up in November. He was easy just one on one—no teasing, no sarcasm, no sullen silences.

"He's a tender soul," I wrote home. "And a fierce competitor." *A beautiful boy*, I thought. Short for his age, small-boned, ninety-four pounds at most, fragile but fast. He'd made first string on the football team playing both quarterback and halfback. He was built like the senator and played the way I imagined he had—quick off the line, cunning in the field, wild to reach the end zone. To help him gain weight and get stronger, we set up barbells and a

David, thirteen years old, shows his quarterback form on the grounds of Hickory Hill in Virginia. Max scampers off chasing a dog.

diet program. The broken wrist set him back a week or two, but he got permission to play, and I didn't miss a game the whole season. The weekend he chose me first for a touch game, I knew I'd passed another test.

Chapter 13

BECOMING FAMILY

FRIDAY NIGHTS WERE MOVIE NIGHTS, AND AFTER DINNER DOWN IN the pool house, there'd be jostling for seats on the pink sofas, a possible fight over the big armchairs, and then the movie would roll and calm descend. If it were a new release, the adults might join us—Mrs. Kennedy had dinner guests every Friday and most Saturdays—but usually it was just the kids, their friends, the dogs, and me. In those first weeks, we watched a combination of first runs and old standbys, all G- or PG-rated: *The Umbrellas of Cherbourg* and *Inspector Clouseau*, *Mutiny on the Bounty* and *Paper Lion*. Sometimes Mrs. Kennedy weighed in on new movies she wanted to see, but mainly it was up to Sally Irish to find the weekend entertainment.

Sally had connections around town, like the ones I was developing at Saks and the baby store in Hyannis. Individuals and businesses wanted to cater to those in power—or who might be in power; it could be advantageous to supply favors. The Robert Kennedys had had political power since 1961 when he was attorney general in the Kennedy White House, then later when he became a New York senator, and most recently as a presidential candidate. Sally could have borrowed films from the library, but she was more likely to tap connections like George Stevens Jr., who was developing the American Film Institute, or other DC distributors. But as time passed after the senator's death, first-run films became harder and harder to obtain. Sally muttered after putting in call after call trying to find a copy of a film Mrs. Kennedy wanted, "How am I going to explain to her that it's just not like it used to be?"

WHO RAN THE PROJECTOR ON Friday and Saturday nights? Joe-the-Butler? Freddy Bacon? John Yaxley, the friendly gardener and maintenance man? Someone threaded it up and rewound it and somehow got it back to the library or film institute or distribution company. But like many jobs that kept the household running smoothly, the worker remained unrecognized. I was no different than the kids in expecting to be provided for, in enjoying the privilege of being served.

After the novelty of movie night wore off, when the film was too old or too ridiculous to watch, I'd escape to the big house to catch up on chores, replacing a lost button or sewing in name tags, or to share a final debrief with Joe before he headed home for the night. Voices drifting up from the pool signaled when the film was over, and I'd wander down to herd my crew toward bed.

Saturdays were our play days—tennis, riding, swimming—and the main event: touch football. These were serious games with carefully constructed teams. Dave Hackett came over almost every Saturday that fall. He'd been the senator's best friend since prep school and became, along with Uncle Teddy, a surrogate father. He seemed the most like I imagined their father—athletic, physical, funny, and familiar. Senator Ted came some Saturdays,

A September Saturday at Hickory Hill taking a break between touch football games with Courtney, Michael holding Freckles, and Kerry, nine years old.

but he had a bad back and couldn't play as hard as Dave. Other players showed up, teachers and classmates from the Potomac School, overnight guests. David might captain one team, Michael the other. A coin toss would determine who got first choice. Quarterbacks designed elaborate plays that involved two or three runners following patterns. Others of us ran interference, blocking the defenders. Even though it was touch, the touches could be rough, and the blockers were expected to knock people down. It didn't take much to fire up my competitive spirit, and the rough and tumble, the shouts and arguments released a lot of pent-up energy. I took hits every weekend and sometimes nursed bruises until Wednesday, but I scored touchdowns and knocked more than a few runners out of bounds. In a tape home, I detailed a few of our plays and my scores, knowing that my father would be pleased.

More casual games might pit boys against girls or make room for Christopher and Max on a few plays. David would sketch out the plan for Christopher, drawing his finger on his palm: "Run forward three steps, turn out and run five steps, then turn around and look at me, and I'll throw you the ball." Michael would do the same for Max. Simple instructions, a little hand sketch, and a "Ready, hut." They were kind, these big brothers, in the informal games. A loose game played in bathing suits and interrupted with pool splashes might last for half an hour, but a serious game could go on for an hour and a half, with a break for lunch, before resuming later out on the broad, sweeping side lawn.

One Saturday morning Dave Hackett arrived with his kids just as we were finishing breakfast. He'd brought along his Olympic hockey jersey, the one he never got to wear at the Olympics because he broke his ankle in training. He also brought his friend from prep school, John Knowles, the man who'd written *A Separate Peace*, the book I'd read the year before, the one that had left me in tears, its story touching a deep core of truth within me. Finally, an opportunity to meet someone famous I actually knew about, a writer whose novel I'd admired and taught.

A lot seemed at stake that morning when two of David's teachers also joined us to play. For the first time, he chose me to be on his team. We ended up winning 24 to 18, and I scored three of the touchdowns. Afterwards, Mrs. K raved about my play, which sent me into lunch all aglow. In contrast, John Knowles had not played well at all. After half an hour of lackluster play, dropped balls, and sloppy blocking, he'd begged off and hobbled over to the stone stairs to watch the rest of the game. *What a wimp*, I thought. *How like Gene.* Dave Hackett, though, dominated the field. *He's Finny*, I realized.

When I'd read the book, I'd identified more with Gene, the studious, introspective but flawed narrator. But now it was fun, freewheeling Finny I wanted to be, not that wimp, Knowles. Of course, I was confusing the author with the narrator and myself with a character. Maybe I felt disappointed that John Knowles wasn't how I'd expected an author to be. Or maybe I'd let my not-so-latent competitive spirit lash out. It was easy to feel competitive at the Kennedys', especially when it came to sports.

After the game, David pulled on Dave Hackett's USA jersey, which hung almost to his knees.

"Look, I'm on the Olympic team."

"Let me take your picture," I said, and he posed, silly and proud. He liked to pose, his arm cocked, ready for a long pass or pinning Michael to the carpet in a fake wrestling move or beside one of the big rockets that he, Michael, and John Yaxley built and launched from a nearby park, my snapshots of him more like my mom's than a paparazzo's.

Another weekend several players from the Washington Redskins came to play. Maybe that was the weekend David ran into a player and cracked his wrist, but he played to the end of the game before confessing he was hurt. He instigated my first but not last drive to the Georgetown University Hospital emergency room. I set speed records on that road between McLean and Georgetown over the year.

ONCE WE RETURNED TO VIRGINIA, my schedule regulated with much-needed time off, but never on Fridays or Saturdays. First I had a Thursday and the next week a Sunday–Monday. What joy to fly to New York my first "weekend off" for rest and rehab with

David poses wearing Dave Hackett's 1952 Olympic ice hockey uniform.

my friends, Bob and Helen Burke, who pampered me with food, drink, laughter, and seventeen hours of sleep. Two weeks later I flew off to Camp Lejeune, North Carolina, to visit their daughter, my former teammate, Lynn Burke, who was living on base with her husband and baby girl.

Refreshed and happy to be "home" again on Tuesday, I slipped back into the daily routine. A guest cook, Joe-the-Butler's brother, was filling in for Ruby while she took a week's vacation, her reward for spending the summer in Hyannis Port. As usual, several guests joined Mrs. K for lunch, a fancy soufflé. The dinner menu departed from Ruby's meat and potatoes, and the kids muttered a few complaints, but I dug in, happy to try something new—seafood perhaps, linguine with clam sauce or stuffed calamari in tomato sauce, a crab salad. Whatever it was, Mrs. Kennedy praised it and called the chef out from the kitchen to thank him. He took a little bow, gracefully accepting the compliment. It meant the world to get praise from her...even a little notice sometimes set my heart racing. I hadn't outgrown the need to please a person in authority—my brother, my parents, teachers, coaches, principals—or my desire to exceed expectations. It reminded me of being noticed by my swim idol when I was twelve or thirteen, her nod after a win better than a medal.

Sometime after midnight I woke in a sweat as salty saliva gushed into my mouth, my throat burning. I swallowed back bile and ran for the bathroom, threw back the lid, and vomited before I could even kneel. My breath came in gasps, and my stomach clenched again, hurling dinner chunks into the bowl. I moaned and flushed. *Am I finished?*

Before I could stand, Ena stepped in and patted my back. "Come on, then." She handed me a wet washrag, and I wiped my face. "You're burning up. Let's get you back to bed."

She led me down the dark hall as if I were a little girl, settled me in bed, and pulled up the covers. On top of the sheets, she left a towel then disappeared only to return with a bucket. It's what my mother would have done had she been there.

How long has it been since I've thrown up? I wondered as I lay waiting, unsure if this episode was over. One time in college after too much cheap red wine, my date had to pull over his car and open the door so I could pitch onto the pavement. And in Blackpool, England, the whole US swim team got food poisoning the night after high tea with the lord mayor of Blackburn. That memory brought on another wave of nausea, and I curled over the bed edge and barfed into the bucket.

Maybe I slept again, or maybe I dozed only to be seized by a whole-body wretch that hit so hard, I puked and shat in the same convulsion. "No, no, no," I moaned, too weak to move.

Hall light seeped into my little room, and hands pulled at my shoulders.

"Here, take a swallow of this," Mrs. Kennedy said as she spooned bitter liquid into my mouth. Ena helped me up and walked me down the hall, pulled off my soiled nightgown, and put me in the shower.

"Mrs. Kennedy and I'll make up the bed nice and clean," she said. "You wash up. We'll take care of you."

That night I was too sick to feel humiliated, but in the morning when Mrs. K poked her head in and asked, "How're ya doing, kid?" I blushed and lied, "Much better." Maybe I still had a fever, because it felt like I was burning up. How could a person sink any lower than having vile fluids escape from both ends simultaneously in bed in the house of your employer and she has to clean you up?

I didn't do it on purpose. It's not my fault. Childish thoughts pinged against my headache. It must have been food poisoning!

All day I lay in bed exhausted, unable to eat, although Ena came in with broth and tea. "You need liquids," she told me.

"I got poisoned," I told her. She nodded and assured me that I'd feel better tomorrow. And I did feel better late that afternoon. One by one the kids peered in to see me.

"Tell me what happened," Christopher demanded when he returned home from kindergarten, wanting gory details, ones that I might share later to gross him out. Courtney wanted to know if I needed anything to read, and Kerry wondered if I wanted to play a game. Michael reported briefly on the results of an Olympic race. The kids were good about tending someone sick and stuck in bed. With so many siblings who at some point had been bedridden with colds or flu, asthma attacks or broken limbs, they knew what to ask and what might help—sympathy, distraction, food, laughter, a cuddle.

Mrs. Kennedy checked in one more time after everyone was in bed. I thanked her for being so kind and apologized for making a mess.

"Not the first time, kiddo. Take it easy. You'll be with it again by Friday."

She'd seemed like a real person, someone you could count on in an emergency, someone who'd come through even in the middle of the night. She wasn't a bit like she'd been that day with Dougie's poop in the bathtub. She'd actually cared for me. I think I fell a little bit in love with her that night.

Ena told me later that Mrs. K had a complete "pharmacy" in her dressing room. She had something for every ailment and emergency that might arise. "She gave you opium drops for the diarrhea. It stops up everything."

When I told Joe on Thursday that I was sure I'd had food poisoning, he defended his brother. "You certainly did not. Nobody else got sick."

"Yes, but it felt like before."

"No." He was adamant.

I squinted at him but didn't argue, aware that it was much more likely the flu than food poisoning. *But it felt like Blackpool*, I thought, and my stomach turned a lazy somersault.

Weekend play wound down on Sundays like an overused toy. We'd sleep late, linger over breakfast, dawdle outside on the patio. Courtney and I might hit balls back and forth on the tennis court. David twirled on the long tree rope while Michael wrestled with Freckles on the lawn. Early in the fall, before it got too cold, we'd all end up in the pool. Guests headed home, and friends, worn out from Saturday, didn't return.

At lunch I'd ask about homework, and by late afternoon I'd be nagging. "If you finish it now, we can play games after Mass." "Last week you stayed up past bedtime with that map, remember? Let's get a head start." "I'm not going to help you at nine tonight. I'm not." These were from a catalogue of parenting skills: suggestions, bribes, guilt trips, threats. Sometimes they worked, but no guarantees.

My Cape Cod trick of confiscating shoes helped me prep the boys for Mass and school on Monday. Saturday night or early Sunday morning, I'd polish them and stow them in my room. At five thirty Sunday night they'd appear, but only after the boys were dressed up in slacks, shirts, ties, and navy blazers ready to go.

Kerry needed some help in choosing appropriately, so we'd confab on "what to wear tonight," and I'd help her dress and comb her unruly hair. Courtney was on her own. We'd be downstairs waiting when Mrs. Kennedy, who always arrived as if blown through a wind tunnel, would shout from the stairs, "Let's get going. We're late." Out we scurried to the Pontiac, Kerry elbowing her way to the front seat next to Mummy and Courtney rolling her eyes while she sped to keep up. David, Michael, and I climbed into the back, and off we drove to Saint Luke's for the six o'clock folk Mass.

One Sunday evening as we walked back to the car after Mass, Mrs. Kennedy turned to me. "Do you mind going to Arlington with us tonight?"

"Of course not." But I wondered what they did there and what I was supposed to do. *Do we drive through or walk in? Should I sit in the car or follow them?* Questions chased each other round and round. *Wait and see,* I advised myself.

Nobody talked in the back seat. David stared out the window, and Michael fiddled with his tie. Up front the girls murmured now and then, but I couldn't catch what they said. It felt like a long ride before we turned up a road blocked by a gate. A guard stepped out, looked in, and nodded at Mrs. K, then pushed open the gate, and we passed through and up to the grave sites.

Mrs. K parked and began to open her door. *I can't go up there with them,* I thought. *This is for family.* David and Michael piled out, but Courtney turned around and whispered, "Come on, Carolyn." I was about to shake my head when Mrs. K leaned back in the car, "Aren't you coming with us?"

"No, I'll just wait here."

"Well, come on now, you're perfectly welcome, you know."

How could anyone say no to Mrs. Kennedy, especially after she'd been so attentive through my illness? I might have wanted to be invisible sometimes, uncertain what to do or what was expected, but I was becoming an adjunct family member, and tonight they expected me to go with them.

It didn't occur to me that the kids might not know exactly what was going on either. They'd been to Uncle Jack's grave before, but had they been to their father's since the funeral? They'd been living up on the cape all summer. Or perhaps they'd gone other Sundays when I was in New York or North Carolina.

I followed a step behind while they marched side by side up to the grave site, stooping now and then to pick English daisies scattered through the grass, which they placed in a small wicker basket set in front of a plain white cross. Then they knelt for a long time, close together, in an arc around the foot of the grave, hands folded in prayer, silent and motionless.

I stood a step or two behind, aware of people gathering, the snapping of cameras. My neck hair prickled, my shoulders hunched. What the family was feeling, what they thought while they knelt there so long, I could not imagine then. Instead, self-consciously, I wondered who the tourists thought I might be and wished I'd stayed in the car.

After five minutes or more, Mrs. Kennedy rose and the kids unfolded to trudge with her uphill to Uncle Jack's grave. I followed and this time knelt with them briefly on the cold marble. A chill wind blew in the darkness. On the walk back to the car, Courtney came up and slipped her arm around my waist. I hugged her close as we walked back downhill. "It's awfully cold, isn't it?" she said.

What kind of solace did the visit give Mrs. Kennedy or the kids? No one talked about their father; no one cried. They had to feel the ache of his absence, but love and grief surely bound them, as did memories and the powerful sense of being a Kennedy.

We had settled back in the car when Mrs. Kennedy announced, "Let's have family prayer time now." She pulled out her rosary, and the kids fumbled in their pockets and purses until they found theirs. Courtney handed me an extra one from the glove kit. I was a convert Catholic, three years new to the faith and unschooled in family prayer or the rosary. Panic struck as Mrs. Kennedy began to recite the prayers. After two rounds she stopped, sounding like a teacher giving a pop quiz, and asked, "Michael, who shall we pray for tonight?"

"Joe and the new baby," he bellowed back.

This felt like my oral exam for Chaucer had. I was completely unprepared and terrified I'd blunder, err, stumble, fail. The prayers began again as each child, after being nudged, recited two rounds of ten Hail Marys. When eight had been completed, they all turned to me and pointed. I was to be the fifth "family member" to start the last series. I think I did a better job than I'd done with *The Canterbury Tales*, but it wasn't until later in bed that I let myself feel anything but relief.

I've wiggled into the litter, I thought, feeling warm, loved, embraced.

ON WEDNESDAY AN AMBULANCE RUSHED Mrs. Kennedy to the hospital following a night of early contractions. She returned to Hickory Hill on complete bed rest, confined to her room for the remainder of the pregnancy—eight weeks.

For a few days I had felt like part of the pack, a big sister padding behind while Mrs. Kennedy led. With her in bed—absent from the breakfast table's discussions of news or the dinner table's nightly quizzes, absent from frantic hygiene checks or speeding drives to Mass, absent from dropping in to feed the little ones or watching football games—life at Hickory Hill would change.

I guess I'll be in charge of downstairs until after Christmas, I thought, hoisting the heavy load of responsibility.

Chapter 14

WHO'S IN CHARGE?

WITHIN DAYS OF MRS. KENNEDY'S HOSPITALIZATION, MISS LUELLA Hennessey (we called her Lulu), descended on Hickory Hill like Mary Poppins floating in on an umbrella. She came with a suitcase full of stories from her years with the Ambassador's family in England before the war to the births of every Kennedy child in the intervening years. Lulu was a nurse who had tended Kennedys since 1936, when twelve-year-old Patricia Kennedy had her appendix out. Under Miss Hennessey's command, Mrs. Kennedy would remain in her room on bed rest until the birth. It became quickly apparent that each of us had our own pack of responsibility—she to keep Mrs. K down and me to corral the kids.

Lulu was in her early sixties, a bit older than my mother, but she reminded me of my mother's bridge friends, who could seem a little giggly and flighty and then slap down a grand slam. She had unnaturally yellow-blonde hair that had weathered too many perms and a perpetual smile that made her appear meek and solicitous, but she took charge of Mrs. Kennedy; the entire new wing became her domain where she was gatekeeper and housemother, suggesting menus and imposing closing hours. Or so I imagined.

Max with Lee Geisen in the downstairs den at Hickory Hill.

Downstairs, all three secretaries, Sally, Lee, and Penny, divided up tasks, although Lee had given notice that October 31 would be her last day. She vowed that she was not going through another Thanksgiving and Christmas at Hickory Hill. I teased that she would surely miss the greens, the shopping, the presents, the exchanges, all the packing that she had warned me about. All I got was a smirk and a "Ha!"

Sally, by taking over Lee's business manager position, was now in charge of household finances, staff, and bookkeeping. When volunteers showed up to help answer letters, Sally assigned the jobs. Other days, Penny handled correspondence, even though she was supposed to be Mrs. Kennedy's secretary and keeper of the Red Book. But Mrs. K was hanging on to Lee as long as she could. She did not want her to leave any more than I did.

They had been through so much together in the past year and a half—family vacations, holidays, the campaign, the death, the funeral. Steadfast Lee did not bow to Mrs. K's whims nor cower to her rages. And besides all that, she helped Mrs. Kennedy finish the Sunday *Times* crossword on Monday mornings. Penny could never hope to match Lee.

A few days after Mrs. Kennedy returned from the hospital, Lulu Hennessey allowed her to receive guests again, a few at a time, and in they streamed, greeting everyone in the secretaries' office and asking how she was doing before climbing up to her room for lunch and gossip, I assumed. On the weekend Ann and Art Buchwald came as usual for dinner and a movie, although they stayed up in Mrs. K's room while the rest of us ate down in the pool house, where we screened the movie a little bit earlier than usual. Downstairs, we breathed easier.

Sometimes I ate lunch with the secretaries in their room, and sometimes one or two of them would keep me company in the dining room with Max and Christopher. The house seemed hushed, the way the world sounds after snowfall. The daily routines stayed pretty much the same—Katherine glided through the drawing room with her dust rag, brushing off photos and paintings, refilling cigarette boxes, looking for evidence of dog. Joe answered the door in his bow tie and black suspenders, waited the table with formality, did Ruby's bidding in the kitchen. The electric prod of Mrs. Kennedy's presence, however, was gone. At first it seemed strange not to have her suddenly appear around a corner or through a door. But then we grew used to it and our shoulders relaxed a bit, we moved more slowly, we forgot some of the rules.

Some nights I didn't make everyone tuck in their shirts before dinner. Fingernails may have gone unchecked, although I did insist that hands be washed. Our conversation wandered all over the place, from possible Halloween costumes to nuclear tests to whether I could beat Olympic champion Debbie Meyer (no!) in freestyle. We talked about homework and teachers and upcoming games. Kerry always wanted to interrupt, bouncing in her chair, "Let me tell you something..." Courtney maintained dining room decorum, her posture erect, her demeanor serious. She had taken over her mother's position at the head of the table opposite David, who slumped at the other end like a lazy patriarch. Michael would be shoveling in his food, seemingly out of it, when he'd pause mid-fork and blurt out some pertinent fact to prove a point or dispute something just said, and we'd look at him and laugh. *This is what a happy family feels like*, I thought. *Loose* and *chatty and kind.*

After dinner I made sure that everyone visited Mummy before disappearing to study or settling in to play games. Courtney and Kerry would go up together and come out half an hour later. Michael usually made his visit just before dinner without any prompting. But David seemed to steer clear and had to be reminded. Mrs. Kennedy wrote in the Red Book once, "David has not been in for two days. Where is he?"

I wasn't sure what the problem was. Lulu speculated that once boys hit puberty, they posed some sort of threat to their mothers. She'd noticed it in other homes where she'd worked. Mothers loved to cuddle their boy babies and toddlers, but when they got older, a gulf developed. Whether it was initiated by mother or son, the result was similar: withdrawal of physical touch, explosions of impatience, frustration, anger...distance. The emerging young men were no longer controllable in the way they had been at three or six or ten.

Maybe that's what I'd sensed with my "bad boys" in English class the year before. Tim, the troublemaker, had actualized my teacher-nightmare when he blatantly interrupted class by snapping the blinds; he had challenged my sense of control, threatened my tenuous authority, and I'd felt an uncontrollable rage. Over the summer at the cape, Bobby and David had roved the neighborhoods outside the compound, out of Mummy's reach, out of control. The girls, Courtney and Kerry, were much easier to manage. They obeyed the rules. And Kathleen, old enough to have worthy ideas and valuable opinions, seemed like a friend when she was home. At least David's biggest infractions so far were dirty nails and not visiting for two nights. Those seemed easy to rectify.

When we first arrived at Hickory Hill, Courtney and Kerry had given me a grand tour of the grounds. I'd kept my eyes open for safe places to disappear, havens where I might find solitude or smoke a cigarette alone, places Mrs. Kennedy would never enter. My bedroom, of course, was one sanctuary, although the kids wandered in and out as if it were an anteroom of their own. A shed out on the grounds looked promising but lacked basic comforts, like a couch or comfortable chairs. It smelled grassy inside, an old lawn mower leaning against one wall. Some tools and hardware—hammers, screwdrivers, jars of nuts and bolts—lay scattered along a work bench where, in December, I would be assembling toys in "Santa's workshop." When I asked Lee where might be a good place to disappear now and then, she told me that the last place Mrs. Kennedy would ever go was the basement, which housed the laundry and Bobby's reptiles.

In the morning after all the kids were off to school and Max was playing with Douglas in the nursery, I creaked down the basement steps into an alternate world, similar to rec rooms anywhere, with a ping-pong table and a foosball table, a couple of couches, a few chairs, wood-paneled walls covered in kid posters of skiers and bands, a life-sized photo of the senator, and a built-in terrarium. That had to be Bobby's. Two industrial-sized washing machines churned and rumbled from around a corner. I didn't see anyone, but before I could strike a match, a deep voice from somewhere near the machines commanded, "Don't startle Carothers."

"What?" I scanned across the rattling machines and driers, the ironing board, until I spotted two brown eyes above a steaming mangle.

"Bobby's turtle. He's shy." The voice came from Geneva, a woman of few words and no nonsense. She came and left without greeting, no time for coffee klatches with Ruby and Ena in the kitchen, no extra duties piled on. She did the laundry. Period. Geneva—Queen of the Laundry Room.

I could sit in the basement, have a smoke, relax, and not have to worry about making small talk with her. Some days when the machines were quiet and she was ironing, we did speak. I might ask a few questions, offer her a cigarette, sit, and smoke and then climb back up the stairs to go back to work. Even though she rarely left the basement, Geneva did know house news. One time early on, she told me to mind myself.

"Ena run off more than one governess," she said while she ran the iron back and forth.

I nodded and thanked her, but I'd already figured out that you pay respect to those who came before you. I was minding myself with Ena and later with Lulu Hennessey. Becoming a peer with

Ena and Courtney vamp in the dining room.

my former teachers had been both humbling and instructive. That ferocious English teacher, Leota Ferrin, had had tricks from her years in the classroom that I needed, not to take her place but to improve my teaching. And before that, when I'd trained for swimming, the older swimmers who were more experienced, had trained longer and raced more, knew things I wanted to learn. I heard Geneva's warning and would make a daily effort to appease Ena and all the other older coworkers. We needed each other to make the household run smoothly, to keep Mrs. Kennedy happy.

In a letter home, I wrote, "I'm still the little darling of the staff, by which I mean that none of the older workers hate me. After three years in a sorority and one teaching, I've learned that diplomacy and politics keep boats from rocking or sinking. Even the most crotchety ladies here have a little secret for me or an anecdote they must tell if I'm willing to stop and listen."

My favorite time of day to laze came after lunch, when Douglas went down for a nap and Ena got Chris and Max to lie down, free time before the big kids came bounding back from school. Some afternoons when I'd head to the basement, Penny would already be there answering the mail, which arrived daily from all over the world, letters spread out over the ping-pong table—condolences, personal stories, the occasional request.

"Look at this one. It's from *him*." In one hand Penny held up an envelope with childish block printing and scribbled drawings of wings, and in the other a thick packet of folded school-lined paper, covered front and back, edge to edge, with the same block printing.

"Who's *him*?"

"The guy who writes 'Ethel Queen of the Heavens' practically every day."

This was the first I'd heard of *him*. She pulled a pile of letters from a manila envelope.

"Where's he from?" I asked.

Penny looked at the envelope. "Oh my gosh, he's on the East Coast now."

Whoever he was, he'd been writing incoherent tomes for over a month, to Hyannis and now to McLean, posting them from somewhere in the Midwest. Up on the cape, Lee might have shown them to the Secret Service, but what could they do?

Penny pawed through the folder and found an envelope from the previous week. It had been mailed in Boston. Today's letter was posted from New York. He was getting closer, and neither Mrs. Kennedy nor the kids had any kind of protection. Hickory Hill wasn't like the compound that had been secured during John Kennedy's presidency and where Jackie, Caroline, and John had round-the-clock protection. Hickory Hill had a hedge and a cattle guard and four rather useless dogs.

"What do you think he wants?" I asked Penny. Together we read the letter with its drawings of angels and one of Mrs. Kennedy, with a halo of pink flowers, floating into clouds.

"Don't tell the kids," Penny warned as we plodded upstairs to show Sally and Lee.

Obviously, we didn't want to frighten the children or upset Mrs. Kennedy, and we couldn't cancel Halloween. Hundreds of people came by the Kennedy house every Halloween night for the pennies, a long-standing tradition. Little kids could reach into a fishbowl filled with new pennies and keep as many as they pulled out. Joe and Sally would be on duty that night while Dave Hackett went out with his kids, Kerry, her friends, Max, and Christopher. Courtney was going to a party at a friend's house, Michael and David somewhere else. All the adults would be on alert, although I'm not sure what any of us really expected to do if a truly threatening person appeared.

One more letter, in an envelope covered in wings, arrived the next day with a Washington, DC, postmark. Sally turned it over to the McLean Police or the FBI, someone Bill Barry, the former agent, had recommended perhaps. It was the last letter that I knew about. How vulnerable and exposed we all were to anyone a little off. Sympathetic Kennedy devotees and leering tourists could be annoying, but somehow the image of Mrs. Kennedy ascending to heaven felt threatening. I didn't want to imagine a deranged man stalking a widow or chasing a child.

Courtney had a big idea for her Halloween costume, and Saturday we drove into McLean to shop for plastic laundry baskets and a couple of cans of spray paint. She was going to make

Kerry and friends ready to head out for Halloween.

herself into the Great Pumpkin by painting the baskets orange and somehow hooking them together. She'd cut out eyes and a mouth in a plastic pumpkin big enough to pull over her head to complete the outfit.

In the basement we spread newspapers and began the spray job while Christopher and Kerry watched. Kerry intended to become Ringo Starr or Sonny Bono, someone with a black mustache and goatee who wore a black-peaked motorcycle cap, psychedelic shirt, and strings of beads. While we sprayed and sprayed the laundry baskets, Kerry practiced drawing moustaches on herself and then Christopher. But he had plans to be Spider-Man, using a hand-me-down costume and a mask he continually flipped up and down until the elastic broke.

Maybe Lee or Sally had mentioned something about an upcoming event, but my world revolved around the children—costumes, carpools and schoolwork, football, field trips with Max, and errands for anyone who asked—so the arrival of sisters Jean Kennedy Smith and Pat Kennedy Lawford a few days before Halloween came as a surprise. Fewer than two weeks had passed since Mrs. Kennedy began bed rest, and now a big event was unfolding at Hickory Hill without her presence. She'd been working with the senator's aides, allies, friends, and family since the summer for a more lasting memorial than the film that screened at the Democratic convention, but I'd been totally unaware. On Tuesday Joe-the-Butler and John Yaxley rearranged the big front room to accommodate a crowd of friends and former staffers, campaign aides, supporters, and journalists. Senator Ted made the announcement for Mrs. Kennedy, who remained in her room upstairs. She was establishing the Robert F. Kennedy Center for Justice and Human Rights to memorialize his goals: to encourage young people, to help the disadvantaged and discriminated against both here and abroad, and to promote peace in the world. The first executive director would be former campaign manager Fred Dutton, assisted by the senator's aide Peter Edelman. Robert McNamara would be the chair of the executive committee. It had only been four months since Robert Kennedy's death, but already Mrs. Kennedy, the family, friends, and colleagues were ensuring that ripples of hope would continue into the future.

Two days later on Halloween afternoon, Kerry and Michael ransacked Bobby's closet until they found a costume for me: a teal-green, pastel-flowered Nehru jacket that I wore over red tights with a Frankenstein's monster mask. As party time neared, Joe-the-Butler floated through the entry smothered in a red curtain,

The kids dressed me up to greet trick-or-treaters. Christopher darts off on a mission.

a towel turban, and an Ali Baba mask. Ena held Dougie on her lap. Lulu Hennessey looked on bemused. Penny and Sally unwrapped rolls of pennies and began to fill the fishbowl.

All afternoon we popped out from behind curtains or chairs or snuck in through closed doors and shouted "Boo!" to one another. Ruby and Joe had decorated the dining room with tissue-paper pumpkins and would serve dinner on Halloween paper plates. The kids hurried through the meal the way I remembered doing on Halloween eve, yearning to be out in the dark with neighbors and friends even when it was still light outside. Black and orange twisted crepe-paper streamers sagged from corner to corner across the dining room.

After dinner and once everyone was in costume and makeup, we paraded through "Mummy's" room for her appreciation. Lulu insisted on pushing Joe and me in after the kids, so we too got our "Fantastic!" from Mrs. K. Panda and Freckles disappeared into Michael's bedroom, and Brumus hid in the basement. Rocky wore a green knitted jacket and shivered on Lee's lap. Halloween was Lee's last day on the job.

The doorbell rang and rang that night. The pennies in the fishbowl disappeared, were replenished, and disappeared again. No truly scary person knocked on the door. Our own trick-or-treaters returned with buckets of candy (that somehow disappeared overnight) and everyone was home and in bed by ten, even David. The next day was a school day. Everyone would be attending. I was in charge of that.

Chapter 15

DAY-OFF ADVENTURES

With the car fan blasting hot air, the tape deck blaring Vivaldi's *Four Seasons*, I sped along the Virginia rural roads in Mrs. Kennedy's Bonneville convertible, top down, headed west toward places that ignited the imagination—Manassas, Shenandoah, the Blue Ridge Mountains. The names evoked songs we'd learned in sixth grade from *The Americana Songbook* and Civil War battles we'd studied in history. But I wasn't going to those places on my two days off—instead, I was going to a cottage in Middleburg, about an hour's drive west of McLean.

Autumn rains had fallen all day Saturday from low gray clouds that reminded me of home. The kids had felt housebound, the lawn too soggy for football, the track too muddy for riding. They tormented each other and tattled. They cried and moaned, "I'm bored." When the drizzle tapered off for a while, Ena bundled Max and Chris in slickers and boots, and we sloshed our way to the end of the driveway. Water coursed in a shallow ditch beside the road, and we tossed in leaves and twigs to see how far they'd sail before they snagged on rocks or got tangled in water-bent weeds. It reminded me of weekend afternoons when I was a kid playing outside in the breaks between Oregon rains.

Saturday night I packed for my two days off, a duffel stuffed with extra jeans and socks, sneakers, a couple of legal pads from the secretaries' office, a book of poems I'd found on a shelf in the TV room. Before everyone had finished Sunday breakfast, I was on the road with a thermos of coffee Joe had made up for me and a peanut butter sandwich, driving that top-down convertible under a bright-blue rain-washed sky.

Roadside trees, their leaves littering the pavement from yesterday's storm, still radiated color: golden yellow, scarlet, rust, and umber. I missed the brooding greens of western cedars and the towering firs—Douglas, grand, white—that shadowed every hillside in western Oregon. Here it seemed to be all deciduous trees—hickories, oaks, chokecherries, and maples—planted along the roadways or standing in loose clusters among the fields. There were no hills, no undulations to the landscape, until I got closer to Middleburg. *Are there hills farther off to the west?* I wondered. *Those could not be considered mountains, could they?*

The farther away from Hickory Hill, the freer I felt. The squabbling children, the laid-low matriarch, the perpetual on-call button faded in the rearview mirror. This was an adventure, a road trip, a step into new territory where nobody would be calling my name. The map and directions, held down by the thermos, rustled in the heater's blast. I may have stopped to check them at some crossroad grocery where I hoped to buy a six-pack of Heineken and a pack of Winstons.

As I remember, the cottage—which belonged to friends of Lee—was really a newish one-story ranch house, out of character with the fieldstone mansions sitting regally behind four-slat horse fences or winding, gray-stone walls I'd passed along the road. Middleburg was foxhunting country, Lee had told me, where the president and Jackie had a farm or where she came to foxhunt during the season or where her friend, Bunny Mellon, lived or some story that made the area seem high class and exclusive. But the house was quite modest and comfortable, and it suited a secretary or a governess on her days off.

It sat on several acres in a small yard cut from broad, open fields that extended toward a scattering of yellow oaks and scarlet maples and a stream. I've forgotten the interior, but it felt snug with views out across the vacant fields. There was a stereo, with a collection of folk songs and movie soundtracks and spoken-word records. Books filled several shelves. It was so quiet, I could hear water dripping from a clogged gutter. I hadn't felt this alone since…I couldn't think when. Maybe when I'd driven up to Mount Hood by myself the winter before. It seemed like people had been clamoring around me that whole first year teaching and then the summer before leaving for Hyannis and every day since then. I liked the silence, the solitude, the emptiness that I could choose to fill now with music or a walk outdoors or a book. Later, when I wanted connection, I'd write. My goal: seven letters and a tape recording to send home.

The peanut butter sandwich and a can of soup from the pantry made for lunch, and I pulled an edition of *Walden* from the bookshelf and thought about writing to my friend Ann. We'd been English majors at Oregon and shared many of the same classes. All through college we'd found times to discuss character motivation or to read aloud to each other from Willa Cather's prairie descriptions or to lament "man's inhumanity to man" or to question social class systems and how they played out in *The Great Gatsby* or *The Sound and the Fury* or *The Grapes of Wrath*. Late-night talks took place in a hideaway study we'd made in the sorority basement, our desks hidden among suitcases and winter coats. It was quiet and private and easy to read or to study until one or the other of us would pose a question and the conversation would begin, ranging from why no one edited Thomas Wolfe to the nature of man to how we would ever get our future students to read *The Scarlet Letter*. During our first year teaching we met up to strategize lesson plans or complain about workloads and classroom discipline.

Now our conversations crept back and forth at the speed of the postal service and at the mercy of each other's work schedule, — time off for me, grades recorded for her. Before going outside to explore, I wrote to Ann:

> *I'm feeling nostalgic for a long conversation with an old friend. No matter what our conversations are about, they're always interesting. What do you think about these quotations?*
>
> *"Human existence should not be a duty or a burden, not a mere means to an end, but a self-satisfying esthetic joy." [sic]*
>
> *"Time is but a stream I go a-fishing in. I drink at it, but while I drink I see the sandy bottom and detect how shallow it is....Every part of nature teaches that the passing away of one life is the making room for another." Thoreau*

Setting aside the paper, I pulled on my sneakers and a rain jacket. Outside, rain-laden clouds were huffing away the blue sky, but I wanted to explore. A path beyond the lawn crossed the bleak field, lumpy with dense clumps of dried grass, and dropped down a steep hill until it ended at an old stone wall beside a tiny rivulet. I struggled through branches and twigs to a rocky shelf that overlooked a lazy, muddy stream maybe twenty feet across.

Water eddied around some submerged stones and gurgled against a fallen tree. I sat down on a damp log, listening and taking notes: "An unfamiliar, singular bird cry. The only green here: a few tufts of grass, the moss, the lichens and the ferns. The ground squishes with rain-soaked rotting leaves. A crowd of gnats hovers around my head."

Sprinkles began to hiss on the stream's surface, and the gnats disappeared. I stumbled back up the slippery slope, breaking a few live and dead branches in my scramble, and ran sweating and breathless across the field to the house. *How long have I been outside? Is it only midafternoon?* Without the chaos of kids or the demands of chores never quite finished, time seemed to have slowed in the country like a turntable accidently unplugged.

I looked though the record collection and stacked a few on the stereo: Simon & Garfunkel; Peter, Paul and Mary; the *A Man and a Woman* soundtrack; and a recording of Carl Sandburg reading his poems. As each played through its side A, I drank beer and wrote letters. When I flipped the stack, I wrote to Ann: "I'm convinced that as much as I admire Thoreau, I shall never be able to live like him. I cannot shake loose my upbringing. I cannot cut the societal cord. I have no burning desire to discipline myself for Thoreau's goals. I am so lazy that I content myself with halfway trips."

These thoughts and self-criticisms from fifty years ago sound familiar today. How I longed to escape materialism and society's expectations, and how insurmountable the task seemed. A conflict raged between the romanticized version of myself who wanted to live simply, to experiment with life, to observe and question its meaning and the other me who carried the Kennedy credit card. I wanted both worlds—or access to both, not to possess either but to experience them.

For my junior term paper on Stephen Crane, I'd read an un-forgettable story, "An Experiment in Misery," where a young man spends a weekend on the Bowery among the unemployed and homeless, experiencing the violence and filth of the streets and flophouses, the insults and condemnation of the more well-off. I'd wanted to do something similar, to experience a world totally different from my own, but an experiment is not a commitment; it doesn't require abdication or renunciation of one's values or status. Although I wanted new and varied experiences, I did not want to surrender the values and the privileges familiar to me.

It got dark early in the country, and there were no neighbors, no lights over the fields or through the woods, no locks on the doors. I wrote to Ann, "It's spooky as hell, and I keep hearing things." In the morning I drove into Middleburg and found a café for breakfast, bought some snacks for lunch, and returned to lie about reading and napping and listening to records. I wanted to stay as late as possible, past nine thirty or ten so that David would be asleep when I returned. I didn't want to end my two days of refuge in conflict with him over bedtime.

I spent three or four overnights in Middleburg at Lee's friends' cottage that fall and winter, following much the same pattern of walk, write, listen, nap, read, drink, write, nap, and return refreshed. Ann saved all my letters from that year, and during a difficult period in my life, she returned them, a thoughtful and generous gesture. That twenty-two-year-old had such optimism and confidence: "I need a big problem to solve, to suffer a little, and then to perceive the pain releasing and subsiding," I'd written. "Thank goodness for dissatisfaction."

Chapter 16

NOVEMBER 1968

IN THE LITTLE ROOM DOWNSTAIRS WHERE MOST NIGHTS THE KIDS and I played games or tussled or watched a TV show after dinner, Joe-the-Butler, Lulu Hennessey, and I sat slouched on the sofa as the presidential election results dribbled in. Lamplight pooled at either end of the couch, leaving the rest of the room dark and shadowy. Upstairs, Senator Ted sat with Mrs. Kennedy. He'd arrived while we were eating, chatted with the kids a while, his shirt collar open, tie loosened. Then after we'd finished dinner, he climbed the stairs and disappeared into Mrs. K's room to watch the returns with her.

Downstairs, Courtney, Kerry, and Michael wandered in then out of the TV room, curious but not interested enough to stay. They tried halfheartedly to get our attention until each gave up and went to bed. Only David would sit with us for a few minutes, leave, and return to stand or sit again. Around ten the senator came down from upstairs, sat on the arm of a chair, and watched with us for a few more minutes. What did he say as the states fell to Richard Nixon one after the other? Did he disparage him? Did he denounce the nomination of Hubert Humphrey? I don't remember now. He must have felt his brother's absence that night, the ache of loss. All the what-ifs, the what-might-have-beens, the if-onlys seemed to murmur from dark corners. I could not imagine what Mrs. Kennedy felt.

After Senator Ted left, we turned off the TV. Disheartened and reluctant to move, we sank deeper into the sofa, and Lulu began to tell us a story from the 1960 election.

"I sat in here eight years ago, the night after Jack was elected. Right here on the couch with Ethel beside me. Only one light on," she said. "The president sat over there"—she pointed to the left—"and Bobby was there"—she pointed to another armchair. "And the Ambassador over there. For five hours they brought up names for the cabinet, talked them over, until they made the entire cabinet. When they had their list, I said to Ethel, 'I don't think I've ever been so quiet in all my life.'"

"I don't think I have either," Mrs. K had answered. Lulu shook her head, remembering.

I thought about David then, his restlessness, his inability to watch the results yet his return again and again to sit with us. It reminded me of another story Lulu had told on one of the first nights we talked together. The weekend before the June primary, David and his siblings had been flown out to California, the same weekend I'd been asked to accompany them to Disneyland and the beach. On the night of the California primary, she said, David had stayed up alone in his room to watch the returns and his father's victory speech, which devolved into the chaos after the shooting.

The horrific images must have seared into his brain like a brand, yet he never talked about that night, about what he saw or how he felt or whether he dreamed about it. I asked Lulu if she thought the kids should have counseling, because it seemed to me that talking with someone would be a help. Did she tell me that the Kennedys weren't ones to air their laundry? Or maybe she said that surely a priest was counseling Mrs. Kennedy? But I knew of no time the children were offered or given emotional support other than the comfort of their family or their gathering together to pray the rosary. And I, inexperienced in death and loss, did not ask if anyone wanted to talk or offer anything other than companionship and play.

I don't think anybody in the Kennedy house that night could bear to watch Richard Nixon celebrate the election. David may have paced in his room. Courtney and Kerry were probably already curling together with their mother, Michael with the dogs. In the morning I brought in the *New York Times*, and as usual David pulled off the front page first. Nixon and his family were pictured under the headline "Nixon Wins By a Thin Margin, Pleads for Reunited Nation." He pushed the paper aside and opened the sports page.

ON FRIDAY AFTERNOON BEFORE VETERANS DAY, Courtney, Kerry, and I boarded the northbound train in Washington, DC, for the three-hour ride to New York and a four-day weekend with cousins Caroline and John. They were curious about Aunt Jackie's wedding to Aristotle Onassis in Greece the previous month, but the big event that weekend, the reason we were going, was the National Horse Show at Madison Square Garden. *You can have your horses,* I thought. *I want to see inside Jackie's apartment.*

On the train we played Battleship and tic-tac-toe, tried to read, and ended up gorging on snacks Ruby had packed for us. A driver met us when we arrived at Penn Station, and soon we were headed up Fifth Avenue to the apartment. It took up the entire fifteenth floor of the building, with five bedrooms and multiple bathrooms, a drawing room, dining room, living room, and library, and three fireplaces.

When we entered, the little elevator opened into the kitchen, where Caroline and John were waiting for us with their Swiss governess and cook. Whatever she'd prepared for dinner, it smelled good. The girls took their luggage to Caroline's room, and the governess showed me to mine, a tiny servant's room like the ones in the attic at the haunted house on the cape, with a single bed, a tiny closet, and a short walk down the hall to a shared bathroom. *It's good enough for a weekend, but I don't think I'd want to spend a lot of time in here*, I thought. Soon we were all gathered around a table in the kitchen, where it felt homey and warm. Of course, I wanted to explore, feeling curious but acting nonchalant. I'd already spent a couple of weeks in Jackie's Hyannis house, and there were three more days for exploration here.

In the morning, the governess gave me a grand tour before Jackie's young stepsister and her husband, who were house-sitting for Mrs. Kennedy-Onassis, got up. They kept the fashionable hours of the beautiful people, the governess told me, rising at eleven or noon for breakfast, dining late, long after the kids had finished, keeping the cook on duty. She led me through the front rooms, the ones that faced Fifth Avenue, each with a fireplace: the dining room off the kitchen and a living room with gloomy, floor-to-ceiling drapes, deep red and gold, and dark-brown velvet chairs. Large paintings in ornate gold frames and clusters of smaller prints framed in natural wood—many with horses—hung on wallpapered walls. To me, it looked like a mishmash of French antiques and overstuffed furniture with clashing coverings of stripes and big floral prints. I preferred the pastels, the greens and pinks and whites, in "my Mrs. Kennedy's" house. Hickory Hill felt like springtime, 1040 Fifth Avenue like the dead of winter. Parquet flooring covered the entry hall; enormous silk carpets spread over hardwood everywhere else. From a living room window, I could see Central Park and people jogging around the reservoir. *What a view! But if I were a kid, I wouldn't want to grow up here. Too dreary.*

The governess and I spent most of the time talking in the kitchen while the cousins played in the back bedrooms. She told me that Caroline and John played well together—she was very imaginative and together they liked to make books, she writing and he illustrating. I couldn't imagine Courtney and Kerry writing a book together or Courtney and David. They were too combative with each other. I thought of Freddy's observation that Caroline was the best rider because she practiced. She had asked me to help improve her flip turn before the summer swim meet and then how to do the butterfly. Hadn't the Irish nanny last summer told me that she was working on a strategy in Battleship so that she could beat me? The John Kennedy kids were competitive, but they were also polite, disciplined—maybe a little too perfect. Caroline had been in the public eye all her life, been watched and watched over, and it made her careful, although she wasn't so hesitant that she didn't ask for help.

She could use some time at our house to roughhouse and let loose, I thought then. But now I think she'd have hated it at Hickory Hill. She had a different personality, a different upbringing. She was being raised to be cultured, a lady, a world citizen—bilingual, creative, observant, and quietly assertive like her mother. I shouldn't have worried about her. I told the governess that my kids were a bit more physical than hers. What I thought was: *They are impulsive, spirited, undisciplined, wild—and a lot of fun.*

On Saturday night the Secret Service man drove us to Madison Square Garden for the horse show. We sat in a box close to the ring. All I remember is the smell of sawdust and the ridiculous prance of Tennessee Walkers. We must have watched the competition of hunters and jumpers, but I've forgotten it all.

Sunday after Mass and breakfast, cousins Stevie and Willie Smith joined us to go to an early movie, *Finian's Rainbow*, a too-long musical with Petula Clark and Fred Astaire that bored us all. Afterward we took roller skates and bikes to Central Park, and I pedaled kids up the hills so they could skate down. We finished the afternoon with a short game of touch. I remember chasing after Caroline, who tossed a nice lateral to her Secret Service guy just as I was about to tag her, and he scored. After dinner on Sunday night, all six of us, cousins and governesses, piled onto Mrs. Kennedy-Onassis's bed to watch *To Kill a Mockingbird* on TV. I thought Atticus Finch (or Gregory Peck) might remind the girls of their fathers with his rugged good looks and his quiet wisdom, his fight against injustice. Robert Kennedy's vision seemed similar to Atticus Finch's. They shared a profound empathy for the underprivileged, and both had worked to eradicate injustice.

But Kerry quickly lost interest. She was used to full screenings in the pool house or at Grandpa Joe's, and this was black and white on a small television screen with a story she didn't quite follow. Soon she and John were off to play. I can't be sure whether Caroline and Courtney stayed to the end or if they too bailed out. I'd wanted Courtney to stay for those final scenes when Atticus comforts Scout, to see how a young girl processes violent events, how a father's final message is an invitation to walk in someone else's shoes. But I don't think she and Caroline stayed for the whole movie either. Maybe it was just me and the other governess watching to the end.

Late Monday morning when I walked through the dining room, the stepsister was sitting alone. We exchanged greetings, and for some reason (had I mentioned that I was an English teacher?) she told me that she had been doing a study of *Winnie-the-Pooh*. I don't think I laughed. Later I wrote to Ann, "Imagine. Not only did she have nothing to say, she didn't even say that well: never raising nor lowering her voice, but speaking in a monotone, without excitement, enthusiasm, or humor." Was she kidding? A study of *Winnie-the-Pooh*? What kind of people go out every afternoon to shop or meet for tea and converse about *Pooh*?

My middle-class values erupted in a mini-tirade to Ann: "These dull bores have everything yet nothing. Their conversations sound like bad movie scripts. They have nothing to do, no decisions to make. They sleep late and expect to be waited on, eyebrows raised, noses lifted." What a snob I was in my self-righteous rant. Maybe by getting away from Hickory Hill, where the casual atmosphere concealed the same privileges, I began to suspect a similar indifference toward those of us who worked to make their lives easy. But I wasn't ready to confront that yet. I still felt lucky to be serving, to have been chosen to provide something, something that the senator had sensed in our short encounter that he wanted for his kids even if I didn't know what that was and didn't even wonder.

We were back in Washington by late Monday afternoon. Nothing bad had happened while we were away, no emergencies, no trips to Georgetown University Hospital. The girls hurried in to tell Mummy all the news, and I reported first to Ena, then to Lulu, and late that night the real gossip to Joe.

Two weeks later David and Michael were altar boys at the morning Mass celebrating their father's forty-third birthday. Courtney and Kerry presented the bread and wine. We sat

Courtney and Michael multitask before bedtime with Scrabble and television.

together—Uncle Teddy, Christopher, Max, and Ena—and afterward drove up to Arlington to pray at the grave. Two days later for the fifth anniversary of their Uncle Jack's death, the boys served again for an after-school Mass in a small chapel with only about eight attending, including three nuns.

The magnitude of the Kennedy losses weighed heavy in November. I certainly didn't know any way to alleviate the pain other than to do my job. Maybe playing games together at night helped. Maybe our pig piles on the couch during commercials, giggling and tickling and bumping into each other, satisfied some physical need for connection, an outlet for stored-up energy.

There is a physicality in a big family that I'd never known growing up seven years younger than my only brother, who left for college when I was ten. With the Kennedys you were always in contact. Michael and David roughhoused together in fake wrestling matches. The minute I sat down to talk to Sally or Penny, someone would plop in my lap—Christopher, Max, Kerry. If I turned on the TV and sat down, Courtney would immediately wiggle in on one side, Kerry on the other, Michael slowly sliding over the armrest and half onto Kerry's lap. Before the first commercial, Max would be pulled onto Courtney's lap and Christopher onto mine. Or so it seems now: a crowd of kids, a wriggling litter. I liked being included in the pack, the comfort of the bodies. Of course, the spell could be broken with an accidental pinch or an intentional bump, something that prompted a howl of protest or a cascade of tears.

I didn't want any scenes, no incidents where someone might run up to "tell Mummy" and I'd be held responsible for not controlling things. It could happen, especially with Courtney, whose emotions sometimes spilled out like dropped marbles, scattering out of control. When she launched into an unprovoked scene, puffed up over a misplaced blouse or the locked bathroom door, her voice rising and her freckles dissolving to red, I'd announce the arrival of Sarah Bernhardt, and usually she'd stop and laugh. Other times I'd untangle fighting combatants and sit on one of them until he cried uncle. Sometimes I'd get up and walk away. It all depended on who was involved and what the provocation. After four months I usually knew what was needed, sensed what to do in that way you know things after you've lived with someone long enough.

ONE BY ONE, IN LATE November the older kids arrived at National Airport coming home for Thanksgiving. Joe-the-Butler and John Yaxley drove back and forth on the pickups. By dinnertime all three were home, had checked in with their mother, and had thrown their bags into rooms, Joe with David, Bobby with Michael, and Kathleen in her own room in the new wing. Lulu Hennessey kept her place in the guest room, close to Mrs. Kennedy. Sally Irish had somehow managed to get a print of the Beatles' new movie, *Yellow Submarine*, and we all jammed into the pool house to see the most colorful, outrageous film that ever careened across a screen. Christopher could not get enough of the Blue Meanies, and Michael asked for a psychedelic tie for Christmas.

The Washington weather cooperated all Thanksgiving weekend with clear skies and not-too-cold temperatures. Thursday morning, friends and relatives converged for a late-morning football game before our one thirty feast. Joe-the-Butler had set the table for at least twenty: Dave Hackett and his family, Uncle Teddy and his, Jean and Steve Smith and their boys, and all of the Kennedy kids. The table, set with silver and porcelain and candelabras, looked fancier than any I'd ever seen, at least until the kids sat down and started to eat. Ruby had prepared a traditional meal with roasted turkey and stuffing, mashed potatoes and gravy, sweet potatoes, green beans, cranberry sauce, and biscuits with butter. Then came the desserts: pumpkin pie, apple pie, a pear torte, and ice cream. We rolled through the afternoon in front of the television while the grown-ups climbed the stairs to keep Mrs. Kennedy company. In the pool house later we watched *I Love You, Alice B. Toklas*. When Peter Sellers offered marijuana brownies to his parents, I began to wonder what Sally had been thinking when she ordered this film for Thanksgiving evening.

My double-day-off fell on the weekend, but there was no way I'd be given time off at Thanksgiving with everybody home. A friend from Portland—Barbara Fealy's daughter who was living in New York—called to see if we might get together when she visited Washington over the weekend. Sally and Lulu suggested that I take an hour or so off on Friday. I think she wanted to see Hickory Hill, but it seemed too presumptuous and unprofessional to ask permission. Instead, we met somewhere in McLean for coffee, where she told me about the dance scene in New York and I spun a few tales about my job. I couldn't have been gone for more than two hours, but as soon as I opened the big red front door, I knew something had happened.

Courtney ran up. "Where were you? Michael got hit in the head, and Joe drove him to the hospital."

Guilty! I'd failed my mission, left my post. Guilty! Lee had warned me, hadn't she? "Things happen when Bobby's home."

Sure enough, the kids had been playing out on the hill and up in the tree—capture the flag or rock tag. A stone thrown by Bobby caught Michael in the middle of his forehead, cutting a gash. Lulu had patched him up with some Steri-Strips from Mrs. Kennedy's "pharmacy" and sent him off to the ER for real stitches.

She probably consoled me that no one could have stopped it happening, but I felt sick with failure and guilt, sure that Mrs. Kennedy would be having words with me. I'd let her down, been selfish, irresponsible. Michael returned from the hospital like the soldier in *The Red Badge of Courage*, smug with his forehead bandaged. I don't remember Bobby's response nor any words from Mrs. Kennedy. It seemed to be a given that something would happen at Hickory Hill when everybody was home.

A group of us was back outside playing football Saturday morning when John Yaxley came running onto the lawn shouting that Kathleen had fallen off her horse on the CIA grounds. "She's hurt. Come quick," he yelled. Dave Hackett ran for his car and took off. I grabbed the keys to the station wagon, ordered

Courtney to run and get Lulu Hennessey, and all together we raced the two miles to Langley and up the drive into the CIA campus where we spotted Dave sitting on the ground under a tree next to Kathleen. She had abrasions on one side of her face, a huge lump on her forehead, and blood leaking from the corner of her eye. She was very groggy, and Lulu said she must have been in shock as we helped her into the car. I drove quickly and steadily to the emergency room with the second Kennedy to visit in two days. Apparently she'd hit a low-hanging branch, which had knocked her off the horse and caused a bad concussion. She'd spend two nights in the hospital and would need bedrest for at least another week, the doctor told us. On our way home, Lulu complimented my driving, and I felt partially redeemed for my Friday lapse.

Sunday morning after nine o'clock Mass and breakfast, we played one last game of touch before I packed the older boys for departure. Bobby had a one thirty plane to catch, and at twelve forty-five he left with his hawk and his monkey, escorted by Dave Hackett, who was charged with getting him off safely. Courtney and I were setting up a game of Scrabble when Kerry wandered in with Bobby's plane ticket.

"I found this on the bathroom floor," she said, waving it at me.

Up I jumped, ordered Joe-the-Butler to page Dave at the airport that the ticket was coming, and ran out of the house, Courtney right behind me. We hit Chain Bridge Road at 1:12 p.m. Eight minutes later, Courtney raced into American Airlines with the ticket. We'd set a new world record from Hickory Hill to the airport, and we congratulated ourselves all the way back to McLean.

When regular school schedules resumed on Monday, Courtney and Kerry returned to classes at Stone Ridge School, David,

Michael, and Christopher to the Potomac School. At the house, Sally and Penny, Joe, John Yaxley, and Katherine began decorating for Christmas. I took Max to Great Falls to run the paths and watch the river. When we returned, greens covered the banisters and wreaths hung from every window.

Chapter 17

GETTING IN THE SPIRIT

DECEMBER 1968

For a few mornings I sat with Kathleen in her darkened room and talked, glad to share stories with a teenager instead of a three-year-old. She told me about Putney, her job shoveling out the stables, her hopes for college. Her friend Ann wanted to go to Stanford, where my friend was in graduate school. "If she wants a campus tour, I'll call Gretchen. She could show her around," I offered. By midweek when Michael got his stitches taken out, Kathleen was fed up with lying around all day. She'd been listening to new Beatles songs on the radio. Everyone was talking about *The White Album*. She wondered if I could find her a copy before she headed back to school.

Joe gave me directions to the Georgetown record store, and Sally gave me the money and an order for a house album too. By that afternoon Christopher and Max knew the words to "Rocky Raccoon," and by evening David and Michael had belted out "Why Don't We Do It in the Road?" so many times, I wanted to lock myself in the basement. Anytime I hear a cut from that album, whether "Ob-La-Di, Ob-La-Da" or "Blackbird," I'm back among the wreaths and garlands, the dogs and children, the ever-present workers who kept that ship sailing toward Christmas at Hickory Hill.

Lulu Hennessey predicted that the baby would come right after Thanksgiving because she knew the holiday would be stressful for Mrs. Kennedy. But the first week of December slipped by with a lot of orders from upstairs but no contractions. Penny and I met with Mrs. K every morning as she read out orders from the Red Book, specifically for me: Was everyone ready for Sun Valley? Had I gotten presents for everyone yet? Had the order been placed for baby clothes from the shop in Hyannis? What about the Stork Set on Connecticut Avenue in Washington?

She rattled off items that every child would need for Sun Valley: antifog goggles, warm gloves, travel alarm clocks, two parkas each. Hats. Long underwear. Long underwear that fit.

Penny made stars in the Red Book and nodded. And hand warmers. One for each child.

"You need to get on this, kid. I don't know what you've been doing."

That stung. What did she expect? We were only a few days past Thanksgiving, and we'd had a pretty full house for the past week. But when I told Lulu, she laughed. "That's the baby talking." And I remembered Lee's advice months before: "If you take it to heart, you'll have a nervous breakdown."

Max's and my "kindergarten" was on recess in December while I drove all over the city shopping or hid out in the backyard shed assembling, boxing, and wrapping presents. In between, I disappeared to the attic to make teetering piles of ski gear: seven kids' plus mine. Each pile needed multiples of long johns, turtlenecks, sweaters, parkas, snow pants, hats, gloves, goggles, ski boots, après ski boots, skis, and poles. We'd leave on Christmas Day and return sometime after New Year's, so that meant packing play clothes too. Outgrown clothing moved down the line from Joe to Bobby, Bobby to David, David to Michael. Courtney's clothes bumped over to Kerry, but Kathleen's were still too big for Courtney so she would be getting lots of new gear, from the Franconia Olympic racing sweater (a request that appeared in the Red Book) to new red Raichle ski boots. Lists grew for what needed to be purchased, and soon I was off to Abercrombie & Fitch and Saks and specialty ski stores.

That Christmas all hope of attaining Thoreau-like simplicity vanished. Weeks after I'd written to Ann about antimaterialism, I wrote home that I was spending two hundred fifty to three hundred dollars at a time buying clothes and presents for the family and loving it. Even though my take-home pay amounted to eighty dollars a week, I'd started spending on myself too. While searching for a coat for David at Best & Co., I found myself wandering into the women's department searching for a warm, wool loden coat. For ten minutes on an audiotape home, I described shopping and finding an authentic "Austrian royal-blue, brushed-mohair coat with dark-green braided trim" detailing its lapels, belt, and buttons. "It's a bit dressy for me," I said into the tape, "but it looks beautiful, and it's real. Not like the cheap, processed wool ones that cost a lot less."

Listening now, I know exactly what I was hinting at on the tape: in another department I'd found a heavy German three-quarter-length brown Loden with an authentic plaid lining and rope toggles securing what I thought were deer-horn buttons. "It was on sale," I explained, "but might be a bit too tight if I wear a sweater. The clerk is checking to see if they have a bigger size in New York." In the end I bought both coats, sure that my mom would offer to pay for one as a birthday present.

MRS. KENNEDY HAD A FEW ideas for presents for the kids, like the travel alarm clocks. She thought Kathleen would like a painting from some gallery in Georgetown. And every child would get a framed photograph of their father.

"Find cute pantsuits for the girls, something wild," she suggested.

At dinner one night, I handed out notebook paper and, with a wink to the big kids, asked that they write a letter to Santa.

"Be sure to ask how things are going in the workshop and thank him for good presents last year. Then list a few things you might want this year. Fold it up and give it to me, and I'll be sure Santa gets it." By dessert time I had six letters. Max dictated to Courtney, Christopher to Michael, and David invented a list for Douglas.

"Items the children have requested" headed a sheet of typing paper.

David
"The Duke" football
Pro-football game
Casual pants (Levi's cords)
Beatles records

Michael
A squirrel monkey to keep Courtney's company
An official soccer ball
A wetsuit like Jean Smith's

Courtney
Backgammon game

Kerry
A Zoom Loom knitting machine
Pantsuit

Max
Airplanes and rockets
Racing tracks

Kathleen
A roll of twenty-four curlers
Hat

Christopher
Kookie Kamera

Douglas
Twelve-inch white musical bear

Bobby
Tape recorder

Joe
Dog collar for a baby Newfoundland puppy

Also on the list was a Veg-O-Matic, but who it was for remains a mystery. Ruby perhaps?

Courtney went with me on a Saturday to pick out a few sweaters for the ski trip and to look for artwork for Kathleen. Mrs. Kennedy thought a Sister Corita would be nice, and we'd found one in a Georgetown gallery. I looked out the side-view mirror watching for a break in the traffic. All of Washington, DC, seemed to be out shopping that Saturday.

"Dang these cars," I said, frustrated with being stuck. "Why is everybody out?" But it was more than the traffic that was bugging me. I was thinking about how much we would spend that day. The new Raichle boots were $135. Four new sweaters would be another hundred. The art piece we'd chosen was over a hundred dollars. What seemed like fun a couple of weeks before had begun to feel sickening.

"That print is as much as I make in a week's work," I said.

"What do you mean?" Courtney asked.

"I mean, I get a hundred dollars a week to work at your house twenty-four hours a day. Eighty, actually, because they take out taxes. That's as much as this one present."

I felt myself getting a little emotional. Something about being on call twenty-four hours a day, about not getting days off. How long had it been this time? Three or four weeks? It was fun spending from the Kennedy purse, but it also felt wrong—hundreds of dollars for every single kid. I wanted this twelve-year-old to know something about the people who worked for their wages, to think about how a pair of ski boots that might sit in a closet for fifty weeks out of the year cost more than a week's wages for the two upstairs maids who cleaned up after her and her brothers and sisters every day.

One of Lulu Hennessey's stories came to mind then, a time up on the cape at the Ambassador's when the president was still alive. She'd told me that a movie was scheduled for the grown-ups to be shown at nine o'clock.

"The help always sat in the first three rows of the little theater, the family in the back three. All of us were in there waiting for the movie to start," she said. "Rose, Jackie, Ethel, Joan. We were waiting for the men to arrive. At nine thirty the president, Bobby, and Teddy still weren't there. Finally, around nine forty-five they came in and the projectionist started the film.

"A little shadow appeared on the screen," Lulu said. "A little shadow and a big voice. 'Stop the cameras. Stop.' The lights came up, and Rose Kennedy stood pointing. 'Now, boys, I want to tell you something. There are people here who have to get up tomorrow morning early to make your breakfast and wash your clothes, so I don't care who you are. Jack, are you listening?' He nodded. 'When the movie is scheduled to be at nine o'clock, I want you here at nine o'clock or the movie goes on without you. Do you understand that, boys?' All three said, 'Yes, Mummy.'"

I wondered if Courtney had ever heard that story. Or if anyone but Miss Hennessey remembered that night. Maybe I'd tell Courtney some other time when I felt another teaching moment arise. I'd said enough already, and now she looked at me from the car seat as if she couldn't fathom that I was being paid *anything* to live at her house, as if all this time she had thought I was doing the job because I liked them, loved them. Or that's how I interpreted her look before I pulled the big car out into a break in the traffic.

I did love them, each differently. Part of the fun of Christmas shopping was to fulfill each kid's request but also to find that one thing they hadn't asked for but might enjoy. I liked feeling as if I knew them so well that I'd pick the right present. But enough was enough.

At the dinner table in between current events and the who's-who quiz, we speculated on when the baby would come and ran through possible names. Once the calendar passed December 8,

I'm pretty sure Mrs. Kennedy and Lulu knew the delivery date since she was having a C-section (her sixth or seventh), but they kept it secret. All we knew was that Kerry and Michael were to be the godparents and would present the newborn for christening sometime in January.

On a Monday, a beautician came from Elizabeth Arden to give Mrs. K a manicure, a pedicure, and a facial. The next day her favorite hairdresser spent all afternoon on a shampoo, set, and brush-out. On Wednesday, she set out with Lulu Hennessey and Senator Ted for Georgetown University Hospital, and the next day, December 12, 1968, Rory Kennedy was born.

Before they came home from the hospital, a new employee arrived: Nou Nou Mills, the baby nurse. Lulu would stay a week or so to look after Mrs. Kennedy, but now Nou Nou was the new upstairs general in charge of baby, feeding schedules, and sleep routines.

Unlike Miss Hennessey, who seemed so quiet and meek, Nou Nou took up space—a big woman in body and personality, from her henna-red hair and aquiline nose to the gold cuff links on her starched, Irish linen uniform. A powder-blue cashmere cardigan matched her bright-blue eyes that always hinted, *I've got a secret you want to know.* Which was true.

She and the new baby, Rory, took over Kerry's room next door to me on the third floor, and Kerry roomed with Courtney until Lulu left, when she moved into that room. Night cries might have wakened me now and then, but the ever-blowing window fan muted most sounds, and I slept through the nights.

Nou Nou ate some dinners with us and some with Mrs. Kennedy, whom she always called Madam. She spoke fluent French, although she was Irish, or so she told us—an Irish girl

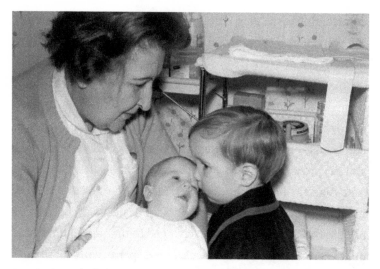

Douglas kisses his baby sister, Rory, good night in Nou Nou's room.

who'd been fostered in the States and then had moved to France, where she'd been working in a factory when Germany invaded during World War II. In the Alsace warehouse, her coworkers hid her nationality, and she passed for French. I don't remember how she ended up back in the States or the story of how she became a baby nurse, but like Lulu, she had greeted new Kennedy babies for years and years. I loved when she had time to sit and chat, to pass along anecdotes from her life, stories of other times, other babies.

From the middle of October when Lulu Hennessey arrived until the middle of February when Nou Nou left, these two older women, storytellers both, provided welcomed camaraderie and perspective. They were women who had lived through traumatic times in history and within the families they worked for. In households far beyond their economic means or social status, they held their own, their confidence coming from strength and experience. These were women I admired, generous with advice and entertaining with story, who carried themselves as professionals, the way Leota Ferrin and Barbara Fealy and Congresswoman Edith Green did. They were a benefit that came with the job.

Mrs. Kennedy gave me two presents—a one-hundred-dollar bonus check for Christmas and a fur ski hat with bonbon tassels for my birthday the week before. I knew that one of the volunteers had been given the task of buying presents for the staff and help, and she probably thought anyone going to Sun Valley would love a Russian fur hat. I burst out laughing when I tried it on and modeled it for Nou Nou and Sally Irish. The next day it went right back to the ski shop, where I exchanged it for a pair of navy-blue, pullover, nylon quilted Edelweiss snow pants with full-length side zippers and boot guards. They would keep me warm in Sun Valley when the temperature dropped below zero and on Mount Hood and Mount Bachelor skiing for the next forty years, and at rainy soccer games and spring track meets all through the 1990s. The waistband elastic is shot, but everything else works—snaps, zippers, and warm-as-toast quilting. My grandmother and mother had taught me about quality and practicality, their gifts to me, long before I came to the Kennedys'.

Downstairs, Sally loaded the turntable with Christmas records from Andy Williams to Bing Crosby, Perry Como to Burl Ives, but upstairs the Beatles played on with "Piggies" or "Sexy Sadie" or "Don't Pass Me By" or "Birthday." David and Michael caroled in the halls, "Why Don't We Do It in the Road?"

Chapter 18

CHRISTMAS VACATION

WHAT STARTED AS EXPRESSIONS OF LOVE OR THE FULFILLMENT OF someone's desires became a glut of meaningless gifts to be ripped open, jerked around, and quickly discarded in waste heaps throughout the drawing room on Christmas morning. I'd not been the only one sent off on Santa's missions. Mrs. Kennedy had recruited friends and volunteers to buy for her. She'd made phone calls to stores and talked to the older kids for ideas and more ideas.

When Kathleen and Bobby returned ten days before Christmas, they too were sent out on spending sprees. Boxes packed the little shed—ribbons and tissue reached toward the rafters. I recruited Penny to help me wrap and John Yaxley to assemble the Big Wheels for Chris and Max and a workbench that I couldn't quite figure out.

On Wednesday night the week before Christmas, Dave Hackett arrived for dinner where he took the head of the table, dominating the conversation with questions and stories, engaging the boys with sports questions, delighting Lulu Hennessey. Before dessert, Courtney and Kerry excused themselves and left the dining room, an unusual occurrence, but Dave kept talking, deep in a political argument with Kathleen. Michael abruptly got up, walked to the side wall, and flipped off the lights just as the kitchen door swung open and Courtney and Kerry entered carrying an enormous, candle-covered sheet cake—twenty-three candles blazing on a blue-iced swimming pool, the Olympic rings over the center. Ruby and Ena looked on from the kitchen while the kids shouted: "Surprise!" before howling out a rousing version of "Happy Birthday to You."

Could anything rival a surprise party celebrated with my kids? My cheeks radiated red, and I grinned like a fool. Joe, who'd followed behind the girls, snapped a photo of me with Christopher on my lap helping to cut the cake. Max had scrambled onto another lap, and Courtney hovered over my shoulder waiting for me to open the present from all the kids—a wide-banded, royal-blue, patent-leather watch. Very mod. Kerry said she'd picked out the Yellow Submarine stationery, because I wrote so many letters and she liked the Blue Meanie whose image filled the entire sheet of paper, his blue tongue licking a red-and-pink rose. Later, Courtney gave me a little drawing she'd made, a bouquet of psychedelic flowers. These three presents, gifts from the heart, I've kept. The wind-up watch still works for a couple of hours at a time, seven sheets of the stationery lie in my desk drawer, and Courtney's drawing is filed with the letters and memorabilia from that year. The Doctor Zhivago fur hat from Mrs. Kennedy came and went the next day, exchanged for the snow pants.

THE WEEK RACED TOWARD CHRISTMAS, but few memories remain. In photographs I see the tall tree heavy with gold ribbons and ornaments but have no recollection of who decorated it or when. I presume we went to Mass on Christmas Eve, and I have a vague

My surprise twenty-third birthday party in December with a frosted cake decorated as a swimming pool, lane lines and all. Left to right: Christopher on my lap,
Courtney behind, and Max on a secretary's lap.

notion that the children were sent upstairs when we returned, not to come down again until morning. That night, Santa's helpers hauled presents out of hiding, wheelbarrow loads from the shed, stacks up from the laundry room. We—John Yaxley, Joe, and I—heaped them into ten separate piles ready for morning.

My photographs reflect the wrapping-paper chaos, the opened and discarded gifts lying on top of each other. Michael sits in his pajamas in a much-too-small Big Wheel. David spins the handle on a mini-foosball game. Christopher poses in front of the tree holding an almost life-sized angel. But I don't remember any of the morning frenzy or our drive to the airport or the long, long flight on the Skakel jet to Sun Valley. Two out-of-focus pictures show Bobby playing cards with Michael and cousin Stevie Smith, and someone under covers and asleep on a fold-out bed aboard the plane. We must have played the new board games: Yahtzee, Risk, backgammon. Did we bring along a picnic that Ruby had packed, or did the plane have a kitchen? I don't remember.

We stayed in Averell Harriman's "cottage," which had enough bedrooms to house Tim-the-Tennis-Teacher—on vacation from college—and me as chaperones, our seven kids, Pat Lawford, and Jean and Steve Smith and their kids. Several times my letters mention that it cost $250 a day, an astronomical amount it seemed. I don't remember how we got to the slopes and back each night or who cooked or where we ate. It's as if the same memory train that hurtled through dark subway stations on my 1967 trip to New York and Montreal carried me to Sun Valley. Only two vivid scenes and foggy traces of chairlift conversations remain from the ten days we were gone from Hickory Hill.

The first scene begins with me in the gate at the top of a not-too-steep giant slalom racecourse set by Jim Whittaker, Mount

Everest summiteer, and Willy Schaeffler, US Olympic ski coach, for the Annual Kennedy Christmas Team Ski Race. It was intended to be a snap for the experienced skiers like the older Kennedy kids and Jim Whittaker's sons but a challenge for the rest of us—the younger kids, the help, and guests like singer Andy Williams. We inexperienced skiers were paired with a "pro" (Steve Smith was my partner), and our combined times would determine the winners.

Ever since watching the 1960 Squaw Valley Olympics, I'd imagined ski racing, romanticized the rush of speed, the slip of ski edges on an icy course. Here I was at the top of the hill, like Oregon Olympians Jean Saubert or Kiki Cutter, ready to race, my stomach tight with nerves. The long slope wound downhill off to the left, red and blue flags barely fluttering.

Three. Two. One. Go.

I made it through every gate. No tips caught on a pole. No out-of-control, one-legged skate off course. I climbed back up the hill and watched the rest of the crowd. Kathleen, who raced for her school team, blazed down the run low and professional looking. David and Bobby zoomed ahead. Courtney zipped through the flags only slightly slower than I did. Andy Williams fell on the first gate, got up, and tried again. Kerry giggled her way down. My time put me tenth overall behind all the experts, and together Steve Smith and I finished with the fastest combined time. Two nights later at the awards ceremony, our teams had been shifted, and someone had paired me with crooner and slowpoke Andy "The Klutz" Williams. *It doesn't matter,* I told myself when they awarded me a special prize: Fastest Governess On or Off the Slopes.

Why do I remember this incident after all these years? Had it been an affront to my sense of fair play? They said I was Steve Smith's teammate, and then they changed it to pair me with the worst possible grown-up. Or had an infantile delusion been exposed, the belief that because I wanted to be good at something, I would be? A reminder that what you expect, even what you think you deserve, you don't always get. Or maybe I simply remember the event because it was a moment when I felt totally present up there at the top of the run, in that familiar race mode, senses heightened for a start.

For most of the week, Courtney and I skied together, being well matched in ability and experience, while Kerry skied with her cousins on little Dollar Mountain and Kathleen and the boys headed off for the steep slopes. On the morning ride up the chairlift, I told Courtney about skiing Sun Valley for the first time three years before. For ninety-nine dollars in late March they offered a dorm bunk, two meals a day, and a week of lessons and lifts. I was just a beginner with only one winter of lessons, but my ski-racer boyfriend convinced me I'd improve over spring vacation if we drove to Idaho. "As soon as we arrived, he took me up this very chair," I said. I'd barely gotten my skis untangled when he spotted fresh powder in a back bowl and took off, signaling me to follow him. I had no choice since I didn't know the area or any of the runs. Within seconds I was down and up to my neck in powder. When I pushed on my poles to try to stand, they sank like lead-weighted lines. Thank goodness he stopped and sidestepped back up to help me, even though he was laughing, which made me madder. I screamed and swore so much, I bet the snow melted.

Courtney laughed with me, imagining the scene. The lift cranked on toward the top of the mountain before she asked what happened next. I told her I thought I'd plowed out of the powder eventually and onto a packed run, angry and blind with tears. "I told him I'd never, ever ski with him again."

"Did you?" she asked.

"Only after a week of lessons with someone who knew how to teach."

On our rides up the butt-chilling, foot-freezing chair, we alternated ski stories, bouncing memories one after the other—bad-day stories when the winds banged the chairs into the poles or when fog fell so thick, you couldn't see the ground or when you accidently got on a too-steep run and ended up side-stepping down or worse, taking skies off and walking while better skiers zipped past. We both had those stories even though she was twelve and I was twenty-three.

When we wore out our ski stories, she asked about college, not classes or what I'd studied but where I'd lived and who with. These were the experiences she hadn't had, and I became the storyteller like Lulu Hennessey and Nou Nou. As the cable pulled us up Bald Mountain and winds buffeted our chair, I described the house where I'd lived in Eugene, its many shared rooms that we decorated ourselves with fresh wallpaper and paint each fall. We each were assigned house duties, I told her. One time a California girl who had never run a vacuum sweeper and couldn't figure it out got a demerit for not completing her job. "Be sure to learn how to sweep and iron before you head off to college," I might have advised her.

I told her how we all slept on a sleeping porch with open, uncurtained windows, rows of bunk beds with girls who talked in their sleep on one side of the room and were answered in gibberish from someone on the other side. "You learn to go to bed early and fall asleep fast," I told her. My stories seemed to end with lessons either stated or submerged in subtext. When we were almost frozen through and through, I described the hidden haven Ann and I created in the basement among the coats, where warm lamplight pooled on our school desks and the outer world disappeared while we read the novels and poems of twentieth-century literature. Car rides and chair lifts offered a kind of side-by-side companionship that led to conversation, storytelling, and sometimes intimacy, which seemed unavailable among the hustle and bustle of daily life.

On New Year's Eve before the grown-ups departed for dinner and dancing and whatever else, everyone lined up for group photos in the Harriman cottage, the last pictures from 1968. The adults had no sooner left than the older kids followed out the door and vanished to who knows where, well beyond Tim's and my control. Courtney, Kerry, Michael, and the two Smith boys stayed behind to play games, determined to stay awake until midnight. Sometime in the midst of a Yahtzee game, I took a break to telephone Gretchen, my long-time friend from grade school, the one who was now in graduate school at Stanford. We shared some hurried gossip and wished each other happy new year. As we were saying our goodbyes, she lowered her voice and whispered into the phone—as if the FBI might be listening—that she'd tried marijuana.

"What?" I envisioned Audrey Hepburn sitting down to eat a five-layer brownie cake and a quart of ice cream. Grandma Green bringing home a six-pack of beer. Barbara Fritchie dropping the flag. No one I knew had ever smoked dope, certainly not Gretchen or me. At least that's what I had thought until now. Stunned, I hung up the phone. When the kids were all tucked into bed, I said to Tim, "The straightest arrow I know went off to grad school and now smokes dope."

"Want to smoke a joint to greet the new year?" he offered with a sly smile.

Of course. If Gretchen had tried it, I would too.

In the bathroom, he locked the door and sat on the toilet seat while I scrunched in the bathtub. He carefully shook out leaves from a tin onto a cigarette paper, licked the paper and rolled it, then twisted both ends. Before he lit it, he demonstrated how to inhale and hold. I was already a smoker, but when I took the first drag I coughed and had to puff again.

"I don't feel a thing," I remember saying, holding out the joint. "Is this real?"

Tim assured me it would kick in pretty soon. I think I expected the room to go all Yellow Submarine or to feel my eyes spin around in my head, or maybe I expected to have some secret of the universe revealed. I repeated, "I don't feel a thing" about two more times and then snorted a laugh, which sent Tim into giggles.

"Shhhhh! Shhhhhhh! I don't feel a thing," I whispered, and we both cracked up. It was the most hilarious thing I'd ever said.

The grown-ups seemed to revolve in an orbit that rarely crossed the kids', Tim's, and mine while we were in Sun Valley. Without Mrs. Kennedy to worry about, it had been a stress-free vacation, but as soon as we returned to Hickory Hill and she joined us downstairs for dinner for the first time since October, it felt a bit like starting all over again. The vacation was over.

Chapter 19

HOME

JANUARY 1969

RAIN PATTERING ON THE SHINGLES AND GURGLING IN THE DOWN-spouts outside my window wakened me. A slice of gray light leaked along the edge of the window blind. It smelled like home, the ancient pink sheets washed almost white, the heavy Hudson's Bay blanket over an unzipped down sleeping bag—rough, natural, a far cry from the French linens in the Kennedy house. Somewhere down the street, a school bus rumbled and stopped. Then kids' voices called out. *Are they coming home from school?* As if in slow motion, I struggled to lift the blankets and swim up to wakeful-ness. Away from Hickory Hill, fatigue filled my arms and legs and brain like warm JellO. *What time is it anyway? Six days off and already one lost to sleep,* I scolded myself. Downstairs a note on the kitchen table read: "Honey, I didn't want to wake you. Had to go down to the store to work on payroll. So good to have you home! Love, Mom."

After the Sun Valley trip, Mrs. Kennedy owed me over ten days off, and I negotiated with Sally Irish for consecutive days in January so I could fly home for a week. Nou Nou was scheduled to stay with Rory and Mrs. K for two months, and she promised she'd help Ena with the kids.

Portland had been smothered in snow for most of December and January, but rain greeted me on that first day home. At dinner Mom peppered me with questions about the kids and how I felt about Mrs. Kennedy and the house—everything I thought I'd already told her in letters and on tapes. But she wanted more, as everyone would throughout the week. More stories, more inside scoops, more details.

I told the story of ski racing in Sun Valley and having my team switched. Since I didn't feel any loyalty to Andy Williams, I could joke about his ski inability. My father loved hearing about the touch football games and how I'd scored a few touchdowns off passes from David. Dad had dressed up for dinner that first night wearing the new tie I'd given him for Christmas with the *PT-109* tie clip. He praised my mom's meal and wondered if anything was ever as good at the Kennedys'.

"Bet they don't have Dungeness crab back there, do they? Or Oregon shrimp?"

I think I realized in some new way what good people they were. My father was a lot like John Yaxley—reliable, good-natured, able to fix or jury-rig almost anything while chattering away to keep you close while he worked. Most of my life he'd gone to work at six thirty or seven in the morning six days a week and hadn't come home until after six at night. It was a brutal, relentless schedule, I thought, like the one all the people who worked for Mrs. Kennedy kept. And it hadn't been his choice.

He'd given up his career as a teacher and coach when the war came, and he moved to Portland with plans to train the troops, but somehow, he'd been coerced into working at my mother's father's market because all the younger men had been drafted. They needed him at the store, so he stayed and made the best of it. He'd sacrificed for the family, for the war effort, hadn't he? It's what grown-ups did, I thought. What choices had I already made or might make in the future that would change my life? I wondered. But conversations with my parents did not lean toward the speculative; they stayed in the here and now.

Dad couldn't wait to show me the new store. "I don't have to stand all day on wet cement," he said. "I tell you, I don't miss that old open-front store with the cold off the river."

"He spends more time in the office than out back filleting fish," Mom added.

After they'd asked their Kennedy questions, they chatted on about life in Portland. If I pull back and watch us at that dinner table, I hope I see myself listening and nodding, engaged with their reporting and their stories—my mother telling me how warm pantyhose are under her slacks down at the office, wondering if I know how easy they are to put on and how warm they can be. Or my father's analysis of how Oregon State would do against University of Oregon in the basketball season. They were sharing with me over peas and potatoes and fresh halibut important things about their lives and the world they inhabited. I heard a report on each cat's adventures and health, the neighbor child's tussle with mumps. Then they would pause, and it would be my turn to bounce the ball back: a story of Michael's two days home with a cold when he constructed, flew, and crashed innumerable paper airplanes or a detailed accounting of Christopher's pronouncement that he was going to tell Mummy to call the president to fix the bumpy road going to his school.

I hope I appreciated this table talk and recognized that my parents, while not deep political thinkers or arguers or philosophers, were wonderful conversationalists. They were reporters and storytellers of the day's events, Mrs. Meier's order for caviar or Betty Baller's new job driving the Welcome Wagon. They predicted an unpretentious future: who would win a basketball game, where the next-door neighbor would go to college, when the crab season would close. Ours was not a table where parents dropped in to pose twenty questions or grabbed hands to check for dirty nails. Nor was it a table filled with six or eight children, I reminded myself.

My father had grown up with ten brothers and sisters, raised in a wee ranch house without running water or electricity until after he left for college. His mother, dead long before I was born, had cooked on a woodstove all year round, even in the hundred-plus-degree summer heat of the San Joaquin Valley. When my mom went there for Thanksgiving dinner the first time, Dad's mother had complained that the gathering of twenty or twenty-five was too small. I thought of our Thanksgiving at Hickory Hill and how many people it had taken to serve the twenty or so who sat at the table that afternoon. In my Grandmother Wood's home, the only help were the children and an unmarried sister who lived in a shack a few miles away. If it takes a village to raise a child, my father's family itself was the village.

A longtime friend often told her story of growing up with eight siblings. They shared two second-floor bedrooms—three boys in one, six girls in the other—the parents downstairs, with one bathroom for them all. Diapers hung from laundry lines that crisscrossed the basement or backyard depending on the season, her story went. When she turned nine, the new baby became "her girl," her job to change, bathe, entertain, and sometimes feed. School offered respite for kids and mother, a nearby park their grounds. The church community, parents, and siblings were nurse, nanny, governess, cook, laundress, chauffer, butler, maids, gardener, secretary, and accountant. If I thought about how many people supported the one woman and her family at Hickory Hill, if I counted us all up, and I did, there were more employees than my father had at his store. That Christmas of 1968, there had been as many workers as occupants of the house.

WHILE I WAS HOME, I met with the Beaverton High principal early one morning to ask about my placement for the next year. He'd somehow neglected to tell me the previous June that as a first-year teacher I really had not been "on leave"—I'd quit the district when I broke my contract for the Kennedy job. Had he forgotten to tell me that, or had I been too excited to hear it? He could not guarantee that I'd have a job at Beaverton or even in the district in the next school year, although he was pretty sure something would open up.

How did I like it back East? he wanted to know. Who had I met so far?

I told him Colonel John Glenn was very nice and that I'd played football with Rosey Grier. They were good people to mention to this principal, who had a special interest in the military and in football, as many principals did who had come up through the good-old-boy networks in those days. I wondered if he was still requiring teachers to measure boys' hair length and refer long-hairs to the vice principal. We finished our conversation with his opinion that there'd probably be an opening in the English department, but he wouldn't know for sure until March.

My older self would have felt very nervous about this situation. She would have made calls to the district office, written letters to the principal and department head of the other high school in the district. But the one-year-of-experience me headed into the teachers' room to find my colleagues Dale, Linda, Leota, and Coach Harman. I'm sure I hung around all day drinking coffee and smoking with whoever had a free period. Linda told me how the new curriculum was working with the juniors and a silly story about a boy who had come up during reading time for *The Catcher in the Rye* to ask what "chrissake" meant. He thought it might be a Japanese drink, but why was it in this book? She stifled her laughter and whispered to him: "For Christ's sake. He thinks it fast so he says: 'chrissake.' Get it?" It was a stupid story, and it made me miss teaching. Every week there was an amusing incident from the classroom that could delight for a year. Even the Terrible Tim tale had its humor now, and I could crack up retelling the slapping-blinds story that had me seeing red.

Dale, who was recovering from pneumonia, seemed quiet except to ask what I'd been reading lately. If Lee hadn't given me Solzhenitsyn's *In the First Circle* for Christmas, I'd have had to admit that I'd pretty much read nothing except a few essays and poems in the Middleburg cabin on my very few days off. I brought up a Dag Hammarskjöld essay nobody had read and Steinbeck's *America and Americans*, but our discussion kept returning to questions about living with the Kennedys. Who had I met? What were the kids like? Was Jackie Kennedy really nice? When Rod Harman had his break, he gave me the rundown on the swim team, including the splits for both girls' and boys' relays. He told me that our boys' team was going to be really good next year, and his use of the plural possessive assured me that he'd advocate for getting me back to Beaverton. Before I left, Dale, like the principal, said he was pretty sure there would be openings in the English department, not to worry. And I didn't, too confident and naïve to be overly concerned.

On another day, Gretchen R.—my friend whose husband was in Viet Nam—invited me to drive with her to Seaside on the Oregon coast where her in-laws lived. We hadn't spent so much time together since we were roommates in college, two hours over and two back. It's a beautiful drive from Portland to the Pacific Ocean. The road runs due west for thirty or so miles before it climbs up from the Tualatin Valley and into the Coast Range, where Douglas fir, hemlock, and cedar crowd out the sky. The fierce winter storms had left three or four feet of roadside snow at the summit, and we crawled along in the two open lanes talking, catching up.

She told me about Army housing and the letters she'd gotten from Viet Nam. Some of the men had sent disturbing photos home to wives: skulls lined up on jeep hoods or armloads of captured rifles and knives. We talked about the horrors the men were suffering, had caused. What would they be like when they came home? How would they be changed? I wondered if my friend watched television news at night, if she searched to find faces she recognized or feared she'd see someone she knew carried away on a stretcher.

I thought again of David and what he had witnessed on television, his helplessness all alone in his room as he watched for news of his father, but for some reason, I didn't think about the damage done to Mrs. Kennedy. She seemed to me then so impervious to pain, so charismatic and powerful, untouchable. A scene from Hyannis, the morning she pulled at the soiled carpet and screamed at the boys, returned. She was mere months past standing beside her husband when he was shot, when he fell to the kitchen floor in that California hotel. What might have triggered her rage that morning? Some stain on the rug? Some shadow cast across it that unleashed a memory? We didn't know about post-traumatic stress disorder then, didn't have words, diagnoses. World War I soldiers had "shell shock." World War II soldiers had "battle fatigue." We hadn't yet labeled the brutal consequences awaiting Viet Nam veterans. We knew nothing of the recurring nightmares of ordinary people who witnessed murder, who had experienced trauma. That sunny morning on the cape, I had seen a woman seemingly out of emotional control and escaped as fast as I could. But now I wondered how I could not have imagined the trauma of standing beside her husband and hearing—feeling—the gunshot, the blood, the collapse.

I'm pretty sure that Gretchen R. didn't tell me everything that came home in letters and tapes from Viet Nam, just like I didn't share everything I knew from living in the household day and night. My stories were curated from a sense of loyalty and protection. I had no motive to hurt or to damage reputations, only to entertain and convey that the Kennedys were people like us. The images projected in magazines and newspaper photos were as true for those moments as any I could reveal from a typical afternoon or weekend. But away from Hickory Hill that week in January, I had time for reflection instead of reaction, and I began to see and feel things I'd ignored.

When she asked about the kids, our conversation lightened. David was small but a competitive and agile athlete, I told her, like her brother who'd played ball at Beaverton. Michael was quiet and pensive, a kind boy who paid attention to the dogs and his younger siblings. Kerry reminded me of myself as a kid, I told her, always trying to keep up or beat the older kids. She had a wild and stubborn streak, which I recognized but that could drive me crazy at the same time. Courtney, the twelve-year-old, reminded me of her, the freckles and friendliness, I told her. Courtney always wanted to hear about my friends…swim team stories and college. She knew all about how we drank beer up in our room behind a locked door, how my roommate and I dressed up as Chickenman and clucked our way through the house. She knew about Ann, who I'd be seeing over the weekend, and our study hideout in the sorority basement.

Ann sat in an armchair, reading glasses perched on her nose, her legs tucked under her, a stack of student papers set aside on the floor and a glass of wine on a side table. She'd pulled on a loose cardigan over her turtleneck even though the little apartment felt too warm to me. We'd been sitting and talking all afternoon, and now the streetlights were on. From the kitchen the stove clock glowed, but I couldn't read it.

We'd talked about Ann's school and the teachers she admired and why, including the one she was dating. I told her about my new friends on the staff and summarized some of the movies I'd seen. We each had funny stories to share, observations about books that kids liked and the ones they wouldn't read, whether they were in high school or in middle school like my kids. When the wine came out, we made our confessions.

She wasn't sure she could continue teaching. It was too hard, too demanding, impossible to get everyone to succeed. Every paper could take hours to correct if you did a thorough job. There simply wasn't enough time, she said.

"But you're making a difference in their lives," I argued. "You're making them think."

Mrs. Kennedy had asked me months before if I missed teaching, and I'd told her that I was too busy to miss anything. But I did miss classroom discussions about our reading, the ones where we talked about characters, questioning whether humans were basically good or evil, arguing about fate and choice, about the impact a person might have on another or on events. We had added *Man's Search for Meaning* to the junior curriculum. How would that lens clarify characters' behavior? I wondered. I wanted to be back with a classroom of juniors asking them to consider how they were like Holden Caulfield or Ethan Frome or "The Unknown Citizen"—how they might react if they were falsely accused like John Proctor. Maybe some kid would make a connection between the Beatle's song "Piggies" and *Animal Farm* or Buffy Sainte-Marie's "The Circle Game" and *The Catcher in the Rye*. There was so much I'd do differently my second year teaching. We'd only read bits of *Walden*, but I had an idea that in my future classes I'd ask students to design an experiment that they could do for a week or two and document what they discovered about themselves or the world.

Maybe Ann had entered the school-year doldrums, the long, wet stretch between winter break and spring break when you begin to question where you are and dream about where you might go to escape. Maybe that's where I was heading too. I told her that despite all the funny stories I could tell, the job had become pretty boring. Before Mrs. Kennedy was confined to her bed, all I wanted to do was keep her happy. It had been a challenge to please her, to talk to her, to keep out of her way. But it was fun too. Her explosive, erratic personality kept me on my toes, I told Ann, and made every day exciting in the game I called Keeping on the Good Side. When she first went on bed rest, I missed her—or missed the game. The daily routine felt monotonous, the isolation deadening, I complained before adding, "Except for the holidays and the kids and the trips."

"It'll change now, won't it?" Ann said.

Yes, it probably will, I thought. *When Nou Nou leaves, I'll be alone again with Mrs. Kennedy.* Bob's advice from months before came back to me: "Just stay out of Mrs. Kennedy's way," but it wasn't as easy in the house as it had been on the cape.

Before I returned to Virginia, my mom did my laundry, and I thanked her. Had I ever done that before? I made a promise that I'd thank Geneva, who did my clothes along with all the rest of the Kennedy laundry. And Ruby for feeding me throughout the year. The week at home among family and friends had provided respite, like stretching out on a warm tile floor after an overnight flight crammed into a middle seat. I had breathing room again, but even so, when my mom asked at the airport if I thought I might stay for another year I answered, "Hell no!"

Chapter 20

COLD HARD WINTER

Nou Nou poked her head in my door. "You want to look in my room. Lauren Bacall's in there holding the baby." She led me back to her room where Ms. Bacall sat on the bed rocking and cooing with Rory.

Even after meeting so many famous people, I probably gawked. She'd come for the baptism, along with Pat Lawford, Jean Smith, and countless other New Yorkers, DC politicians, and journalists. Nou Nou introduced me as "the indispensable and much-beloved governess," which rushed blood to my cheeks. If I'd had my wits about me, I'd have mentioned seeing her the previous year in *Cactus Flower*, but that would have required more poise than I possessed. The three of us focused on Rory, whose only trick was to burble and stare, before I excused myself to check on Michael and Kerry, the godparents-to-be.

Downstairs in the TV room, I fussed with Michael's breast-pocket handkerchief and arranged Kerry's mantilla before we left for Saint Luke's. Nou Nou, dressed in her starched white uniform and baby-blue sweater, now with a starched nurse's cap atop her red hair and holding Rory, had to be the centerpiece of a photo, and I ran to get my camera. In one snapshot Nou Nou, her lips pursed, hums *whooooo* to Rory, who stares straight into her blue eyes. In another photo, Michael stands at attention, eyebrows raised, in his navy blazer, white shirt, and narrow black tie beside Nou Nou. No psychedelic ties at this important event. On the other side Kerry looks grown-up in a white wool coat piped in black, her smiling face framed by the mantilla. Between them, Rory lies on Nou Nou's lap, her fists tiny balls inside a long-sleeved lace gown and fine cashmere cloak, her lace bonnet secured by satin ribbon.

The Kennedy children didn't have any real responsibilities. They were supposed to make their beds, comb their hair, and scrub their hands, but everything else in their world was done by others, just as it had been in my childhood. My mother and father took care of every need. I didn't have younger brothers or sisters to look out for. At least in the big Kennedy family, whether after school or at breakfast, in outdoor play or indoor games, at birthday parties or overnights with cousins, the kids were caring and gentle with each other—mostly. But being a godparent connected them to *their* child in a significant way. It was a weighty and lifelong duty. In the packed Saint Luke's church, standing before Archbishop Cooke of New York as he poured holy water over Rory's forehead and administered the sacrament, Michael and Kerry looked a bit older, more serious, proud in their new responsibility.

The weekend of the baptism, Courtney, Kerry, and Caroline spent an afternoon with Joe hanging confetti and decorating the table for Matthew Maxwell "Max the Ax" Taylor Kennedy's fourth birthday party. He sat at the head of the dining table like a little prince, Mummy to one side and Ena helping on the other as he blew out candles on another massive sheet cake, Ruby's

Max's fourth birthday party. Left to right: Christopher, David, Kerry, Max, Caroline, Courtney, Michael (behind the streamers).

birthday special. David and Michael looked on behind him while Christopher edged in a little closer to the cake. I watched them all jostle and joke and then settle down to cake and ice cream. Here were my kids growing up in front of me—in mere months they all looked older. The previous year, scrambling to create lesson plans and to stay on top of things, I hadn't noticed how my students matured throughout the school year or seen the changes wrought over a summer. But here was Max, still number nine among eleven but looking older than he had when I'd first arrived. Soon he'd be attending preschool at the Potomac School. *What will I do with my mornings?* I wondered, feeling a twinge of sadness.

Max's birthday signaled the official end of the Christmas holiday season. When I returned from my Portland vacation, Mrs. Kennedy had completely recovered from her "maternity leave" and was beginning to plan for the future: weekend dinners for guests, a Valentine's Day party perhaps, a ski trip to Waterville Valley in New Hampshire for Washington's Birthday, and another for spring vacation. We had lots to look forward to until Sally announced one morning in late January that the accountants would be coming to the house, and it would get ugly. Apparently, spending alerts arrived every January from New York, but this year everything in Mrs. Kennedy's fiscal world had changed for the worse.

On a dreary January morning in my half-imagined memory, we peered from behind the drapes in the secretaries' office and watched a black limousine with tinted windows inch up the drive. It sat parked for several threatening minutes before two ominous-looking men in long black overcoats and with sleek leather briefcases emerged. Joe opened the front door before anyone knocked. In fact, I don't exactly remember the accountants, only the outcome of their visit.

Sally came out of the hours-long meeting visibly shaken. The household staff had to be cut, expenses reined in drastically. The horses and ponies were to be sold, Freddy Bacon let go. One upstairs maid, cut. The outdoor workman who helped John Yaxley, gone. Sally would be on her own; Penny was being terminated. The entertainment budget, slashed. Dinner parties and events, canceled. Phone extensions in the drawing room and all the bedrooms would be removed. Apparently, the long-distance bill was "over the moon" after every dinner party, when guests took advantage of the free phone opportunity. Even the Coke machine down by the pool would be emptied. No more free sodas.

When my dad was in financial trouble, he took our garbage to work for a couple of weeks to save money on our household bills; my mother complained it was just a drop in the bucket. Now here were rich people plugging up the little holes in a bucket where money could drip, drip, drip away. It didn't matter if you earned five thousand dollars a year or fifty thousand or had a million-dollar inheritance—if you spent more than what came in, you had to budget and make cuts.

But if you didn't write the checks, if you never even knew how much you had, how could you begin to understand a budget? I thought of a story I'd heard that the Kennedys never carried cash. If they were out and stopped to eat or took a taxi somewhere, the senator would pull at his empty pockets, and the aides would have to come up with the money to pay. A dinner out and a taxi fare might bust the week's budget of a staffer but mean nothing to someone who's never written a check or carried cash or worked for a paycheck. Maybe that was what I had been trying to teach Courtney when I'd explained about how one present for Kathleen was a week's wages for me.

When Dave Hackett came over for dinner that Friday night, he assured me that all the "blessed ones" were being kept on, the ones with cheery dispositions and who were good to the kids. That was the criteria. Joe, John Yaxley, and I did not need to worry. Instead, I worried about the horses. Even though the girls didn't ride during the winter, the loss of the horses seemed cruel. What would it mean to Mrs. Kennedy to close the stable? Hadn't that horseman in Middleburg told me she had been a rider? Where would their horses end up, and what would happen in the summer? In my letters home, I seemed indifferent to the employees suddenly without jobs, but I must have worried about them. Where would they go? How would they pay their bills? Only Penny—who could never do anything right in Mrs. Kennedy's eyes and was always getting yelled at—talked about her dismissal, and she seemed resigned. "This whole organization threw me for a loop. I haven't done a damned thing since I've been here," she said before she left.

ON MOST SCHOOL NIGHTS AROUND bedtime, David wandered downstairs to grab a bowl of cereal or a handful of crackers and cheese from the kitchen before he perched with me in the TV room, not to watch a show but to eat with company. We'd chat, he'd munch, and I'd shoo him upstairs and into bed. This Thursday, however, he'd finished his last final after three days of tests, and I was letting him sit up to watch *It's Happening* with me. At around ten forty-five the intercom rang in the TV room.

"Where's David?" Mrs. Kennedy demanded.

At the first ring, he'd jumped out of his chair and run up the stairs, knowing who was on that line.

"He just came down for a snack," I lied.

"Can't you exercise any control over these kids? He should be asleep by ten forty-five. What's going on, anyway? Speak to me tomorrow morning regarding this."

"Yes, ma'am," I answered politely. This was the second time she'd gone after me that day.

You keep Chris and Max and Kerry up an hour past their bedtime every single night, I fumed to myself.

For three months I hadn't had to deal with her rages. I'd taken care of things, kept a careful routine. She may not have known it, but I had my four in bed on time every night. We'd read together, say prayers, and I'd tuck them in. Ena did the same with Max and Chris up on the third floor. But now Mrs. K had everyone off schedule. When I'd start to herd Kerry toward bed, she'd break for Mummy's room. As soon as Ena got Chris and Max into PJs, down they'd run and disappear into her bedroom for an extra half hour or hour. After fifteen years in the household, Ena was used to the inconsistencies, to the ebb and flow of emotions, the ever-changing weather systems. But not I. My whole life had been regulated by school bell schedules and swim team training programs. While Ena's patience stretched like warm taffy, mine began to crack.

At dinner that night, Mrs. Kennedy had reprimanded me because David had dirt under a fingernail.

"I asked him four times to rewash his hands, Mrs. Kennedy," I explained, and she turned to David and let rip. When she raised her voice and attacked, we all winced.

Tonight I felt angry—at David for not washing up to standards, at myself for blaming him, and especially at her for being so petty. *What a pleasant way to start dinner*, I thought sarcastically. We'd had three months without any dinner scenes, but now everyone stared at their plates. Courtney, with her usual poise, dissipated the tension. "Are we going to Waterville to ski over Washington's Birthday, Mummy?"

After the night's eruptions, I stewed in my room, angry and self-righteous. *She doesn't even know her kids. David's in bed on time almost every night. He's bright and witty and needs a little attention.* My thoughts flew toward accusation and grandiosity. *I bet I know her kids better in these six months than she ever will. One dirty nail or one late bedtime and I get screamed at? It's not right!*

Later, still seething about the unfairness of it all, I wrote what I called "a therapy letter" to Ann. "When the accountants ordered a

60 percent cut in expenditures, they caused a 60 percent increase in irritability," it began. I added that if I thought about the kids, I could detach myself from the unfair rants. I speculated that maybe it was good for me to have "to take it." Did I think it might teach me humility? Or help me develop empathy for those who couldn't fight back against injustice?

Coaches hollered and yelled at us when we were training, but they were driving us to work harder than we thought we could. Maybe Mrs. Kennedy wanted me to do better, but her yelling felt battering, and it butted against what felt right. I'd made a judgment to let David stay up as a reward for a week of hard work. I was right, and she was wrong. It seemed so simple.

My letter concluded that one thing had become clear that night: I was working for *my* kids and for the senator who had hired me, not for her.

Now, with fifty more years of life experience, I see a more complex picture than I did when I was twenty-three. Mrs. Kennedy, widowed at forty, must have felt totally alone that year, so out of control of her life and everything going on around her. She'd been confined and inaccessible to her children all fall. She'd been unable to attend games and performances and school fairs like she'd done in previous years. She'd missed the annual ski trip with family and friends to Sun Valley. How presumptuous to think I knew more about her kids than she did. I hadn't been there the previous year to deal with David and Bobby's problem behavior. For all I knew, maybe they'd snuck out of their room on an escapade at the end of finals before, so that when she didn't find David in his room that night, she worried about it happening again. This year she was dealing with budget cuts that she didn't want or even know how to make. The accountants were dictating what she had to do. And nobody was talking about what had to be looming in her mind: Sirhan Sirhan's trial for the murder of her husband, which would begin in Los Angeles in two weeks. All the memories, the losses, the suffering would be reawakened.

And what did I know of grief? How could I imagine the images that must have played and replayed in Mrs. Kennedy's memory night after night when the house became still and the night quiet? What last conversations, hopes, dreams? What fears? How does a person meet such a tragedy? I didn't ask those questions that year, at first too absorbed in discovery and mastering tasks, too exhausted each night to reflect. Yet even as the year went on, I remained too inexperienced in life's inevitabilities—love, relationships, violence, parenthood, death—to understand Mrs. Kennedy's state. Perhaps if I'd been twenty years older or had worked for them for five or ten years, I might have been more like Nou Nou or Lulu, assertive and instructive. Maybe I'd have stood up for myself or defended the child being reprimanded. I'd know to suggest the value of sharing the load of grief for children who'd lost a parent.

The next morning Mrs. Kennedy never mentioned the evening's incidents, but I was still processing. I finished the letter to Ann: "As much as I love the children, I could not stand another year of lost independence because of Mrs. Kennedy. One thing I have learned, to humiliate or even to try to humiliate another can serve no purpose. To be artificial, to be ultra-demanding, and to give no compliments on work accomplished is to kill respect, devotion, and happiness. What goes on here goes on in the classroom, but it will never happen in mine."

Like a winter storm, the heavy clouds dumped their load, lightened, and moved on. After a few weeks of austerity, the parties resumed in February, first to celebrate Joe-the-Butler's permanent resident status, his green card. He was on his way to citizenship, and Nou Nou planned the party. She had Ruby send him off on a series of errands while we dashed around decorating the TV room. Chris and Max, patriotically dressed in red turtlenecks and navy-blue pants, planted little flags on tabletops, in picture frames, and atop the lamps. David and Courtney, still in school uniforms, pulled a banner across the fireplace mantle, where Nou Nou had placed an Uncle Sam top hat and cocktail glasses with the Union Jack on one side, the Stars and Stripes on the other. When we heard the station wagon crunch up the drive, everyone crammed into the TV room (except Mrs. Kennedy, who was back in bed with bronchitis, and Ena, who was watching Rory). Kerry held Douglas, Michael held Freckles, and the rest of us held our breath as we heard Joe walk past our closed door on his way to the kitchen. Ruby must have sent him back for something, because he returned and pushed in the doors to be greeted by our shout: "Surprise!" I hope we sang a boisterous version of "God Bless America" before Nou Nou popped the cork on the champagne and I opened the ginger ale.

The best thing about getting the green card, Joe told me later, was that now he could travel out of the country. He could go home to England and see his parents, visit his brother in the Channel Islands, return to his grandparents' farm in Italy. "It opens up the world again," he said.

After Joe's party came a small Valentine's Day dinner party for grown-ups. In a photo, the dining room has been reconfigured

Joe and Nou Nou celebrate Joe's "green card" day, becoming a lawful permanent American resident.

with round tables set for ten with fine linens, china, and crystal. Each table has an ice-sculpture centerpiece filled with pink and red blossoms created by Joe and his brother, who was chef for the night. In the pool house, the kids and I probably shared pizza and gobbled boxes of Sweethearts brand candy hearts before watching *The Lion in Winter*.

I kept two special valentines from that day. One was hand-made at school by Christopher, a red heart glued to a lace doily. He'd printed on it: "I LOE YOU Criz"

The other was a card from Joe and Nou Nou. On the outside Joe had drawn a map of Europe with skiers on a mountain in Switzerland, two people on a scooter in Italy, and a bull's-eye over Paris, where Nou Nou would soon be moving. Inside he'd calligraphed this message:

Would you beleive a trip around
The woeld?
Would you beleive a trip to
EUROPE ??
OKAY THEN — HOW A'BOUT A SUMMER AT THE
CAPE ?????????.............

It was their initial enticement, and I smiled but didn't respond.

To save money, I was left behind on the first Waterville ski trip over Washington's Birthday weekend. My four kids flew up to New Hampshire with Mummy on Thursday, and I lolled around Hickory Hill with Chris and Max, Nou Nou and Ena, and the babies. After school we played in the basement, and I sent several tapes home with the boys singing songs and telling stories to my mom and dad. At dinner we could breathe easy and chatter without fear of a sudden nail check or an outburst of emotion. After the boys went to bed, I read chapter after chapter in my book.

Sunday afternoon Mrs. Kennedy called to tell us that they were caught in a storm. Nothing was moving in the Northeast, not even the snowplows. Nothing would move for four more days because the storm, later dubbed the 100-Hour Storm, dumped almost four feet of snow that blew into massive drifts that paralyzed all traffic,

Douglas records a message on my tape recorder.

air and ground. I hung up the phone and danced to Nou Nou's room to announce: "We've got a snow day! We're on our own here."

That evening shortly after dinner, the phone rang and I answered, "Kennedy residence. Carolyn speaking."

"Allo, Caroline. This is Ari. Is Ethel there?" It was Aristotle Onassis.

"No, I'm sorry. She's still in Waterville." I explained her plight, and he laughed and laughed. He was calling to encourage her to join Jackie and him for a Caribbean cruise in April.

He pattered on with a few more pleasantries as if we knew each other before he hung up.

Two minutes later the phone rang again.

"Cah-ro-lin? This is Jackie. Do you have Ethel's phone number up there?"

So began the lobbying effort to entice Mrs. Kennedy onto their yacht to cruise the Caribbean, "a little birthday outing for

Peace and quiet at Hickory Hill after the February snowstorm.

her," in April. If she went, it would be like a few more snow days for the staff.

Calls came daily from Mrs. Kennedy describing the massive drifts, the fabulous skiing, how great she felt. Maybe she'd send the kids home when flights started up again, she told us, and she'd stay a bit longer with Tommy and Roberta Corcoran, the founders and owners of Waterville Valley Resort. But by Friday she'd gotten a little crazed. If she couldn't get to the airport on Saturday, she'd miss her chance on the Skakel jet and have to fly commercial. And it looked like another storm was on its way. On a tape home I say that I have "a feeling they'll make it through the drifts soon. But maybe not. There's always that hope." Like a kid listening for the radio to announce school closures, I waited to hear whether or not they'd return. Each delay became a gift, the house so calm and quiet.

Nou Nou's going-away party went on without Mrs. Kennedy or the kids. She and her husband were moving to France, and she'd already extended her stay by two weeks. This was her last job before retirement. Lee Geisen came back to see her off, Lulu Hennessey called from Boston to wish her well, and Ruby gave her a vibrant caftan from Elizabeth Arden—"For life in Paris," she said. Mrs. Kennedy called from New Hampshire, and they talked for a long time, and then one by one Nou Nou farewelled the kids. She'd probably held them all at some point. Many she'd cradled, comforted, and fed their first months of life. But Nou Nou was completely unsentimental. It was a job. She'd done it well. And now, adieu. Before she left that afternoon, she pulled Lee and Joe and me aside. "Come visit me this summer in Paris," she said. "I mean it. We'll have a time together."

First the valentine and then the personal invitation: seeds of temptation planted in the furrows of discontent.

Chapter 21

SPRING FEVER

THE DAY BEFORE SIRHAN SIRHAN'S TRIAL BEGAN IN FEBRUARY, JUST before the Waterville trip, Mrs. Kennedy called me into her room. "When the trial starts, I want you to cut every article out of the paper before it comes to the breakfast table," she told me. No one was to see or read anything.

The first two days were easy because the family was preparing to leave for their Waterville ski trip. I snagged the papers off the front porch before any of the kids came down for breakfast and stashed them in the office, where later I could clip out the photos and articles. But when they came back and returned to their routine of checking the paper, the cut-outs and missing sections were obvious. One morning David rushed into the dining room a bit late, as usual. He stood at the end of the table, his shirt still untucked, his tie not yet knotted, and filled his cereal bowl before grabbing for the *Times* or the *Post*.

"Where's the front page?" he asked.

"Your mom wants me to cut out the trial articles," I told him, unwilling to make up a story that would have to be repeated for weeks to come. He looked at me as if I might say something more, then he sat down and fished for the sports section.

I can understand Mrs. Kennedy's desire to protect the children, to divert their attention, to hide details that could be distressing. I don't remember if I'd been instructed to destroy the stories or to hand them over to Sally to be filed away, but every day as new details emerged, we talked among ourselves in the office when the kids and Mrs. Kennedy were away. We learned that Sirhan blamed Robert Kennedy for supporting Israel in the Arab-Israeli War, what we now called the Six-Day War, the conflict that had so frightened me when I'd been a mother's helper on Long Island. He'd chosen June 5 because it coincided with the anniversary of the war's onset. Five other people had been wounded that night, including Liz Stevens, Mrs. Kennedy's friend. Sirhan's defense argued he was mentally incompetent; he asked to plead guilty, but the judge denied his request. We wondered if Mrs. Kennedy wanted the papers removed to protect the children or if she herself wanted to avoid reading the daily accounts. Unlike now when there are multiple news sources, all she had were the papers, the nightly news, and her friends and family to inform her of the daily proceedings.

Could she have been subpoenaed to testify? Was there talk of her going to Los Angeles? Any conversations about the trial that she may have had with Uncle Teddy or Dave Hackett or an attorney happened far from the downstairs world. It was as if when I cut the articles out of the papers, the trial itself no longer existed. But in fact, it went on for over two months—while the family was stranded in Waterville, when we skied there again in March, when Mrs. Kennedy joined Jackie and Aristotle Onassis in April just as the trial ended and Sirhan Sirhan was sentenced to the death penalty. By the last week of April, the newspapers were again delivered to the breakfast table full and uncut.

Two weeks after the family dug their way out of Waterville Valley, we were all back on the plane heading north for spring vacation. The bags practically packed themselves. All I'd had to do was empty the long johns and turtlenecks, liners and socks, haul them downstairs to Geneva in the laundry, and pack them right back into suitcases for the next trip.

Everyone was going to Waterville, despite the budget cuts, including Christopher and Max, Joe-the-Butler, and me. Kathleen, Joe, and Bobby would meet us there. For a while there'd been talk that we'd stay only a few days, but too much was going on to limit the visit. Top skiers were coming to race in the 1969 North American Alpine Championships, dedicated to honor Robert F. Kennedy, which would be the World Cup's final event, the last chance for racers to win World Cup points. One of the best American skiers came from Bend, Oregon: nineteen-year-old Kiki Cutter, who'd been one of the youngest US skiers in the 1968 Grenoble Olympics. This season she was tearing up the slalom courses. I felt a special bond of us being young Oregon Olympians even though we'd never met. Courtney, Kerry, and I followed her practice runs and races all week as unofficial cheerleaders.

Tommy Corcoran, the resort developer, provided the biggest house he could because the whole clan would be there the weekend of the race: the Lawfords, the Smiths, Caroline and John. I might have been "the fastest governess" on the slopes of Sun Valley, but I had the most responsibility in Waterville, and Joe had the job of cooking for us all. When I wrote home, I added up twenty children and three or four Kennedy adults all in one ten-room condo.

I don't remember having any special duties on the slopes. We skied together, pretending to race some sections and loafing some on the sunny, broad, almost treeless runs, so different from those carved through the trees on Mount Hood. The steepest runs were cordoned off for the racers, and we often paused to watch them scream by at speeds I could barely fathom. You'd hear a slicey sound uphill—then a sklish—a swoosh—and they were past.

The younger kids were all taking lessons or skiing with instructors on easy slopes. The older kids, all experts—Kathleen and her friends, Joe and his, Bobby, and David—skied by themselves on the black diamond runs. Mrs. Kennedy and the middle group, including me, spent most mornings skiing together on more moderate slopes. Joe, who served as a second chaperone in addition to being cook, skied with us in the mornings and early afternoon before he'd return to the condo to prepare dinner. We traded off riding the lift with the kids, waiting at the top for the group to gather before we sailed down.

One day toward noon, Joe and I rode up together. "Want a little nip?" he asked, unzipping his jacket and pulling out a leather bota bag that hung from his neck.

"Are you kidding? We're skiing with Mrs. Kennedy."

"She won't care. It'll warm us up." He squirted a mouthful then aimed the bag at me. "Open up."

We'd been playing follow the leader all morning on the wide-open slopes, letting our skis run a bit before slowing and waiting for everyone to catch up. Late-morning sun had softened the snow, and on the last run we'd slalomed through moguls as if on a flagged racecourse. Mrs. Kennedy had even complimented my style.

"Sun Valley Ski School," I'd said, crediting my college spring vacation classes.

How many swigs did Joe and I swallow before the lift arrived at the top of the run? Courtney started down first, and Mrs. Kennedy followed, then the rest of our group peeled off one by one, and down we sped. But the wine in me resisted follow the leader and awakened the racer. I pointed my skis downhill as if I thought I was Kiki Cutter and schussed past one skier after another until I caught an edge on a mogul and tumbled head over skis over head in a snowy explosion. Afterward Joe told me he thought I might have broken something. Mrs. Kennedy sidestepped half the slope to get back to me. Courtney was almost in tears.

"Very dramatic, Carolyn," Joe said.

I think I was knocked out for a few seconds because I don't remember what happened or how I got my skis back on or how I got off the slope. All I remember is that night in the bathroom standing up from the toilet and experiencing the wall crashing into my head. Or so I thought. "The bathroom wall knocked into me," I said and someone walked me back to my bunk.

No more bota bags on the chair lift, but Joe had other temptations. He talked ceaselessly about going to Europe for the summer. Nou Nou had a place for us in Paris. The senator's longtime secretary, Angie Novello, was now secretary for the US ambassador to Denmark, and we could visit her in Copenhagen. Joe brother's employer had a chalet in the Swiss Alps, where he was sure we could to stay if no one else was using it. He had cousins in Rome and his grandparents' house in the Calore River valley. It would be an extraordinary adventure, he promised.

Joe had worked out many of the trip details, leaving in June and returning in August, but he lacked companions: Lee Geisen and me. We could split the costs of a car and camp along the way. It would practically be a free trip once we got over there, he vowed.

Here was the snake offering the apple—it wasn't just a trip to Europe; it was a trip that would also cut short my not-so-idyllic commitment. My arguments began to develop. Maybe I could join them in August, although I knew that with a job teaching, most of my August would be spent preparing for classes. "I could never hope to travel with a more diverse but natural and loving group," I wrote home to Ann. "What different types of people I've met here, not only the rich bastards, the intellectual elite, but the 'help' who I'd never have found in Oregon."

On the first race day in Waterville, a few of us watched from the slope several gates up from the finish line. Joe let me test the camera that he hoped to sell to me, a Beseler Topcon with a telephoto lens, because he was upgrading to a Nikon for the Europe trip. The roll I shot is filled with photos of red and blue blurs streaking against a white background. In one, a tiny speck crosses under red, white, and blue finish-line banners where a few spectators stand behind yellow plastic web fencing. It's labeled, "Berni Rauter, Austria, winning the women's giant slalom." Upgrading my camera would not make me into Margaret Bourke-White, but I liked its weight and loved the leather-cased telephoto hanging around my neck. If I did go to Europe with Joe and Lee, I'd be able to document our travels.

The whole Kennedy family and friends who had come for the finale packed around the finish line for the final race of the season, the women's slalom. Mrs. Kennedy was to hand out the awards for the race and for the top three finishers of the World Cup season. From start to finish, Courtney, Kerry, and I chanted, "Kiki," and practically jumped out of our skis when she actually won, beating a German by two-tenths of a second.

ONCE AN ENTICING IDEA GETS planted, it's hard to eradicate. Nou Nou's invitation for escape and adventure gnawed away. Joe talked to Sally about a summer break. Or maybe he told her he was going to take a leave, because he already had the plans. When I asked her if she thought I might be able to depart before August, she went right to Lem Billings and Dave Hackett, who responded: "Not a chance. She can't be replaced."

It's so flattering to think you're indispensable. When Dave and Lem said I couldn't leave, that I was irreplaceable, part of me believed them. The kids adored me, they said. And even though Mrs. Kennedy never complimented me directly—except for my athletic skills—I heard from others her opinion: how good I was with the children, how much I'd taught them, how well they worked with me. Even so, I knew that Mrs. Kennedy had insisted she couldn't manage without Lee, had kept her on for months after she wanted to leave. In fact, after Lee left, Mrs. Kennedy got along fine. It might have been inconvenient or uncomfortable for her, but...

I made the case to myself: the kids would be busy all summer with their lessons and sleepovers, their beach barbecues and island picnics, movies at Grandpa's, the constant presence of cousins and friends and guests on the compound. Summer plans off-compound for Kathleen, Joe, and Bobby were in place by late April, and David had been invited to England with his cousin Chris Lawford, whose father was shooting a film there. With the official year of mourning over, Mrs. Kennedy and the kids might join the Whittakers on a river raft trip or the Onassises in Greece. *What would I do then?* I wondered. Hang out with Christopher and Max, Dougie, and seven-month-old Rory? It would be as bad as my father's summers that he'd spent alone with cattle. I was hungry for adult companionship, intellectual conversation, new adventures. "I'll go buggy, buggy, buggy with the same dull routine," I wrote home to Ann, further developing my arguments for leaving early.

But was it early? I'd never signed a contract, never been given specified dates of employment. They'd asked me to come in August, "for a year," I thought they'd said. *Did that mean August to August or a school year?* I wondered now. I recalled how I'd thought my principal had told me to "take a leave" when I'd been offered the Kennedy job. In fact, I'd resigned with no guarantees. If it wasn't written down and agreed upon, everyone could have her own version of an agreement. You could hear anything, remember what you wanted to remember.

On my off Thursdays that winter and spring, Lee and I would meet for an afternoon film in a DC art house. I saw my first foreign films with her—*Belle de Jour*, *Weekend*, *The Magus*, which mystified and intrigued me. Afterward we'd stop for a drink somewhere and discuss the film, Lee providing an older and more worldly perspective. Actually, she would try to answer my inevitable question: "What the hell was that about?"

One Thursday she said she'd heard from Nou Nou, who was urging her to join Joe for the summer visit in France. "She told me to persuade you too." When I insisted that the kids needed me, she laughed. "They'll find someone to take your place. There's always someone."

The next time I saw Lee, she'd heard from her friend Lowell, who was living in Oxford, and she dangled the lure, "We can visit England and stay with Lowell and her husband. Her uncle is Robert Lowell, the poet." Lee added that she had also heard from Angie Novello in Copenhagen, who had room for all of us at her place. Obviously, Lee had made up her mind. She and Joe were going; the trip was beginning to solidify. It was going to happen, with or without me.

Isn't this how we make decisions? Incrementally. An idea presents itself, and the imagination gets triggered. I wrangled with my thoughts in letters home. "Perhaps it's the time of year because every spring since 1959 I've longed intensely for an adventure and a challenge. When will I ever be happy and content? What can I do next? Where can I go?" I wrote Ann, knowing full well the answer but not quite ready to commit. I still didn't have a job secured for the next school year. "I have an itch to move, to change, to travel, to do anything but what I'm doing. I love my children. I enjoy my work and my colleagues despite the boring routine. I'm just not affecting enough people. I need to influence more. I want to teach again."

A few days after that letter to Ann, the Beaverton School District offered me a position in the English department and Dale Harvey called me in McLean. "I've taken a job at Flathead Valley Community College in Montana," he said. When I'd visited the school in January, he had already applied for the job and was advocating for me to replace him. "I told the principal you were the only one I'd recommend to take over Advanced American Literature. Are you up for it?"

"Yes! Yes!" I couldn't believe my luck. The news lifted me out of Hickory Hill and shot me into the future.

Chapter 22

COUNTDOWN

SOMETIMES IN OREGON A FEW DAYS IN FEBRUARY OR MARCH WILL remind you that spring is coming. Robins return in flocks, spreading over lawns and fields to pull worms from the water-soaked earth. Flickers drum on chimney flashing seeking mates. But the rain always returns. Not so in Northern Virginia. After our Waterville trip, spring arrived and stayed with longer, warmer days. The nets went up on the tennis courts, and Mrs. Kennedy began competitive play with Mrs. McNamara and her women friends on weekdays and mixed doubles on the weekends. The thwack-ponk-thwack of tennis balls drifted over the lawn from the courts, punctuated now and then by shouts and howls, players lamenting bad shots, arguing calls.

Our after-school family touch football games resumed, but for a while the boys took greater interest in rocketry. The NASA Apollo program had been in full gear throughout the fall and winter of 1968, sending up rockets in October and December. Two more spacecrafts were launched in March and May in preparation for the attempted moon landing scheduled for July 1969. We watched the launches on television, and Max and I had been twice to see Colonel Glenn's space capsule at the Smithsonian.

Rocket boys, Michael, John Yaxley, and David, prepare the *Apollo* for blastoff.

His favorite Christmas present remained his blue space-program jumpsuit and hard hat.

In early April, David and Michael spent afternoons assembling model rockets, launching them on weekends. I wasn't involved in the construction—I think John Yaxley helped them out in the shed—but for several Saturdays we drove to an open field by the Potomac School where they set up a mini-NASA site: Cape Potomac. The first rockets were twelve or fourteen inches long and would fire up to a thousand feet before breaking apart when a parachute would open and float the nose cone back to ground (or into a tree). These launches required a spotter and lots of legwork for retrieval of the nose cones. Fortunately, David, who was training for the track team, chased them down, the rest of us trailing behind.

The last launch that I remember that early spring, a massive two-and-a-half-foot replica of the Apollo Saturn rocket with

Max and Courtney patiently await the rocket launch.

multiple stages, drew a bigger audience. Courtney, Kerry, Max, and Christopher jammed into the station wagon with John Yaxley, Lem Billings—who was visiting for the weekend—and me while David and Michael rode in the far back, protecting the rocket. We parked on the far side of the soccer field, the kids spilling out to race across the grass. The rocket boys disembarked cautiously, David carrying the battery-packed launcher, Michael cradling the rocket, attached to each other by a couple of feet of tangled wires. They set up the launch pad at the center of the field, tinkered with the wire attachments, and set the rocket on its pad. Michael narrated for us how they'd assembled it, how every stage would separate, where it might land.

There may have been more than one countdown and failed ignition. Here, memory dissolves into mists the way it did from the Montreal World's Fair. In a photo, the boys lie stretched on the grass while John Yaxley rewraps wires around the battery posts. In another, Lem Billings, wearing his gray suit, kneels beside them, all four men and boys fiddling and diddling with the wires and pad and rocket. Meanwhile, the rest of us milled on the sidelines, waiting restlessly as audiences do, wanting them to speed up the action, unconcerned whether it would result in success or catastrophe.

The rocketry fad ended after the Potomac Apollo Saturn launch. Nothing could top that feeling of blasting off the biggest missile. Or perhaps John Yaxley's work schedule changed with the warming weather. Spring opened up all around us so that no one wanted to be cooped up in the shed assembling rockets any more than I wanted to be up in the attic sorting clothes or driving off to Georgetown to pick up Easter presents. We all wanted to be outdoors playing in the warming spring air. On the weekends, Chris and Max followed behind the tractor-drawn mower while John Yaxley groomed the grounds, Brumus and Panda lumbering along behind. Freckles chased after Michael while he swung back and forth from the tree fort rope before jumping and rolling down the hillside. Music drifted up from the pool house jukebox, drowned out now and then by shouts of "Marco! Polo!" from the girls and their school friends playing in the newly cleaned and heated pool. David pounded tennis balls over the net with his instructor or played doubles with friends.

THE WEEK MRS. KENNEDY LEFT to yacht in the Caribbean with Jackie and Aristotle Onassis, the household relaxed the way a school does when the principal's gone for a conference. While she was away, the Sirhan Sirhan trial ended with a guilty verdict. To have it over was to finally put away the long, bleak winter.

It was also the week when my mother and her best college friend, Georgie, came east to sightsee in Washington, DC; Virginia; and New York. Really, they were coming to visit Hickory Hill. I felt embarrassed that I had a mother who'd fly from Oregon to see where her daughter worked, but more so because I knew that she and Georgie could hardly wait to peek inside the Kennedy world and that no doubt Sally and Joe and Mrs. Kennedy all knew that too. Of course, Mrs. Kennedy gave permission for them to drop by when I asked her. She even acknowledged that she'd kept me so busy, I'd probably not had time to write all year, forgetting that I'd gone home in January. But it was a nice gesture. That she wouldn't be there when they visited eased my discomfort.

Mom and Georgie rented a car at the airport and followed my directions out to Hickory Hill, where they arrived all dressed up in almost-matching chartreuse double-knit suits, circle pins, and pearl clip-on earrings. Wearing cat's-eye glasses and subdued smiles, they posed before the big red Kennedy front door, each with a white sweater draped over one arm and a wildly printed handbag over the other, looking the epitome of well-dressed tourists. I snapped the photo using my mom's camera. In another picture, she's holding Douglas, and then one of Georgie with Max on her lap. In a final photo, the four of them seem to be marching down the hill together to the pool house. The older kids, when they came home from school, first the boys from Potomac and then the girls, came up to stand beside me and greet the older women. They shook hands formally and shyly, as if they were on the campaign trail, then looked at me to be excused, and I shooed them up to their rooms to change.

Late in the afternoon, I drove with Mom and Georgie out to Middleburg for the night and then on across the Blue Ridge

Mountains and down to Jamestown. Sally had given me three days off to travel with them before they continued on sightseeing in Washington, DC, and New York, pleased with their special time in McLean.

I must have brought up the potential Europe trip on the drive, practicing my arguments for leaving the job in June. My mother would've listened and clucked a bit of disapproval, but Georgie might have commented on how much time I'd already given the family and what a chance I'd be missing if I didn't join the secretary and the butler. Georgie had always been an influencer, so if she supported the idea, my mom would too. I worked to tip the balance in favor of the decision I wanted to make.

Back at the house a letter had arrived from someone I'd met in Hyannis the previous summer. Throughout the year I'd been in sporadic contact with a few of the household workers from there: the Irish cook at the John Kennedys', Tim-the-Tennis-Teacher, and a nanny who'd worked for Fitzgerald cousins who were related to Grandma Rose Kennedy. She had spent a few August evenings up in the haunted house with me sharing stories over beer. Now an upperclassman at the University of North Carolina, she was looking for a summer job on the cape. Did I know of any families who needed a nanny?

Her letter was the gift I'd been waiting for: someone to replace me—someone not unknown who'd be acceptable to the gatekeepers, clued in to the summer routines, the family dynamics, and the sometimes-difficult personalities. By the time Mrs. Kennedy returned, I'd made up my mind to travel with Lee and Joe. Whether I talked to Sally or informed Dave Hackett or Lem Billings, I'm not sure. Nor do I remember breaking the news to Mrs. Kennedy. But I can imagine myself racing to the kitchen waving the letter and shouting to Joe, "I'm going to Europe. I've got a replacement!" Or maybe I ripped the letter open in the office and whooped the news to Sally before picking up the phone and dialing Lee's number.

I'd snagged some more luck. Stanford professor Tina Seelig says that luck is constantly blowing around us, but we need to set out a sail to catch its wind. That spring I felt like once again I was raising my sails, trying to find a breeze to lift me out and away, not because I was unhappy or dissatisfied so much as I was ready to launch into a new adventure.

COURTNEY SAT ON HER BED, her wet hair wrapped in a towel, math homework spread out beside her. "When are you leaving?" she asked without looking up.

We hadn't bought plane tickets yet, but we'd promised Mrs. Kennedy, Sally, Dave Hackett, everyone that we'd stay past June 6. The house would be overflowing with people that weekend, and the whole staff and more would be needed. "After your dad's memorial," I answered.

She sounded dejected and hurt. I was choosing to leave, not like other governesses forced out by the kids or fired or blasted away by Mrs. Kennedy. We'd become friends over the year. Until that night I hadn't imagined that my departure might be taken as an affront or a betrayal, a loss. Now I wondered if maybe she felt personally rejected, as if I were deserting her.

The luck my sail had caught might have felt like misfortune to a twelve-year-old who'd found a friend in someone ten years older, a big sister almost always available to talk or help with schoolwork or setbacks or questions. We'd shared talks and stories about friendships, menstruation, college, diets, freckles, fashion, and music.

I scrambled to make her feel better, reminding her how much fun she'd be having with Sydney and Maria back at the cape. I'd be the one left behind then, I told her. Besides, who else would provide her with reports on Nou Nou's new house or Joe's grandfather's castle in Italy? When you know a few details of someone's future plans, you can share imaginatively. My parents always mapped out trips before long drives, telling stories about what we'd see and where we'd stop to eat ice cream or to wade in a roadside creek on our long drives to California or up into Canada. So with Courtney, I showed her our trip plans, shared a bit of the unknown future.

"I know what you'll be doing up on the cape this summer, but here's what we're going to do. We'll fly to Iceland and then on to Belgium and rent a car," I said. Her social studies book had maps, and we traced the tentative route that Lee, Joe, and I were planning. When she asked questions, I knew she'd gone past moping to curiosity. "We'll stay with your dad's secretary, Angie," I went on. "What's she like?" I hope I asked, because acknowledging that kids have something to teach, honestly asking them for information, confers power. Courtney would have had Angie Novello stories, as would David and the rest of the kids. Seeing Nou Nou in France and reporting on her new life made our departure less a betrayal and more a supplement. We were taking a field trip and sending home dispatches, or so I wanted to imagine.

If David cared whether I stayed or left, he didn't say anything. *Easy come, easy go*, he may have thought, but for a while his teases came more often, his football hits felt a bit rougher. We still maintained a wink and nod about dinnertime hand washing and bedtime snacks. When a copy of *The Raja's Ramrod* appeared under his bed among a pile of clothes I was gathering for Geneva in the laundry, I took it down to show Joe, who laughed. "Don't let Mrs. Kennedy see that." Later that night, using suggestion as I had the year before with the boy whose hair had grown to his collar, I returned the book. "You might want to keep this someplace where your mother or sisters won't 'borrow' it," I said.

Courtney and David felt closest to me because they were closer in age or more matched to my personality. I'd miss them most. Michael had always been more independent, more self-sufficient—no need to worry about him. And the younger ones, even Kerry, found Ena for comfort, me for play. I was sure that the new governess would be a good playmate for them.

How Mrs. Kennedy might have felt did not enter my mind. She was losing two key staff members, people she knew, had broken in, people she could count on through emergencies and outbursts, people she could trust. Why didn't I wonder what she felt? The woman who'd come to my assistance when I was sick so many months before seemed distant and unfamiliar now. Did she too feel abandoned? Did she even care? Since she'd had her baby and returned to her social life, her attention and her feelings shifted quickly, like a nervous bird flitting from branch to stem to ground to air. I couldn't help but think that our departure was simply a vexation for her.

One last day off, I drove into DC to visit Congresswoman Edith Green and to say goodbye and thank her once again for helping me get this opportunity. She wasn't in, but the aide asked me to leave a message. In a tape home, I described our interaction: "Whatever I said to her, she looked up and said, 'You're famous around here. What do you do?' When I told her that I worked for the Kennedys, she shrugged. 'No, that's not it. I'm not sure why, but I've heard your name from the congresswoman.'"

I wonder now if it could have been related to my swimming and my decision not to go on competing past high school because colleges had no athletic opportunities for women. In 1969 Congresswoman Green was working on legislation that would later change girls' and women's high school and college experiences, creating a future for women in sports. Title IX, designed with Senator Birch Bayh and Congresswoman Patsy Mink, passed into law three years later in 1972. I'd like to believe that the inequity of my sports experience provided a ripple that, as Robert Kennedy had written, combined with others, built into a current that eventually swept away one form of gender inequality.

As soon as Mrs. Kennedy returned from the Caribbean, her social calendar filled, not only with lunches and tennis games but also with preparations for a formal dinner, the Kennedys' Annual Pet Show, a memorial Mass at Arlington, and the dedication of Robert F. Kennedy Memorial Stadium in Washington, DC. Her best women friends came daily to meet, their heads together planning. Midmorning, Ena would bring Rory out to a shady spot by the pool and put her down for a morning nap in the playpen. I'd follow Douglas here and there on the lawn while the women sat poolside discussing the guest lists.

For days they shuffled dinner invitees from table to table, anticipating who would be the conversation leader, who needed a controller, sharing information on who was seeing someone or who wasn't talking to someone else. Just when they'd have the tables set, a new RSVP would arrive and they'd have to rearrange again. As the big night approached, an emergency arose when a journalist from New York called to tell Mrs. Kennedy that Gloria

Steinem was coming as his date. What a kerfuffle ensued! Where should they seat her? How far ought she be kept from Cardinal Terence Cooke, the Archbishop of New York?

"What's the big deal?" I'm sure I asked. Sally explained that Steinem was for abortion and that Mrs. Kennedy would prefer to keep her out of the house, but now they had to keep her away from the archbishop—they needed to corral her.

"Someone will be assigned," Sally said.

It reminded me of sorority rush then, when we met prospective members. I remembered being assigned to talk to a particular girl for a while and then another pair of house members would take over. Everything was decided and choreographed before the rushees arrived. I had no idea then that we were being trained for galas and parties, lobbying and fundraising, politicking, any of those jobs that necessitated social arranging—meeting and moving people around.

Now I can appreciate what savvy "social workers" Mrs. Kennedy and her friends were. What an asset she must have been to her husband in those years when Hickory Hill had been an informal meeting place for cabinet members and politicians, journalists, intellectuals, and entertainers during President Kennedy's time in office, when Bobby was attorney general and again when he was New York's senator. She knew everyone, and those attentive eyes that could put me on edge were advantageous to her in a party crowd. I remember her telling one of the kids at the dinner table a trick she'd learned about party protocol from the Ambassador. "Have one drink," he'd told her, "and then keep your glass full with water...but don't let anyone know what you're really drinking. You'll hear all kinds of things at a party that you'll want to remember for later." What she was saying was basically that people who drink talk too much, and people who don't gather useful intelligence.

Before the big dinner party, the caterers arrived in the morning to set up: removing the long dining table and replacing it with round tabletops seating ten each. They did the same in the drawing room, where there must have been ten tables for ten. Late in the day, everything seemed ready with linens, silver, china, and crystal. Who knew what was going on in the kitchen all day? My job was to keep the kids busy outside and down at the pool house. We were having pizza and popcorn and an early movie.

Just before the guests arrived, Joe called down to me, "Get up here fast. Mrs. Kennedy is blowing a gasket."

What now? I wondered and raced up the hill to help Joe.

Two days later, on one of my last Sunday–Mondays off before the Europe trip, I flew to New York to visit Bob and Helen Burke and say goodbye, and that's when I first told the story of the blown gasket. I'm sure it started when they asked what the year had been like for me. Like most intense and unique experiences, this one was impossible to convey to someone who'd never been there. I tried to describe getting called up from the pool house on that Saturday night five minutes before a huge formal dinner party was to begin and being given a list of about twenty things that *had to be done* before anyone arrived. Three workers had failed to do their jobs, and Mrs. Kennedy was having a conniption. Even though I didn't know half of what she was talking about, I raced around resetting the tables and bringing in chairs and filling water glasses, all in about four and half minutes, then disappeared back down the hill to rejoin the kids at the movies. A typical ludicrous Kennedy evening, I told them, laughing.

The big Kennedy parties, both before and after, seemed to

be laced with drama. Perhaps I told the Burkes that the day after the party, when the sofas and armchairs, the desks and end tables were returned to their places, Katherine swept through to check for what had gone missing. "They steal the little things like cigarette cups and ashtrays," she said shaking her head with a tsk. "They used to take more," she added. But that was before they started preparty storage of photos and valuables. I thought about all the phone extensions that had been removed in the winter. It would be so tempting, so easy for a guest to wander upstairs in search of a bathroom and to disappear for a few moments into an empty bedroom—to look around or dial up a friend in New York or Los Angeles. "Guess where I am?" the snoop might begin. It wasn't hard to imagine.

Unlike my early days off, when I'd slept for hours on end, this time Bob and Helen and I talked well into the night. They had a million stories about their granddaughter, and I had a million more about my kids. Helen had nicknamed each one based on my tales. "How's Sarah Bernhardt?" she asked about Courtney. "And Mr. President?" referring to Christopher. David was "The Stud" and Kerry "The Brat," her old nickname for me. After I'd told her about Michael's impersonations, she called him "Ed Sullivan." Max was always "Max the Ax."

Days raced by in those last weeks, but the weeks felt more like years. It was the same trick the clocks had played at the end of the school year, when minutes either dragged or sped. This fairy tale of a year, one of stories within stories, was winding down. All that I'd worked to learn and to understand and all those I'd come to love would be left behind. The anticipatory excitement of travel protected me from experiencing the bittersweet taste of letting go and saying goodbye.

Chapter 23

THREE, TWO, ONE

ONCE THE DECISION WAS MADE, MY THOUGHTS DURING DOWNTIME ran in two streams, both toward the future. Luckily, Lee was working at the house again as a fill-in for one week, maybe more. Together she, Joe, and I talked about the trip and planned our ever-changing route. We'd fly to Luxemburg and then drive to...Germany first, then down to Italy? Or would we drive north to Denmark to visit Angie first and then to Paris on our way to Italy?

We pored over maps and checked the airlines for prices. Or Lee did during her days in the office. Joe and I found time to complete personal tasks: passport photos and international driver's licenses, inoculations for tetanus and typhoid. Lee and I would share a travel kit for cosmetics, first aid, rolls of film, and two cartons of cigarettes, but I needed to whittle down my wardrobe to fit in one suitcase. We bought a tent that Joe said he'd carry for overnights in between our free lodging. I'd also need to empty my room, pack my things, and ready them for shipping the same weekend as the memorial Mass and the stadium dedication, a time when all the kids would be home and hundreds of guests coming and going.

But times of extreme multitasking had become normal. In many ways, the entire Kennedy governess experience had been a kind of postgraduate training for teaching: multiple responsibilities, varied and volatile personalities, high expectations and immediate consequences, scheduled and arbitrary deadlines, unpredictable emergencies, collegiality, temper control, heightened perception, mind reading, social manipulation, and crowd control. Intelligence, self-confidence, and performance skills helped also.

When I wasn't performing my household duties or planning the Europe trip, I was thinking about teaching. In late April I drove for the last time out to Middleburg and the cottage that had been my refuge, where I'd been able to relax and read, walk the paths, listen to records, and write my friends back home. The oaks and maples shimmered in their bright new leaves. The green field behind the house lay polka-dotted with dandelions and English daisies. I brought along my tape recorder, and instead of dictating something to send home, I recorded myself reading poetry: Gerard Manley Hopkins's "Pied Beauty" and "Inversnaid" with its final line, "Long live the weeds and the wilderness yet," and "Spring": "What is all this juice and all this joy?" My voice deepened and slurred a bit in a final recording of E. A. Robinson's "Mr. Flood's Party." I must have been thinking ahead to the fall and my return to teaching. Maybe I was rehearsing for a class I didn't yet know. Later, with Simon & Garfunkel's "Homeward Bound" spinning on the turntable and my head buzzy with beer, I sat down to write a final letter to Ann. We'd been corresponding about teaching for months, and this night I became evangelical, writing a declaration of my beliefs and an appeal to her to keep teaching:

The teaching of literature must expand the students' world, their sensitivity, their comprehension, their compassion. I believe Faulkner's idea that writers must not just leave a record

*of man, he has the responsibility to help man prevail by em-
phasizing the virtues that have enabled us to endure thus
far: pity, pride, compassion, honor, love. Our responsibility
as teachers is to find and present literature that illuminates
these virtues so that our students can recognize and use them
in their own lives.*

*I want to help students step out of their narrow worlds...to
step into rural Mississippi, war-torn Spain, an upper-class prep
school, slave quarters. Once they can remove themselves from
their own environments, they can then see the universality of the
human spirit. No matter the philosophy of the author, the class,
race, age, sex, or religion of the character, we all share humanity.
Through literature, students can experience others' thoughts and
feelings, others' times and places. Our students' feet may remain
in Beaverton, Oregon, but their minds are allowed to travel.*

*As teachers we have a responsibility not to train our
students into vocations but to open for them doors of understanding. We must teach empathy and compassion and
encourage active commitment. Because we have responsibility
for over one hundred people every year, we cannot waste time
with iambs and sentence diagrams, but we must ready them for
life in our world. We must make them conscious, caring, feeling.*

*Teaching is the most important profession in America
today. It is our duty, Ann, to reach out and try to make a difference. We have youth on our side. We have hope, conviction,
and love. Teaching literature is a job of duty and love: love
of youth, ideas, America, humanity. We owe our work to the
future. I feel evangelical about our profession.*

*Of course, on a personal level my personality comes into
my teaching, my need for recognition. I want the gratification*

that I have left some print on my students' lives—not just that the subject matter hit them, but that I, too, did. That's wrong, isn't it?

But when I look ahead, how do I know where my 130 students of last year will end up? Where they will travel, what they will do. Hopefully they will carry with them something of me, my thoughts, my questions, my insights, my teaching. If all that they carry is some ability to comprehend or to understand themselves and others, then I have been a success, just as some teacher in my past has been a success with me—whether my parents, friends, clergy, coach. All that I am is from the teachers of my life.

Perhaps it is through teaching that I feel a small part of immortality. For good or bad as I may be as a teacher, I have been a part of many lives, and those lives cannot deny that I was there. Most important as a teacher, I must give understanding, for if this comes across to but one in one hundred, I will have made the world a better place.

As teachers we must try to transcend our personal priorities, whether money, security, marriage, in order to establish professional ones. Right now, my top professional goal is to teach self and human understanding through literature. We owe our work to the future.

And that is my present view of teaching. Don't give up, Ann.

P.S. Save this for me when I get depressed next year, ok?

I'd only had one year's experience, yet I sounded like a fanatic. John Kennedy's inaugural words that had echoed through the locker room and hallways of my high school sophomore year still motivated me. I wanted desperately to do something worthwhile, for my country, for my students. His brother Robert's vision and words had stirred me again seven years later. One person seemed so powerless, but his metaphor of the pebble in the pond making a ripple, the many pebbles forming a wave to sweep in change helped form the belief that my role in the classroom to help students understand themselves and others would ripple outward, would help change the world. Idealistic? Grandiose? Maybe. Motivating and meaningful? Yes.

My year at the Kennedys' had not provided much time for introspection or thought. It had been a year of action and reaction and, at times, of mind-numbing routine. But the experience helped me define my own values and determine how I wanted to spend my life. Being raised to value work and not to want or expect more than what I could earn seemed a gift. Although like the Kennedys, I'd grown up valuing athleticism and action, I'd also been taught the importance of discipline and consistent practice, traits essential in sport, academics, and life. By the end of the year, my vocation was clear. In September, I'd be back in the classroom where I belonged, my intellectual curiosity stimulated by being a student among students even when I was the teacher.

BACK IN THE FALL WHEN the kids had been home for Thanksgiving, Kathleen had asked her siblings to write a remembrance of their father. Her concussion put a damper on that project, but now as the anniversary of his death approached, she returned to the idea. She wanted to collect the writings into a booklet.

Courtney wrote hers the weekend I was in Middleburg, but Kerry, Michael, and David needed prodding when I returned.

It's the only time I remember us talking about their father. Just as if we were in class preparing for a personal essay, I offered some prompts: List the things you liked to do with Daddy. Tell some things you miss. Remember one time you and he did something special, and tell the story. Suddenly stories emerged. Kerry talked about going swimming with him when they all made a huge pyramid in the pool. And then she remembered finding Rocky on a summer river raft trip. She and Michael began recalling other episodes from the trip, but Kerry came back to Rocky.

"Daddy brought me a big box that had a hat in it with fake flowers all over it, and Rocky popped out from under the hat. And that's how we got Rocky."

Michael talked more about how his father loved sports and had so many different friends, "some Black, some white, and a lot who were professional athletes."

"Remember when Mummy and Daddy came home from a long trip and lots of people went to the airport to help us give them a warm welcome and we made a huge sign saying 'Welcome Home, Bobby and Ethel'?" Kerry asked.

Michael had some similar stories, but when he wrote, he focused on what his father had tried to do. "In the last part of his life, Daddy did everything he could for this country."

David may have sat with us while we talked, but his essay—unlike Kerry's that focused on specific events or Michael's that stayed more distant—zeroed in on the kind of man his father had been. He loved his family, "all of us, and wanted us to love each other." He went on to explain that even when someone got in trouble and his father scolded them, it was done in a way that they knew was for their own good and that he still loved them.

Every one of the kids wrote or talked about playing football with their father. Michael said that when he was home, they played touch football all the time. Kerry said that if you got to be on his team, you usually won. And David explained what I noticed when we first played at Hickory Hill, his inclusion of his little brothers. He wrote, "Daddy made sure that if we were playing a game like touch football, everyone would be playing no matter how good or bad they were or how old or young they were or how many people there were. He made sure everyone got into the plays." His conclusion summed up what every child felt, "Daddy really loved us all, and we loved him, and we all miss him and wish he were still here."

After a death, memories and stories enhance a person's best qualities. But the honest reflections of Robert Kennedy's kids—his vibrancy and generosity—made him come alive to me. It was easy to imagine his delight when Rocky dislodged the flowered hat and Kerry screamed with joy. Easy to hear David's subtext that even when he got into trouble, his dad showed him love. He taught inclusion by example in touch football games, the old and young, the good and bad, Black, brown, and white, as he would have tried to do in the country had he lived. I wished I'd had the chance to know him.

Throughout the year, Mrs. Kennedy had tried to keep family traditions alive even from her bed those last months of pregnancy. Sunday Mass, of course. Some Sundays she gathered the kids in her room for a family rosary, the way the senator had done. David told me that at Sunday dinner when his father was home, he assigned them famous people to read about and then to report on. A few Sundays we tried, but mostly we played guess who or talked loosely about history or the news. Once Rory was born,

Mrs. Kennedy never missed a Sunday dinner, and perhaps now and then someone presented "research" on an historical figure. But it would never be the same as when Daddy was there.

Another tradition to be kept occurred in May—the 11th Annual Pet Show to benefit the Northwest Settlement House of Washington, DC. Mrs. Kennedy's friend, Kay Evans, served as organizer, and Art Buchwald would be the ringmaster.

David and Michael spent afternoons building an obstacle course out in the pasture to replace the pony rides of previous years. They strung ropes and dug out mud holes, placed cones, and built rickety hurdles. John Yaxley brought in a batch of tires to leapfrog through and created some sort of rope rigging to climb. Courtney and friends planned a puppet show. Kerry and her Lawford cousin Vicky were in charge of a box of baby chicks.

Anyone could enter the contests ($2.50 per person, $0.50 per pet), which once again opened up Hickory Hill—like the Halloween penny grab—to those in the know. Participants began lining up before ten thirty Saturday morning. The grounds became a wild scene with kids and dogs, fish bowls and birdcages, cats and costumes. Wandering clowns teased through the crowds, and muddy boys ran back and forth from the obstacle course. A fortune-teller read the future, which—in keeping with the flyer—included a gourmet picnic followed by a raffle. Max, dressed identically to Art Buchwald in a red blazer and black-rimmed sunglasses, black top hat, and bow tie, followed him everywhere wagging a bubble gum cigar. Buchwald announced the categories of competition through a megaphone, and ladies from the pet show committee judged: longest-tailed cat or shortest-nosed dog, most colorful bird, smallest fish, most attractively dressed pet. There were enough categories for every child to win something.

Art Buchwald as ringmaster for the Eleventh Annual Pet Show, a benefit for the Northwest Settlement House in DC, with Max, his doppelgänger.

Lee Geisen brought the girl from the family where she lived and maybe her own rabbit that she'd rescued from the farmer's market and kept as a pet. We may have sat apart from the crowds for a while to talk about the trip, which was now only two weeks away. Maybe Joe came out from the kitchen to join us. I can't be sure if this provoked Mrs. Kennedy, but something that week drew me to her attention.

First, she got after Kerry for not combing her hair before dinner. When I defended her and said she had combed it, Mrs. K crabbed, "Well, not good enough," and then she got after me for not controlling the kids.

"What has happened to you?" she challenged.

I could have answered like a defiant kid, "Nothing. Nothing's happened to me." Or I could have said, "I just don't care anymore." Or maybe, "I do the best I can, and today it wasn't good enough for you." But I don't think I answered at all.

My attitude throughout the year had shifted from curious and awestruck to competent, from willing and able to defensive and resentful. I didn't like taking the blame for David's nails or Kerry's hair when 99 percent of the time, everything under my control ran smoothly but seemingly unnoticed, and 1 percent of the time when it didn't, I heard about it. But it was more than that.

The year that I taught, I'd felt my students slipping into summer before the school year ended, their thoughts on sleeping late or earning money or working on their tans, while I tried to lead discussions on books they hadn't read. Some of them resented my criticism of their inattention or lackadaisical attitude. Now I was acting like those students, already on vacation driving across Germany with my friends instead of checking the kids before dinner. Mrs. Kennedy sensed my absence.

She called me up to her room, all crabapple pink and green, the morning sunshine filtering in through the new-leafed branches of the big tree outside her patio, the Red Book open on her desk. She let me stand for a while before she said anything. "I don't know if you know this, but Bobby fought hard to get warnings put on cigarette packages. I don't want you to smoke in front of the children."

Everything tightened up inside me. I'd been caught, reprimanded. And it was true. I did smoke in front of the kids, down in the basement or up in my room—places where she'd never see me because obviously I was breaking an unstated protocol. When the weather had changed for the better, I'd even lit up outdoors sometimes. Had Lee and I smoked that day of the pet show? She must have seen us. Defensively I thought, *You shouldn't have them lying out all over the drawing room,* but really I felt ashamed.

Growing up I'd hated my father's smoking, hated the smell that hung over the pool from the parents smoking on the balcony or the coach back in his office. Yet here I was a smoker, smoking her free cigarettes, clouding up rooms, and dirtying the spring air. I was an Olympic athlete setting a terrible example for children, but I wasn't ready to quit yet. I'd have to be more discreet about when and where to smoke.

"It's not good for you, Caroline," she said as I was leaving her room. *Does she actually care about me?* I wondered, feeling guilty suddenly for bailing out on her.

I could justify my departure in so many ways, but really it was because I'd had enough of being a servant, enough of having someone else dictate my daily routine. Teaching felt different. Of course, the school hours and teaching schedule dictated our lives, but within those parameters, I had felt autonomous. I chose the pace and content of each day. Here it felt like being harnessed to someone else's wagon, thanklessly pulling a load they should be pulling themselves.

Mrs. Kennedy never held a grudge or seemed to remember her reprimands. Later that afternoon or another day, she proposed that I meet the family in Sun Valley at Christmas. "Wouldn't that be fun?" she said. I drifted toward the bait. *Yes, it would be fun...some of the time.* Great to see the kids and hear what had happened in their lives over the summer and fall, great to play follow the leader down the wide Sun Valley runs.

Someone had told me way back in the summer that Mrs. Kennedy could chew your butt one minute and twenty minutes later fling her arm around your shoulder all chummy and ask for a favor. "If you take it to heart, you'll have a nervous break-down," Lee had warned back then. The Sun Valley invitation wasn't a personal offer, I thought, but an ask for a favor. She needed a cook, a maid, and a governess that week, and she knew I could do it all.

THE FINAL WEEKS AT HICKORY Hill sped by like the bus between New York and Hyannis in the spring of 1967. Few specific memories remain. David ran in his last track meets, and Michael prepared for field day at Potomac School. Stone Ridge undoubtedly presented a musical or spring fête that I attended. In June, the older children returned one by one from their boarding schools in Vermont, Massachusetts, New York.

Before the memorial Mass for the senator at Arlington, all the Kennedy families arrived from New York for the weekend—the Lawfords, the Smiths, Jackie and her kids. The next day would be the Robert Kennedy stadium dedication, another extravaganza with students and athletes, music and speeches. I don't remember any of it until Saturday afternoon, when half a dozen kids splashed around in the pool and David and Stevie Smith lurked along the gutter, playing sharks with the little ones. In the pool house, Courtney sat wrapped in a towel, her legs pulled up to fit under it.

"Will you come to Sun Valley?" she asked.

She must have talked with her mother, I thought. "I hope so," I may have answered, because when she asked it sounded different, as if she really wanted me to be there, a friend who'd ski with her and listen and share stories on rides up the chairlift. "Yes, I hope so."

One last memory remains from Hickory Hill. I'm hurrying down the driveway clogged with cars, through late-afternoon shadows cast from the trees. I've been sent off by Joe or someone on an "emergency" errand, no doubt. Walking up the drive toward me are Sander Vanocur, the NBC White House correspondent, and Shirley MacLaine, the actress, arriving late to a reception going on at the house. *Hmmm,* runs through my mind before I greet them, "Hello. Everyone's out back," and hurry on. I'd met enough celebrities, seen more than enough of the rich and powerful. Just a few more errands to complete before life's next experiment.

Chapter 24

THREE FOR THE ROAD

We staggered off the Icelandic airplane in Luxembourg after many hours cramped in the plane and gathered our mountains of luggage, including sleeping bags, air mattresses, and tent in addition to clothes enough for almost three months in Europe, camera equipment, rolls of film, cartons of cigarettes, and stacks of books including Temple Fielding's *Travel Guide to Europe*, the extra economy version. At Avis we rented a European model Ford Taunus 12M, a small stick shift unavailable in the States, and jammed all our gear in the trunk and headed out to find lodging.

The next day our first of many snafus began. When we hit the German border, a customs officer demanded a "green card" proof of insurance. All we could produce was a receipt for having paid for the rental, but that wouldn't do. When we tried to open the car's trunk to rummage through our bags, it would not open. We were locked out!

We fussed and swore, fussed some more, and finally paid for another week of insurance, slept in our clothes that night, and spent hours the next day in Hanover at a Ford dealership where they finally unjammed the lock and sent us on our way. By the time we reached Copenhagen and Angie's apartment, we'd slept

Joe and Lee in our tent at a campground in Germany.

in our clothes, had camped out, and hadn't bathed for almost a week. We had the look of road-weary travelers. Refreshed and with beers in hand, we roared with laughter telling Angie the locked-trunk story.

It was only the first of many fiascos that we met, resolved, and turned into a comedy routine, our nightly entertainment as we told and retold the stories to each other over beer, wine, and dinner. The resolution often necessitated us humbling ourselves. One of the many gifts of rough travel: we learned to ask for help, to communicate with whatever language worked—my rudimentary German, Joe's Italian, Lee's French. In desperation, she could have pulled up Swahili and I a bit of Spanish. Whatever shyness I'd felt in high school language classes trying to repeat silly dialogues vanished. This was for real, and my *"Wo ist ein kamplatz, bitte?"* found us campsites along the Rhine. Recommendations from village gas station attendants introduced us to friendly local guesthouses with home-cooked meals and spotless rooms tended by apple-cheeked hausfraus. When language failed, we all knew charades and fearlessly employed them.

The letters I sent home every few days were meant as a travel diary and read much like the ones I'd keep on later trips: records of places and sights; catalogues of flowering plants and trees; details of meals, linens, window views; exact times of waking and sleeping; reports on the weather; distances covered in a day. Any stories worth telling always involved a mistake or a problem that resolved in an episode of giggles or self-deprecating laughter—the schnapps bottle, a gift from Angie, crashing onto a sidewalk grate; the letters dropped into a bank deposit box a second before the error registered; the horrifically expensive dinner ordered à la carte our first night in Italy; the sprint through Heathrow dragging too many bags in an effort to find one of ten possible departure gates.

The first story I wrote in detail happened in Switzerland on our way south. After a dinner where we drank a bottle of wine apiece before bed, Lee read me the perfect setup for mild hysteria, an excerpt from Temple Fielding's guide on Gstaad: "Jet setters descend on the Palace Gran Hotel for evenings of wining, dining and wife swapping. But leave for owned or rented chalets for their beauty sleep, indoor acrobatics and repairs." We fell asleep chortling.

The next night, in another two-dollar hotel, Lee tried to do yoga on her bed. In one pose she'd stretch, teeter, and then crash nose-first onto her pillow, not once but over and over. The third or fourth time, suffocating with laughter, she stammered out a question, "I wonder how many"—giggle—"people"—giggle—"have done"—ha—"yoga...in this"—snort—"bed?"

"What?" I asked, already hysterical.

"You know…'indoor acrobatics.'" She chortled through her tears. We both dreamt nothing but laughter that night.

Nobody paid the three of us much attention in Germany or Switzerland, two women traveling with a man, all sleeping together in the same tent. But the Italians noticed us, and Joe understood the language and the innuendo. "Where are your mamas?" his aunt asked us when we got to Rome. She could not fathom two girls (she did not believe we were twenty-three and twenty-six) traveling alone without a chaperone, not with her twenty-year old nephew but with a *man*. It was not done.

We were first harassed on the Great Saint Bernard Pass as soon as we crossed the border into Italy. By going over the mountain instead of through the more traveled tunnel, we crossed a border frontier rather than an official customs center. They were pleasant enough to begin with but began to get pushy when Joe reported that we had five cartons of cigarettes. We had to pull over, park, and get out of the car. The officer told us that we could each take in only one hundred cigarettes. When Joe pointed out that the handbook said four hundred, he responded that it was different because we were driving, not flying.

All this time, Joe was speaking with the guard in Italian then quickly translating for us. The guard would look back and forth with a smirk when Lee or I said something in English to Joe. When he rummaged through the bag Lee and I shared and began pulling out our film supply (eleven rolls each), we protested, but Joe told us not to talk. We could hear his frustration and anger, see his face tense and dark.

That night while setting up our camp in an olive grove above the Mediterranean, Joe went through the exchange again. He had offered the guard a carton of cigarettes if he'd give us a receipt and let us through. But the guard told Joe that he didn't have any receipts at that station.

"That's when I said, 'Where's the nearest telephone?' and started walking up the road toward that mountain village above the border." Joe waved his arm up toward the olive trees, as if that's where the village lay. "When he asked where I was going I said, 'I just want to make a call.'

"'About what?' he said.

"'That's my business.'

"'Oh, Mister. Mister?'

"Remember?" Joe asked us as if we'd understood everything that was going on. "I turned around and the guy ordered us back in the car, waved us through, remember? He could have had a free carton, but he played too many cards too fast. You know why he did that? Because I have a southern accent. Northern Italians think they're Germans. They hate Southern Italians. And he hated that I was with two American women."

It hadn't crossed my mind that anyone would notice or care about us, three friends traveling together. We had seen tons of students traveling in twos and threes and crowds all over Germany and Denmark and Switzerland, or I thought I had. By dinnertime we were laughing about the incident, but it set a tone that subtly tainted the trip. Italy didn't seem as tidy or as hospitable after that disagreeable greeting, and even though later Joe's relatives welcomed us into their homes, it was really his homecoming, leaving Lee and me feeling the outsiders. We couldn't help with translations anymore or follow conversations because it was all being filtered through Joe.

The evening light in Northern Italy seemed to linger longer and the air, soft and warm, invited us to stay late outdoors.

We had rooms in a cheap hotel with a café where we sat long after dinner one night drinking grappa, the table crowded with beer bottles and wineglasses. At first, we retold our hilarious travel stories one more time — the border crossing, the locked trunk, Angie's schnapps bottle — before Lee and Joe veered into the past with stories of the senator from the campaign. From outside their circle of memory, I listened to anecdotes of dinner parties with influential guests and late-night confabs with campaign workers, of last-minute packing and rushes to the airport.

I imagined the senator arriving home, the swarm of cars pulling up the drive and spilling aides and advisors, the rush of dogs and kids out of the house to greet him. Maybe he handed off his briefcase or pulled off his jacket, tossing it aside. In a whirlwind of energy, they'd run to the side yard tossing a football among them, relaying it from Michael to Kerry to Daddy to David to Courtney and back to Daddy until quickly set-up teams plowed into each other, ending in a heap of hugging family. It was a romantic vision but not hard to conjure.

"He was always coming home to grab a load of fresh shirts," Joe said, breaking into my fantasy, "and then he was off again."

Later, their recollections turned to the assassination and the days that followed when they'd worked nonstop until the funeral was over. Details of those stories blew away along the cobblestoned street on a boozy midnight breeze. All I remember now is that Lee cried when we got to our room, and in the morning we all had headaches. Stories of the senator were locked away again like our bags in the car's jammed trunk.

ALL THE ROMAN SIGHTSEEING I'D not done during the 1960 Olympics, we crammed into three days while we stayed with Joe's family in Aprilia, a suburb: the Colosseum, the fountains, the palazzos and piazzas, the museums. We saved one afternoon for me to visit the Olympic pool. The taxi let us out in the park outside the venue, and it felt like I was sleepwalking. The acrid smell of car exhaust and dust from the foot-worn paths reminded me of the first time the team had been taken there to try out the pool. My gut sent out flutters. Ahead the stadium rose from the park; inside lay the turquoise pools.

We found a table in the café above the diving area. I scanned the scene, the pool still brilliant but filled now with families and kids, splashing and jumping, running along the decks followed by whistles, like any public pool. It was all far away, the pools below, the Games almost a decade gone. *Here it is*, I thought, *where it all happened*. I could almost feel the water, cold and surprising off a start, the skin contraction that prompts speed, pounding legs, thrashing arms. "Welcome to the site of victory and defeat," I said and we toasted to the XVII Olympiad.

THE MORNING WE LEFT FOR Joe's grandmother's home in Foglianise, a small village southeast of Naples, we packed the car and drove into Rome, parked in St. Peter's Square, and stopped for coffee and a roll before we began our last look at the Vatican museums and the Sistine Chapel.

Walking back to the car hours later, Joe fumbled through his pockets. "Did I give you the keys?" he asked.

"Are you kidding?" we cried out, incredulous.

"Maybe I left them at the café," he muttered.

My return to the 1960 Olympic swimming pool in Rome.

But that had been hours before, and of course no one there had noticed them. Avis was closed for siesta until four thirty. It was two. Someone had our keys with the car's license number on the keychain and all our worldly possessions packed in the trunk. Lee and I sent Joe back to guard the car while we found a nearby café for lunch and beer and intermittent cursing. We'd planned to return to the pool to clean up and cool off before driving on. Now we were stuck on the sidewalk, and it was Joe's fault. When a representative from Avis finally arrived sometime after five and got the doors unlocked, there was nothing he could do about actually driving it. It would need to be towed to a Ford dealer to have a new lock system installed. We'd be in Rome for at least another day, possibly more. I could feel lire being siphoned off and draining away.

The Avis guy ripped out the back seat to get into the trunk, and we transferred all our gear into a minuscule Fiat, wiggled our way through rush hour traffic, and consulted Fielding for a cheap hotel, the Lloyd, twelve dollars for a double with breakfast and a bath. Luxury! The next day, while Joe waited for the car, Lee and I returned to the Olympic pool to swim, sunbathe, and seethe.

We didn't turn the lost-key story into a joke. After four and a half weeks of almost constant togetherness, we needed our distance, and we drove south toward Naples in silence. Joe had promised us a castle in Foglianise, his grandparents' home and vineyard high atop a hill, but that had been a child's memory. Like many of the houses we passed, it was made from gray-white stone, and to be fair, it was big—two stories with arched, stone doorways and two kitchens, one separate and slightly downhill from the house, with a bread oven and wine cellar and a pig's carcass covered with black flies suspended above the oven. Farther along the pathway and guarded by both dogs and a hog sat the outhouse, complete with a bucket of ashes, easy to stumble over in the dark. The house did have electricity, one bulb per room, but no running water, and when the lights went off, the hilltop felt shrouded, the stars veiled by haze.

We sat in the house kitchen for two hours the first night listening but not understanding the lively conversation that swung among Joe and his grandma, uncle, aunt, cousins, and friends until finally around ten they prepared us dinner. Lee and I were given a big room on the second floor with a "balcony" that we could access by crawling through the window. The next day while Joe visited more relatives and neighbors, we escaped to the rooftop patio to lounge on our air mattresses, reading, writing, sunbathing, and napping. It felt like an escape, the way hiding out in my room or down in the basement had felt at the Kennedys' when I didn't want to see or talk to anyone.

I think I was still carrying a grudge and ready to punish Joe but at my own expense. His family and friends were wonderfully warm and friendly and so curious. Children came by the house to look at the Americans. We waved from the rooftop. Neighbors, who worked the fields until ten o'clock, came home and invited us over for wine. We sat and sipped while they looked and smiled, telling Joe over and over that they were so sorry we couldn't talk, couldn't tell them what we wanted to eat or what we wanted to do. Anything we asked, they would make happen if they could, they told him.

"You're the biggest thing that ever hit the village," Joe said while eight children sat staring at Lee and me. "They want to know if you'll join them at two a.m. to cut, pack, and carry the wheat?" I couldn't imagine working fields until ten at night, eating dinner, sleeping a couple of hours, and getting up at two or three in the morning to do it again. It seemed beyond any experience I'd ever had or wanted to have. My face must have conveyed incredulity because Joe explained that it was harvest time and that's what the people did during harvest.

The invitation did not sound like a lost opportunity at that moment, a chance to participate in a family harvest under a full moon on hillside slopes in rural Italy where some workers still swung scythes cutting across the night. Now I might pay a tour company to provide the adventure. How many opportunities a person misses for every chance she takes. That night I was already thinking of climbing the stairs to the bedroom and escaping into my book and then sleep, oblivious of any regrets I might later feel.

Over the years, whenever I recalled the visit to Foglianise, I remembered not the book I was reading then but the moonlit tiptoe past barking dogs and grunting pig to the outhouse; the almost-empty church on Sunday morning where fifteen or twenty women, all except me, wore black and only three took communion; Joe's grandmother, in her blue-print apron and yoked gray blouse, frying morning-gathered eggs and freshly baked bread from the downhill kitchen, its wood smoke drifting up into the blue morning haze.

NOU NOU AND HER HUSBAND met us at the airport in Nice to drive us back to their daughter's house in Biot, a hillside village above Cannes where Lee and I rejoiced in the promise of a hot bath, a private beach, an old friend who spoke English, and our first communiqués from folks back home.

The third letter I opened began:

Dearest Carolyn,

Your father has been in the hospital. He had a terrible hem-orrhage at work and they had to operate. They found colon cancer that has spread to his liver so they couldn't do anything except sew him back up. Give him a good pep talk won't you. He's hoping to get back to work in a week or so but we'll have to see. Anyway, no more lifting. We love your letters so keep them coming.

Love, Mom

The words smashed into my sternum, knocking my breath away. My knees buckled, and before I touched the bed, tears streamed and I shook my head *no no no*, trying to breathe.

"What is it?" Lee asked.

"My father is dying." If I didn't say it to her, it's what I was thinking, what I knew from my mother's letter, the jaunty lines that held the terminal message between them. I don't remember if I called home. It wouldn't have changed anything, and long distance from Europe was so expensive. But we'd run through our travel budget and begun talking about cutting the trip short, so it was a relief to reschedule the return flight. I'd be home soon, I wrote to my parents, uncertain what that would mean or how I could help.

Nou Nou tended to us like her babies, feeding us extraordi-nary meals, driving us to the beach each day, folding us into her family who was vacationing from Paris. The house and grounds were beautiful with the pine forests and yellow-sand beaches, but

I retreated into books, first reading Sartre's *The Age of Reason*, a novel of waiting and paralysis that deepened my own sense of resignation and numbness.

I had no idea what awaited me, how my father was really faring, or how my mother was coping. Although I'd lived for a year with a family whose father had died, it hadn't prepared me for the anticipation of my own father's death. As the shock of his illness sank in, the trip went a bit out of focus, like a View-Master slide stuck between two images, as if I could see the warm blue waters of the Mediterranean but catch a glimpse of my father floating by on an air mattress just beyond the swimmers. Or as if outside a Jersey fish and chips shop I could see my father drive by in his delivery truck. In London's St. Paul's Cathedral, there he was again, disappearing behind a pillar just beyond a sarcophagus. After that letter arrived with his diagnosis, my father traveled with me like a shadow.

Lee and I said goodbye to Joe when we arrived in London; he planned to stay longer with his parents before returning to the States. We toured the city for three days and then traveled on to stay with her Peace Corps friends in a cottage outside Oxford. My letters home are filled with exacting detail of every site we visited, the paintings we saw in the Tate, the plays and films we attended, the tower, the palace, the tea shops. I detailed our riverboat's collision with a yacht on the Thames and the excited swearing that followed. I wanted to share all of London with my parents because I knew they would never travel out of the country now.

"I wish my dad could see the changing of the guard," I said to Lee outside Buckingham Palace, remembering the night he'd taken me to see the Royal Highland Black Watch pipers play in Portland because I'd begged to go.

Early on a July morning, Lee, her friends, and I walked two miles in to the local pub to sit with a crowd of Brits and watch Neil Armstrong step out onto the moon. We watched on a little black-and-white television set up on a shelf above the bar, four Americans among a crowd of Brits, while outside, the moon, still visible in the morning sky, had a man from Earth standing on it and looking back at us. Time and distance somehow shifted. Surely my father was watching back home in Portland, seeing and hearing everything we were in Oxford, and for a moment he seemed close, almost present.

Chapter 25

HOME AGAIN

1969–1970

SCHOOL STARTED IN AUGUST 1970 MUCH AS IT HAD TWO YEARS before when I'd been a first-year teacher, because in fact that's what I was again. On those hot August days that preceded Labor Day weekend, nothing seemed new or intimidating. The student handbook remained the same: fifty-five-minute classes, thirty-minute lunches, pep assemblies for home football games. We got a special warning about drugs, to be alert for drowsy kids or that "funny smell" on their clothes, to report frequent tardiness or too many missed classes. Attending a war protest would not be an excused absence.

Unlike my first year, I had my own classroom, an interior one on the first floor not far from the auditorium and a lobby with doors to the outside. Light filtered in from a wall of windows facing an enclosed courtyard between my room and the art wing, which pulsed with music all day long. With the windows and hall door open, a cross breeze could cool the room and distracted students could nod to the music or watch classmates splattering paint or throwing clay. Green chalkboards on the east and west walls were soon dusty with scrawled assignments, random vocabulary words, student graffiti. On the north wall corkboard

I hung huge Sierra Club posters, one with a passage from Henry David Thoreau, "In Wildness Is the Preservation of the World" and another from Robinson Jeffers, "Not Man Apart."

My plans for the three American literature classes were easy because I'd taught them before. Linda and I had already divvied up the books for the first weeks of school, but the advanced class required more attention. For several days I read and reread Dale's lesson plans from the previous year—imagining the assignments, pace, discussions—reread the stories he'd taught first, and tried to think ahead nine weeks for what we might accomplish. Over the long Labor Day weekend, I decided that a good place to start would be with Hemingway's *In Our Time* story collection, its title taken from the Anglican prayer, "Let there be peace in our time."

Times had changed in the year I'd been gone. In the second week of school, a boy on a bad drug trip ran down a hallway smashing every door window with his fist before he could be stopped and his bloody hand bandaged. Second semester the same principal who'd had us monitor boy's hair length, himself now sporting a thick moustache and muttonchop sideburns, designated a student smoking area on campus. Students for a Democratic Society established a chapter whose students organized the school's first Earth Day.

The atmosphere at Beaverton wasn't the only change. I was different also, not so desperate for control. I'd learned how to manage within the dynamics of a large family, lessons that applied to the classroom too. A more casual confidence replaced the nervous uncertainty of my first year, but within weeks, a new version of Terrible Tim tested me in advanced junior English. Charlie, with his thumb-smudged, thick-lensed glasses and unkempt, greasy hair, could have been a model for Piggy in *Lord of the Flies*.

His defense against what I guessed had been years of teasing and harassment in elementary and middle school was mean sarcasm and derisive laughter used against anyone offering an opinion during discussion. He'd blurt out answers to rhetorical questions or butt in when a classmate struggled with expression. He lowered his voice after gentle redirection, but we could still hear his mutters and muffled snickers. His counselor told me that he had already surpassed what the high school offered in math. Clearly, he also excelled in English, reading difficult assignments with skill, but he was killing the class camaraderie I wanted to build.

On a morning when we were wrangling with a section of William Faulkner's "The Bear," Charlie scoffed at a classmate one too many times. I didn't see red or go blind with fury, but I did ask him to stay after the dismissal bell.

"You're too smart for this class," I began. "It must be very frustrating for you. Why don't you spend this period in the library each day reading and we'll meet during lunch or after school to discuss the book together?"

He stared at me through his bangs and smeary glasses, unsure whether I was serious, and then he nodded. Maybe I'd learned from David that hurt boys need to be acknowledged for a strength, not a wound. Or maybe I'd perfected conflict avoidance after a year living with a difficult person.

I'm not sure how many days Charlie spent in the library—maybe a week—before he wandered back into class one morning and perched on the windowsill to listen. The class was working in small groups, and he eventually edged off the sill and pulled up beside one. In that small arena, he found listeners, his ideas mattered. He still had blurt-outs and sneers now and then, but they became part of the class fabric.

By Christmas he'd been folded into the fourth-period-almost-family group that organized a progressive dinner the first weekend of vacation. The kids carpooled from house to house where they'd work in teams to prepare appetizers and soups, salads and breads, meats and vegetables from their mothers' cookbooks. They arrived at my house caroling for dessert. A few brought along guitars and another a recorder. We sang together in the living room, a fire blazing and candles lit along the mantle and then passed around *A Child's Christmas in Wales*, taking turns reading aloud. It felt like the big family I'd left behind at Hickory Hill, but one that more closely shared my values.

That winter while reading Thoreau, about ten kids from the class hiked with me on a Saturday morning deep into Forest Park along the Wildwood Trail. At lunch we sat on a damp bank while Charlie expounded on banana slugs or licorice ferns, waving his sandwich as he lectured. From out of the Oregon grape and sword ferns, my little dog, Kennedy, flew through the air and snatched the sandwich right from his hand. The kids exploded in laughter as she galloped down the Wildwood, bread wagging from side to side. Charlie became the butt of a joke in the same way I'd been when Courtney's horse ran off with me. The story would be told and retold, but I could see now and so could Charlie that the humor came from a friendly place, from within our family. It was our joke, and we were all laughing together. On another weekend in the spring a group of us trudged together up the forty-four switchbacks to the top of Hamilton Mountain in the Columbia Gorge, but Kennedy was not invited along.

A break along the Wildwood Trial in Forest Park with my students and Dalmation puppy, Kennedy. I'm at the far right of the photo.

THROUGHOUT THE SCHOOL YEAR, LINDA and I collaborated on lessons, printed up song lyrics, invited in speakers, and arranged film field trips. One afternoon we piled onto a big orange school bus with our students heading to Portland to see *They Shoot Horses, Don't They?*, a Depression-era story we hoped would enhance their understanding of people's desperation during that time and supplement our reading of Steinbeck's *Cannery Row*. It reminded me of our first year teaching when we'd persuaded our department head to purchase copies of the new paperbound edition of *In Cold Blood* and then to approve a field trip to see the film at the Laurelhurst Theater in Northeast Portland.

Together we'd escorted dozens of students on a Beaverton school bus across town into alien territory on the east side of the Willamette River. For Linda, it was familiar; she had graduated from Grant High School just blocks from the movie theater. But to many Beaverton students in 1968, going downtown or into Northeast Portland was really a field trip, a frightening excursion. The summer of 1967, race riots had swept across America from Minneapolis to Buffalo, Newark to Detroit. In Portland in late July, crowds had gathered in Irving Park to hear Black Power speakers. A heavy police presence and the threat of National Guard mobilization ratcheted up tensions, which ultimately exploded in waves of arson, vandalism, beatings, and arrests. Portland, far from white suburban Beaverton, had big-city racial clashes, but race relations were not something the English curriculum covered then. Reading about two heartland killers had seemed daring enough.

Now, two years later, Beaverton students regularly headed downtown, some engaged in outreach to the homeless in Old Town, others participating in classroom exchanges with predominately Black high schools, many others marching against the war. In May after the Kent State shootings, hundreds of students left school to join protestors at Portland State, and Linda and I brought in antiwar poetry from past wars and typed copies of contemporary song lyrics to analyze and discuss. Every day I felt a part of something that mattered, not sequestered behind high hedges on a compound or hiding out in the Hickory Hill basement.

My job teaching was to motivate hard work, to be curious, to listen, to encourage, and to nudge—to be hungry and to know when I'd asked for enough. Someone told me that good teachers must love their students or their subject matter. I loved them both throughout my years in the classroom—the well skilled, the special needs, the pregnant girls, the farm boys, the suburban jocks, the city sophisticates, the theater and band nerds—all the kids who spent an hour a day, five days a week, nine months of the year reading new books, asking questions, struggling to understand, daring to discuss and to write, to exchange ideas. They brought their sixteen-year-old experiences and perspectives to stories and characters I thought I already knew.

When Mrs. Ferrin told us in sophomore English that great literature would always have something new to say to us with each reading, I couldn't imagine what she meant. But even in my second year teaching, I experienced what she'd predicted. We worked our way through the then-American canon: Nathaniel Hawthorne, Ralph Waldo Emerson and Henry David Thoreau, Mark Twain, Stephen Crane, Edith Wharton, Sherwood Anderson, Ernest Hemingway, William Faulkner, John Steinbeck, J. D. Salinger, Arthur Miller, and Edward Albee. When it came time to teach *The Great Gatsby*, a book I'd read only once in college, the world Nick Carraway described seemed familiar in ways I could not explain to my students. I'd seen how the rich could live carelessly, ignorant or uncaring of the damage that often trailed them, leaving behind messes for others to clean up. Our current politicians acted with similar recklessness. And yet from that wealthy and powerful world had emerged two articulate and inspiring leaders. You could ponder how things might be different had they lived, but it wouldn't change how things were now. In years to come, I'd realize that not only the rich live carelessly—we all create messes. Some of us shoulder the responsibility, work to repair the damage.

JUST BEFORE THE SENATOR'S BIRTHDAY in November, a letter arrived from Hickory Hill not from Sally Irish but from a volunteer I'd known who'd stepped in to help. "Christmas cheer will start after Thanksgiving, and packages have already started to arrive," she began. My thoughts flashed back to the previous year when I'd scoured Georgetown, McLean, ski shops, and Saks for presents. David was away at boarding school where he was "doing well and playing football. He adored you," she added and suggested that he'd love to hear from me if I had time. She didn't include an address. Michael was still at Potomac, the swiftest runner on the team there, and the girls were back at Stone Ridge. The little ones were the same as ever: Christopher still the organizer, Max sweet and loveable, Douglas now talking a lot, and Rory adorable. I could picture them all and felt a tiny twinge of missing them, missing the rough-and-tumble physicality of them, the mindless games and play. But I didn't miss Mrs. Kennedy's volatile temperament. The classroom provided enough intermittent chaos and unpredictability well contained within the bell schedule and five-day week.

The letter proceeded with details of everyone I'd known the previous year. Ruby had suffered a stroke but still lived in her room behind the kitchen, tended by a visiting nurse. Geneva "worked herself out" and left over the summer. John Yaxley was gone. Sally Irish and her husband moved to California, and since then four secretaries had come and gone, the latest after only three weeks. Katherine and Ena were the only workers left who'd been there in June when Joe and I left, although he returned now and then to cater parties. The governess who took my place had given her notice and would be leaving in December.

"Things are as hectic as ever—always a crisis," she ended her letter.

"P.S. There are now eight dogs."

A few days after that letter, yet another secretary telephoned to say that Mrs. Kennedy wondered if I wouldn't love to join them in Sun Valley after Christmas. In June when she had suggested that

I join them in December, it had been moderately tempting. And I'd told Courtney that I hoped to see her over Christmas vacation. But now the answer was clear-cut. My father was dying. This would probably be our last Christmas together. I had a new puppy, a crazy Dalmatian named Kennedy, who was as wild and undisciplined as the kids and who could not be left with my parents. Besides, after four months of teaching and coaching, I needed a break from kids. I knew what would be asked and expected of me during their holiday.

"I'd love to see everyone again," I said. "I'd love to ski Sun Valley, but I can't this year."

Before Joe, Lee, and I had left for Europe, I'd hugged everyone goodbye. "Be good to the new governess. See you in December." Or maybe I'd simply said, "See you later." I made my report to Courtney on Nou Nou's new house in France, and we may have exchanged a few more letters that fall, but I never saw any of them again. At some level I knew that I'd met enough famous people, been to enough resorts, played enough touch games, bought enough presents, polished enough shoes. I'd driven enough carpools and trips to the airport and drives to the emergency room, broken up enough sibling spats, taken enough scolding. I'd experienced enough of that world. That experiment was over.

MY FATHER'S OLDER BROTHER, LOUIS, visited from California soon after I returned home from Europe, the first of many visits that fall and winter from aunts and uncles I hadn't seen since my early childhood. They were coming to say a final goodbye, although they never actually said that. At the table, Louis and my father reminisced about their old ranch house packed with kids fighting over who would haul the water up from the well and who would get up to help Papa deliver a calf. There were stories I'd never heard before, and I wondered that so much of my father's childhood remained a mystery. He was a great talker, but I think now that I had never asked. That night he spoke of his loneliness when camping in the high pastures with the cattle and then the time when he and Louis had walked to a nearby town, three or four miles from their ranch.

"You dared me to roll under the wagon, remember?" Dad said. "You dared me, and the wheel rolled over my leg. Broke it. And you made me walk home. On the broken leg."

I recoiled, imagining his pain and his brother's cruelty. *Who would do something like that?* I wondered.

My dad laughed about it, his voice holding no rancor. Louis laughed too, shaking his head. "Well, you were something."

"I spent that hot summer in bed in a plaster cast to my hip. Couldn't do a damned thing. Didn't stop me running when I got it off." Dad was giving himself a version of the pep talk he'd give over and over until he died. He'd walked miles on a broken leg. He'd lain in bed in a scorching-hot room, and then he'd gotten better. He'd do it again. His gut kept swelling with the tumors, but he never missed a day of work until March, when he and mom flew to Hawaii to visit his oldest living sister. He swam every morning, sure he'd be healed in the ocean water. Toward the end when he volunteered to try the experimental drugs they were testing at the University of Oregon Medical School in Portland, something called chemotherapy, he knew it would work on him.

The first round of treatment knocked him onto the sofa for almost a week. Before we drove him up to the old St. Vincent Hospital for a second round of chemo, he stood at the edge of our driveway gazing west across the long lawn he'd mown so many times and through the three shimmering birch trees he'd planted twenty-five years before. Maybe he felt the weight of the canvas tarp piled with clippings he'd lugged along behind him while he mowed or remembered the heft of dirt he'd flung digging to plant the now-flowering azaleas and rhododendrons, the dogwoods and camellias. What was he feeling in that long stare to the west? He stepped tentatively onto the grass, green and thick from spring rains, and started to walk toward the orange and yellow blooming border before he turned back to the car. He had to know it was his last view of home.

A call from the hospital came in the early morning, and my mother woke me sometime before dawn with the news. "The nurse said she came in to check on him, and he'd already passed away." She cried. And I cried too, feeling helpless and guilty that I hadn't done enough, and relieved that it was over and then ashamed—so many emotions crowding out thought.

I went to school in the morning as if nothing had happened, said nothing to anyone, holding on to his death like a secret. Maybe I typed out Emily Dickinson's "After great pain, a formal feeling comes." Or maybe I read "Do not go gentle into that good night. Rage, rage against the dying of the light" from Dylan Thomas to my classes without explaining why. Death was cold and lonely and kept far away in 1970. My job was to be strong.

My mother and brother handled the funeral arrangements, but I insisted that they play "Take Me Out to the Ball Game" to honor his life as an athlete and coach. A funeral should reflect a person's life, I'd learned from the Kennedys and from e. e. cummings's "Nobody Loses All the Time." We stood together outside the sanctuary and greeted every guest with a handshake or hug on the morning of his funeral, having learned the way to mourn deaths by watching the Kennedy families on television: follow the formal rituals, bear up without tears, greet friends and family—as if the public show would be enough to absorb the grief.

And then? We weren't Irish. There was no wake. Close friends from church and from old swimming days came to the house with potluck casseroles, salads, and homemade cakes. We sat together throughout the afternoon, and the next day I went back to work. I must have felt as numb and unprepared as the Kennedy kids had seemed, somehow incapable of feeling my loss. I didn't know, hadn't learned even in the year after the senator's death how damaging holding back grief can be.

A special delivery letter that arrived a few days after the funeral, handwritten from Congresswoman Green, finally touched me. But my tears may have been gratitude for her recognition of how hard the year had been, relief that I might have made a difference:

You have a host of friends who care and who would do any-thing possible to lighten the burden of concern and sorrow which you and your mother have carried these last few months. You went to Ethel Kennedy when she so desperately needed someone. I shall never forget this. If I can ever be of any help to you at any time, any place, please call me.

Love, Edith

The phone call at the end of 1969 inviting me to Sun Valley was the last I heard from the Kennedys until 1985 when Courtney wrote after David's death, asking for me to send any photos of David and to write a remembrance for a book she was putting together, much as her sister Kathleen had done for their father sixteen years before. I sent three photographs, one of him wearing Dave Hackett's Olympic ice hockey jersey; another of him walking alongside Douglas, his blue oxford shirttail loose, his hand reaching toward but not touching the toddling two-year-old; and a final one of him standing, hand in a cast, head down, hair hanging long from his forehead as he slouched, browsing through the *Washington Post.*

Part of what I wrote for the remembrance:

> *There are no pictures of the sleepy-eyed boy I remember trying to awaken and reawaken every school morning nor of the hungry boy who stayed awake past bedtime in order to raid the kitchen, making cinnamon toast and drinking towering glasses of milk while trying to eke out one more late show like "The Smothers Brothers" or talking sports with Joe-the-Butler and me.*
>
> *He remains the wiry thirteen-year-old of 1968–69, blonde, somber, almost elfish. He was short, slim, fleet, and incredibly strong. He would bring me down with a crash while playing touch football. He could run, fake, hit, and argue. He wanted to win. Always. His greatest compliment to me came in late September when he chose me to be on his Saturday touch team.*
>
> *The David I remember combined a soft vulnerability with a hard offense. He teased me about messing up in the Olympics, accused me of not winning a gold medal, knocked my socks off more than once playing touch. But he'd seek me out after everyone else was in bed. He'd stand patiently while I scrubbed his nails before dinner when he was in the cast. He was delighted by Pat Paulsen's bid for the presidency, excited by the*

six-foot ski ramp he and Michael built in the back yard, proud
of the obstacle course they crafted for the pet show, soft with
Douglas and Ena and Rory. He was the kind of child I most
enjoy: athletic, witty, a bit of a rip, a bit of a soft touch. We
were a good match.

Fourteen years later, news of Michael Kennedy's death while skiing in Aspen came in a *New York Times* article.

WHAT HAD I BEEN THINKING when I wrote to Senator Kennedy in the spring of 1968 offering to teach his kids to swim? That I might have a chance to step into history, to meet important people? Back in the 1960s, the president and later the senator and all their relatives and children had become *the Kennedys*. They represented what we might aspire to, their lofty ideals, their oversized actions, what we might try to emulate. But in the nine months that I lived with them, I discovered instead their humanity with all its flaws and beauty. I had thought they possessed something I didn't have, something I wanted to know, only to discover that they weren't in on some secret, didn't possess superior knowledge. The incidents that made up their daily lives weren't any more or less important than what was going on in every living person's life. Not more important than my father's new store or a teacher's new classes. Not more important than students protesting the Viet Nam War or bus drivers getting kids to school on time. Not more important than my mother's friends gathering to sit with her after my father died.

We all experience worry and jealousy, hope, fear, delight, anger, grief, and love. History is happening all around us every day, wherever we are. In his Nobel Prize acceptance speech, Faulkner said that the poet's, the writer's, duty is to help humanity endure by writing about love and honor, compassion and sacrifice. It is also the teacher's privilege and duty to lift hearts, to awaken curiosity. It's what Robert Kennedy meant when he urged us to stand up for ideals, to act to improve the lives of others, to send out ripples of hope. What I wrote to Ann about teaching English, I believed throughout my career: literature provides a window through which we learn compassion and understanding for ourselves and others; writing enables us to share our questions and our discoveries. My role was to motivate students to read, think, write, and act—to create ripples day after day, year after year.

EPILOGUE

AFTER I HAULED THAT LONG, RED-AND-WHITE BOX DOWN THE ATTIC ladder, I worked my way through the letters and journals, postcards, and articles from the Kennedy time, talked with former colleagues, reconnected with friends. Memories and stories returned from that extraordinary and ordinary year. When the audiotapes came back from the lab digitized, I sat at my desk for several minutes before clicking play, reluctant to hear what might or might not be on those recordings.

Through a back window, my computer open before me, I looked out onto the same green plot where my parents had built their home some eighty years before and watched the limbs on a grand fir lift and drop, ferns tremble under a spring rain. And then I listened. The high, young voice that came forth, so confident and funny, made me doubt that it was really me. But when my parents spoke—my father's voice, deliberate and formal, his expressions so familiar, and my mother, interrupting him with laughter and meandering stories—time overlapped for a moment, with me at my desk and back in 1968 simultaneously. I was eavesdropping on ghosts.

The ghosts remind us how time pushes onward, circling round and round the seasons. My first of year teaching wasn't the only one that began with excitement, slogged through a long winter, ended in summer escape. Nor was the year with the Kennedys.

An artist walking the Camino told me she stopped every hour to capture the scene in front of her, behind her and one close up beside her. Such a good idea, whether teaching school, writing a memoir, or getting through a pandemic—stop, notice, reflect. Be present in the history that's happening. Up ahead today, scents from the coming summer. Behind, the long COVID winter. Outside, trillium blooms on the south side of trails. A little girl shows me her first lost tooth. Somewhere a teacher prepares to welcome students back from a year of quarantine, finding energy for that final lap of the school year.

Pay attention, I remind myself. There's no time to waste.

ACKNOWLEDGMENTS

THANK YOU TO THE BANFF CENTRE FOR ARTS AND CREATIVITY for providing time, space (extraordinary scenery), and writerly fellowship over two three-week winter retreats. Likewise, thanks to my friends, Jenny and Dana and Tom and Priscilla, who loaned their beach houses weeks at a time for uninterrupted writing. Something about that unstructured time to write, think, and walk without interruption provides the momentum to keep on going.

Andrea Carlisle once again read multiple drafts as this story progressed and offered important editorial suggestions and difficult questions. Anne Fleming and Anakana Schofield, my Banff mentors, gave encouragement and useful tips. Emilly Prado and Perrin Kerns, workshop leaders with Portland's Literary Arts, fostered new ideas. I'm grateful to each of these women.

Thank you to the Multnomah County Library, which allowed me to work in the Sterling Room for Writers for two years, and to the wonderful research librarians who helped me fact-check dates and events from long ago. Additional support came from the Oregon Historical Society, A/V Geeks, ProPhoto and Melissa Flamson of With Permission.

When I first met Ali Shaw, founder and editor of Indigo: Editing, Design and More, she said that I had important stories to tell. I'm so grateful that she has continued to believe that they are worth telling and has helped me bring each to life. Her ongoing support has been motivating and kept this old bus from getting stuck. Thank you.

I am also grateful to the rest of the team at Indigo, who together got *Class Notes* out on the road: proofreaders Kristen Hall-Geisler and Sarah Currin, cover designer Olivia Croom Hammerman, and interior book designer and publication consultant Vinnie Kinsella.

Lee Geisen and Joe Pirozollo: Thank you for befriending me so long ago when I arrived on the cape and for staying in touch over the years.

Throughout the process, I've been encouraged by former students Boaz Frankel, Leander Star, Kate Rood, and Donna Darm; friends Patricia Raley, Jim Blashfield, Melissa Marsland, Laura Foster, and Elise Blatchford; and all the book club members who invited me to their meetings to discuss *Tough Girl* and kept asking, "What's next?"

Finally, unending gratitude to my parents, especially my mother, who kept the archive, and my son, Michael, who's always willing to listen.

ABOUT THE AUTHOR

CAROLYN WOOD HAS LIVED IN OREGON ALL BUT ONE YEAR OF HER life—the year she worked as the governess for Senator Robert and Ethel Kennedy's children. *Class Notes: A Young Teacher's Lessons from Classroom to Kennedy Compound* recounts the serendipitous path that led her to Hyannis in 1968, months after the senator's death, and provides a glimpse into a world few of us encounter.

Over the course of her career, Ms. Wood spent more than thirty years in Portland-area high school classrooms, encouraging students to read broadly and to write. After retirement, she traveled, trekked, backpacked, and gardened, then heeded her own advice and began to compose. Her first memoir, *Tough Girl: Lessons in Courage and Heart from Olympic Gold to the Camino de Santiago*, came out in 2018. The publication of *Tough Girl* brought her back to teaching students of many ages in workshops and school visits. Carolyn's essays have appeared in *Teachers as Writers, Elohi Gadugi Journal, Curve Magazine,* and *REI Co-op Journal.*

CPSIA information can be obtained
at www.ICGtesting.com
Printed in the USA
FSHW010656280921

9 780997 782820